Foreword

The Series

The Community Studies series is intended to provide a body of original Canadian case materials suitable for students of the social sciences and for the interested general reader. The term "community" in the title is used in the broadest sense; books in the series may focus upon a village, town, neighbourhood, region, economic or occupational category, ethnic group, or other societal unit. Authors from various disciplines will be encouraged to treat their subject matter from perspectives that seem appropriate to their context rather than being bound by traditional models. Although the focus will be upon issues of contemporary interest, historical studies may well find a place.

It is hoped that the series will contribute both to the understanding of Canadian society and to the development of Canadian social science.

G.B. Inglis
Memorial University of Newfoundland

Foreword to this Study

This publication by my colleague Gerald Gold on the small industrial town of Saint-Pascal indicates an important phase for the anthropology of Quebec. Just as Everett Hughes generalized to all of urban Quebec in *French Canada in Transition* (1943), this study tells its readers that rural Quebec is also industrialized. The folk society to which Quebec was overly identified after the publication of Horace Miner's study of the neighbouring parish of Saint-Denis, has been successfully withdrawn from the conceptual framework used in Saint-Pascal. The non-Québécois reader, familiar with the now classic works of Hughes and Miner will here find an image of Quebec that is not only different but also much more contemporary and realistic. He will find that this is not a classic monograph that covers superficially every level of social reality. Instead, this is a study that stops to describe in detail the economic transition that Saint-Pascal has experienced, particularly in the last twenty years.

The first merit of Gold's study comes from its reliance on a solid diachronical analysis of the different stages that characterized the socio-economic evolution of Saint-Pascal and of the intervention of different elite groups: seigneurs, professionals, curés, merchants, and entrepreneurs. The essence of this historical plot comes out quite clearly to be the recent emergence of an entrepreneurial elite. Inspired by recent anthropological studies of entrepreneurship by Fredrik Barth and Robert Paine, the author explicitly describes the strategies used by this entrepreneurial group and the networks that they have activated to meet their ends. Perhaps one of the most original aspects of this research is the manner by which the author singles out certain "voluntary" associations such as the Jeunesse Rurale Catholique and the Club Richelieu and their role in the rise of the new Pascalien elite. The entrepreneurs benefit both as a group and as individuals from their external contacts, information exchange and cooperation — resources that are centralized in these common interest associations.

Moreover, this study escapes, through its methodology, from some of the pitfalls of community studies. That is, far from presenting the community as a closed and largely autonomous entity as Miner and numerous other researchers have done, Gold constantly strives to situate Saint-Pascal in the context of Quebec society. In my opinion, this interrelationship is essential for anthropological community studies to continue to have any meaning. The anthropologist must take an interest in larger territorial units than the little community if he wishes to account for the macro-societal forces that often determine the socio-economic life of smaller territorial units.

I hope Gerald Gold's pioneer work bears fruit in motivating other researchers to analyze "from the inside" the economic evolution of Quebec and the role of the agents and of the networks that make up its dynamics.

Paul Charest
Département d'Anthropologie
Université Laval
Québec.

SAINT·PASCAL

Changing Leadership & Social Organization in a Quebec Town

Gerald L. Gold

Cultures & Communities: A Series of Monographs
Community Studies
General Editor: Gordon B. Inglis
Holt, Rinehart & Winston of Canada, Limited
Toronto   Montreal

Printed in Canada

1   2   3   4   5   79   78   77   76   75

Cover Design: Carol Noel. (Henri Fortier and his workers in 1958
                          with executives from his out-of-town
                          suppliers.)

The Book

An underlying objective in writing this case study of Saint-Pascal is to situate the social and economic upheaval of post-Duplessis Quebec within the context of Saint-Pascal, a small town in rural Kamouraska County. Québécois have long considered this region to be traditional and agricultural, and social scientists shared a similar view when they associated the region with Horace Miner's study of the "peasant" community of Saint-Denis. Without denying the continuing importance of rural life in the Lower Saint-Lawrence, this study documents how the mercantile elite of an agrarian service centre has been replaced by an industrial capitalist elite. The new elite, many of whom are sons of local craftsmen, have used national associations to assert their identity at a regional level. Their industries have weakened the close relationship of the regional economy with agriculture and forestry.

The Author

Gerald Gold received his B.A. from McGill University in 1966, and his doctorate from the University of Minnesota in 1972. He has taught at the University of Guelph, at Glendon College — York University, and is now an associate professor of anthropology at Université Laval in Quebec City. His fieldwork has been on regional economic change and stratification in eastern Quebec and in central Mexico. His principal publications are two collections of studies of Francophone communities in Quebec and in Canada (edited with Marc-Adélard Tremblay) and a documentary film on the new economic elite in Saint-Pascal.

Preface

Saint-Pascal has changed a great deal since 1970, the year in which most of the material in this book was gathered. Several revisits and the shooting of a film have given me time to reflect on my initial report (Gold, 1972) and fill in the gaps of some events that concluded when I set aside the full-time task of fieldwork. My analysis of the entrepreneurial group and of the problems of industrialism has held up reasonably well over these several years of fires, new enterprises, failures, elections and institutional additions.

This was only possible because of the patience and cooperation of the people of Saint-Pascal, to whom I owe my deepest gratitude. It is unfair to single out townspeople who helped me more than others, but I will be ungrateful if I fail to mention the unfaltering assistance of the members of the Club Richelieu of Saint-Pascal. My analysis of their social life and of their businesses is meant to provide a better understanding of the problems of community leadership and economic growth in Quebec. Any errors of interpretation or of fact are unintentional, although some changes were made to protect the identity or privacy of people in Saint-Pascal. For this purpose, pseudonyms are used throughout the volume for the names of living Pascaliens. On their request, I have not changed the name of the town.

Contents

Acknowledgements

A number of friends and colleagues have given me suggestions and critical comments. I am particularly grateful for the counsel of Gordon Inglis, the editor of this series, Vincent Lemieux, Frank C. Miller, Robert Paine, Pertti Pelto, Robert F. Spencer and Yves Turcot. Less direct but invaluable encouragement was received from Jean Burnet, Noble Irvine, Ray Pollard and Ken Westhues and many others whom I have not forgotten. My initial fieldwork in Saint-Pascal was sponsored with a doctoral fellowship from the Canada Council whose funding is deeply appreciated. Finally to Barb, my thanks for encouraging my work while excelling in her own field of interest.

My hope is that *Saint-Pascal* will help others to better see and understand themselves. For this reason I would like to see a French version available in the very near future.

à Gilles Picard
un Pascalien extraordinaire

Entrez donc, dans la ronde,
C'est le 25è, c'est le Carnaval,
Buvons, rions, chantons, car,
C'est le Carnaval de Saint-Pascal.

Hélène B. Pelletier
Saint-Pascal

Chapter One
Fieldwork with an Entrepreneurial Group

> It is easy to see that the French are a conquered people. The rich
> classes mostly belong to the English race. Although French is the
> language almost universally spoken, the newspapers, the notices and
> even the shop-signs of French tradesmen are in English. Commercial
> undertakings are almost all in their hands. They are the ruling class
> in Canada. I doubt if this will be so long (*25th August, 1831*).
>
> (Alexis de Tocqueville, 1960:184)

The facade of Quebec society has changed appreciably since de
Tocqueville's perceptive observations on the eve of the bourgeois-
led popular rebellion of 1837-38. The subsequent union of the
two Canada's and then Confederation did little to achieve Lord
Durham's goals of assimilation for the French minority. Yet of
Canada's two charter groups, French Canadians have been significantly less involved in the economic control of Canada (Gagnon,
1965; Porter, 1965:938) and of Quebec where they have always
been numerically dominant (Saint-Germain, 1973:110). Not that
all French-Canadian elites have been impoverished or powerless;
but no matter what individuals have done, for well over a century
business and industrial technology were not held in high esteem.
French-Canadian capitalists unlike their Anglo-American counterparts, had little impact on cultural values (Falardeau 1965:33;
Kluckhohn, 1958). Much of this changed after 1960 with the
emergence of a new French middle class of business managers and
technocrats. This shift, sometimes referred to as Quebec's "Quiet
Revolution", is reasonably well studied on the national level, but
with few exceptions (for example, Moreux, 1970) little has been
written about change on the local and regional level.

This book sets out to fill the gap with a study of the transition
of leadership in the small Quebec town of Saint-Pascal — one of
many rural service centres where traditional agrarian French
Canadian society has intersected with industrial and urban Quebec.
In Saint-Pascal's past can be seen an era of leadership by priests,

lawyers and small merchants. In its present, is the rise of an indigenous commercial-industrial bourgeoisie which I will refer to as an entrepreneurial group. Although this circulation of leadership occurred throughout the wider society, Saint-Pascal is not a "typical" town of French Canada or of French Quebec. No town can faithfully mirror a complex industrial society, just as the social system of a complex state cannot be an enlarged version of its components. Furthermore, loss of identity is the last thing that Saint-Pascal's leaders have ever wanted either when their milieu came to be known as "leathertown" or when it was no more than an inland extension of the Seigneury of Kamouraska.

As such, Saint-Pascal is strikingly different from Cantonville where Everett Hughes (1943) documented the transition from a rural service centre to an Anglo-American controlled industrial centre. As Hughes discovered, the deployment of local resources in Cantonville created a dependence situation for traditional professional and merchant elites:[1]

> I saw more clearly the model of the region or community industrialized by outsiders, cultural aliens. The local region furnished labour, raw materials or power, or all three. The newcomers furnished enterprise and technical knowledge.
>
> As development proceeds . . . the native non-industrial middle or upper class, or both, finds many of its functions usurped by the alien industrial leadership.   (Hughes, 1963:229)

Before beginning the study of Saint-Pascal, I had hypothesized that the new regional economic leaders should not be studied only as individual entrepreneurs. From the national to the local level Quebec seemed to be organized along occupational and class lines which were stronger rallying points than the charisma or power of specific persons. These group interests were reflected in national coalitions such as the business and technocratic interests that succeeded the Duplessis regime in Quebec City. New organizations such as the Club Richelieu and the Centre des Dirigeants d'Entreprise (C.D.E.) provided arenas for sociability and for the affirmation of industrial capitalist values. Whether in the private or public sector, entrepreneurs worked within the framework and support of entrepreneurial groups.

Entrepreneurs and Entrepreneurial Groups

Joseph Schumpeter popularized the concept of the *entrepreneurial function* where individuals reorganized resources through technical innovations (Schumpeter, 1934:77). Some anthropologists have modified this concept to apply it to a wide range of allocations and place it more firmly in a group context. The entrepreneurial function became part of the role of a "social accountant" (Belshaw, 1955). In Fredrik Barth's terms, entrepreneurs "take the initiative, and in the pursuit of profit in some discernable form manipulate other persons or resources" (1963:6). Accordingly, for Barth the study of social change concentrates on the "chain of transactions between the entrepreneur and his environment" (1963:7). Barth translates the manipulation of social resources into economic terms such as "goods", "profit", and "cost", and uses the concept of "spheres of exchange" (Bohannan, 1955) to explain the restrictions on entrepreneurial transactions between discrete domains of social activity (Barth, 1963:10-12). In choosing a *niche* in the environment entrepreneurs might seek "liquid assets" that could be readily deployed to other forms or areas of activity. In this way they maintain some "liquidity" in their "assets". (*Ibid.*) Thus, placing resources into political and status investments such as group membership may be the only way for individuals to gain access to production resources; however, such non-tangible assets are also difficult to reinvest elsewhere.[2] In another example, it is precisely the non-convertibility of investment that makes the family business both an aid and a deterrent to socio-economic change (Benedict, 1968). Using this argument it follows that an uncertain financial and political climate directed some French Canadians to the protected niche of the liberal professions and toward the maintenance of rural ideologies and others to the security of family enterprise (Falardeau, 1965; Rioux, 1973).

The degree to which entrepreneurs keep profits liquid and free from social control is important when we turn to the objectives of taking on an entrepreneurial role. Robert Paine (1962) introduces this problem in his study of Lappish entrepreneurs whom he typologizes as either "freeholders" or "free enterprisers". "Entrepreneurs of the freeholder type . . . are prepared to accept responsibility in associations in order to help raise the productivity of the community" (Paine, 1963:52). They work in the traditional

3

productive activities of the community (in this case farming and fishing) and maintain a conservative preservation ideology. Despite the availability of outside resources and outside values, a freeholder is the type of person who "continues to identify himself with the home group in every way" (Belshaw, 1955:145). The profits of such local-level entrepreneurial activities are channelled into networks of reciprocal obligations within the community. It would seem that only under exceptional circumstances could an outsider become a freeholder in a small community. When freeholders constitute an elite they are akin to Pareto's lions, entrenched and resistant to major change (Pareto, 1968 (1901)).

In comparison, "free enterprisers" are more speculative, and will if necessary, disregard local values in their search for power and status or in cooperation and even in partnership with freeholders. They are in this way akin to Pareto's speculative elites of "foxes" who either have no established position or who do not seek community attachments that direct the profits of their activities. Cosmopolitan and nation-orientated free enterprisers seek short term gain. They may dominate local leadership and command greater "expertise" as brokers with outside agencies. Among the Coast Lapps, such brokerage comes from literacy in Norwegian; among rural French Canadians from ties with government and English-speaking businessmen.

Ultimately there are social costs for those who choose to circumvent the normative rules of their milieu. Either their efforts are undermined, or they seek an appropriate power base and social legitimacy to sustain a tenacious exploitation of "new" values. It is at this juncture that the "entrepreneurial function" is institutionalized in class terms. Control of the means of production is secured through the redefinition of economic opportunities or through the secondary step of taking advantage of the changes initiated by others. The convergence of interests leads to the formation of a new coalition of those who embrace the new economic and moral order. As this coalition acquires an organization, a means of social control and an ideology, it becomes an *entrepreneurial group.*

Some have explained the appearance of new economic groups in terms of a general economic expansion and increased per capita income (Liebenstein, 1957:123-136). Their theory is that economic expansion will dry up alternative activities and "push" busi-

4

nessmen into an entrepreneurial group and on to the route to economic and social mobility. The emphasis on economic expansion probably overly depreciates the importance of cultural factors. The entrepreneurial groups can also be seen as "opportunists" (Glade, 1967:249), being "pulled" into new activities after redefining the use of available resources. The goals of their attempt at redefinition would also determine the type of entrepreneurial profit they were seeking. Some economic historians have hypothesized that these opportunities are limited in practice to "occupationally-related characteristics" that permit access to capital funds rather than the ability to accumulate funds (Aubey, 1969:278). In this way sudden demands on the economy would have an uneven impact on the occupational structure. Some members of some occupations, who may be all of the same ethnic group, will be in a better position to act as entrepreneurs and acquire a niche for themselves and their supporters.

The idea of entrepreneurship as a class phenomenon implies some contradiction between the concept of entrepreneur as an aspect of the roles of *individuals* and the concept of an *entrepreneurial group*. Few writers deny that "around the entrepreneur there arises a corporate group" (Barth, 1963:5), while some have concluded that at least in precapitalist and in preindustrial societies these coalitions will be a major factor in sustaining most entrepreneurial activities (Aubey, Kyle and Strickon, 1974:89, Schneider, 1972:262, Strathern, 1973).

In what kind of social situations can the entrepreneur operate independently of such a coalition? Are the "free enterprisers" liberated from social controls and the power and restrictions that come from class membership? Or are entrepreneurs only brokers who do the primary reorganizing for others who support them — a cycle of innovation and routinization? To answer these questions in my study of changing leadership in the French Quebec town of Saint-Pascal, I have focused my interests on the *entrepreneurial group as a coalition seeking to redirect and redefine existing organization of economic and social resources toward their own control and their own perception of the social order.*

It is my contention that entrepreneurial groups carried out much of the local level organization of Quebec's Quiet Revolution of the sixties. In previously agricultural areas they provided the link between what had been a peasant society and an expanding industrial state. Therefore, in seeking a research site in Quebec, it was all the more important to me to arrive during or immediately after an early phase of industrialization. That way I could study the organization of an entrepreneurial group in an environment of groups with competing occupational and class interests.

John Bennett's (1967, 1969) study of the differential adaptation of Alberta farmers and ranchers suggested that various occupational groups would have very different community-nation relationships as well as disagreements on the use of their ecosystem. The first methodological problem was locating a group of new industrialists in a changing agricultural region.

However, it was not easy to find clues to which occupations and strata of rural French Quebeckers were best placed to acquire the resources and support for capitalist ventures. Geertz hypothesizes (1962:145) that entrepreneurial groups have a traditional extra-local orientation that links them with the national economic system. They are not peasants, but they may still be marginal to dominant elites. Before 1966, few were in a position to form an entrepreneurial group with class interests that were different from those of national professional elites, and regional elites seemed to conform to the national values to an even greater degree than their urban counterparts.

If there were changes in this rural outlook, then Montreal, the commercial centre of Quebec, was as good a place as any to begin fieldwork.

Fieldwork in Saint-Pascal

Networks from Montreal

Like many students of French-Canadian society I had pored over studies on rural Quebec such as Léon Gérin's *Habitant de Saint-Justin* (1897), Horace Miner's study of peasant society in Saint-Denis (1939), Everett Hughes (1943) on the industrialization of "Cantonville" and Marcel Rioux's (1957) analysis of Belle Anse. Therefore, at the outset of a brief trip to Montreal in November, 1968, I made an effort to see both Philippe Garigue who has been critical of those who interpreted rural Quebec as a peasant society (Garigue, 1962), and Marcel Rioux who has both modified and defended the application of the peasant society model to Quebec, placing it in the economic, historical and political context of the Conquest[3] (Rioux, 1964, 1969, 1974). These visits and others led to suggestions that I take advantage of the recent and extensive studies that had just been completed by social scientists working on the "pilot" development plan for the Bureau for the Development of Eastern Quebec (B.A.E.Q. 1966). Eastern Quebec looked promising, but where would I find entrepreneurial groups?

I had considered using census data to select a research site, however I could then think of few census indicators of French Canadian control of regional economic life. More promising were community-nation networks, particularly marketing networks, that might lead to one of many concentrations of externally orientated Francophone entrepreneurs. Undoubtedly, unless a number of such networks are tapped, there is a risk that the community or region selected would not be representative of others in Quebec. Nevertheless I decided that this was a risk worth taking. Academic networks had already steered me to Eastern Quebec — the Lower Saint Lawrence and the Gaspé. My scouting time in Quebec was running short, and I needed a place to set up shop the following spring.

The focus was on industries which could be started with little initial capital and semiskilled labour; in Quebec, as in New England, these had long been in the fields of clothing and leather (Faucher, 1973). Several buyers in the Montreal garment trade then told me of Saint-Pascal, a small town "in the Gaspé" where "this fellow, Gagnon, had built up an enormous tannery in the middle of no-where". I also heard that he was doing a good business in what was a "difficult market". This was a golden fleece in the midst of a part of rural Quebec that I had still pictured as a modified peasant society.

The weight of the social science literature seemed to defy the statistical reality of urbanization. Instead, somewhere I imagined, there were dozens of isolated and tightly organized rural communities somewhat like Horace Miner's (1939), all at the margins of an Americanized, urban Quebec. I find it therefore ironic and fortunate that Saint-Pascal, the community to which my commercial network was orientating me, is only five miles from Saint-Denis. More interesting still was the information that Miner's selection of Saint-Denis had been largely influenced by Georges Bouchard

(Miner, 1939:x), an advocate of rural life in Quebec whose son, René Bouchard, an operatically-inclined postage stamp dealer in Montreal, had long been a personal acquaintance of mine. My networks were converging on Saint-Pascal.

All that I remember about the morning that I left for Kamouraska County was the astonishment of the ticket agent when I asked in faltering Franglais for a bus ticket to Saint-Pascal. He answered: "Which Saint-Pascal?", thinking that I may have wanted a residential *quartier* of Quebec City. "*De Kamouraska*", I stammered.

On the Road to Kamouraska

> ... Far as the eye can reach, a motionless sea of snow, covering country, town and village, man and beast, as one. Erasing every joy and pain. Stifling every scheme the moment it comes to life. And all the while the cold connives its way in and offers the solace of its deathly calm. That man out there on the road to Kamouraska ...
>
> (Anne Hébert, 1973:196)

By the time my bus had reached Montmagny we had long since left the four-lane monotony of the snow-covered Trans-Canada Highway and had begun to follow the circuitous route 2 along the Saint Lawrence. We stopped at a café for a late lunch and I noticed that the fences separating the long narrow strips of farmland were made of small fieldstones. Despite the neon signs, the gas stations and the thundering highway traffic I thought of Marius Barbeau's descriptions of the uniqueness of *Le Pays de Gourganes* (Barbeau, 1918) in Charlevoix on the other shore of the river. I wondered to what extent south shore communities had preserved their idiosyncratic identities and traditions in the face of the urbanization of the countryside.

I looked at a timetable and followed the progress of the bus through the long strip of continuous settlement which is characteristic of the first few *rangs* of lowland settlement. Every five or ten miles the bus would skid to a stop in between rows of slanted tin roofs and venerable snowcapped trees. Cap St.-Ignace, wooden houses, a stone church in Islet, craftsmen in Saint-Jean-Port-Joli, Village des Aulnaies, with its stately Canadien homes, La Pocatière and the spire of the classical college, a centre of nineteenth-century Ultramontane clerical ideology. Then the bus barrelled through the interior of Kamouraska County; Saint-Pacôme, with the tudor style former mansions of the Harding and Power families and rows of small wooden homes; Saint-Philippe-de-Néri, a small sawmill, several wayside crosses. Finally some rocky outcroppings and the frozen waterfall of the former seigneurial mill marked the town limits of Saint-Pascal. After passing a modern looking factory and small stores that seemed to lead to the tall grey stone church, the bus lurched to a stop at an intersection and deposited me on the edge of a snowbank. In the commotion and uncertainty of disembarking I had not noticed a short man in grey cotton work clothes. He edged toward me as though we knew each other.

"M. Gold?"

"Oui." I was taken by surprise. He answered in faltering English. "I am Denis . . . . Rosaire Gagnon sent me to meet you. You're late. I'll take you to the hotel. There's a room for you."

No one knew me in Saint-Pascal and so the reception was unexpected. I followed him to the car and we continued our conversation in French. Denis explained that he works as a shipper in Rosaire Gagnon's tannery. He also handles some special assignments for M. Gagnon as he had learned some English working in "the south of the province". He was optimistic about his future in the tannery.

Denis then drove me to the tannery office, a large white frame home close to the centre of town. A steep flight of stairs led to a panelled waiting room where several secretaries could be seen working in the adjoining room, their typewriters clicking over a not-so-distant rumble and hiss of machinery. Walking about the waiting room was Rosaire Gagnon's retired father, the son of the tannery's moustachioed founder whose photograph conspicuously greets incoming visitors to the office. Soon a rosy-cheeked, thirtyish-looking Rosaire Gagnon emerged from a tiny private office that led to his parents' adjoining apartment. I was ushered in for the first of a series of absorbing encounters.

Gagnon rapidly explained how his father's small craft shop had recently become an industrial tannery, with satellite clothing and glove factories. He turned to others: Henri Fortier and his new tire factory, and others who had gone into producing candy, wool, hogs and setting up a community television system. There were also smaller and "more traditional" firms, one of which made farm wagons and metal products. Gagnon asserted that the new

9

manufacturers were community leaders, "men with an entrepreneurial spirit, constantly reinvesting their profits to increase
production and improve their machinery".

I made a cursory inspection of the tannery and accepted the
keys to the Dodge to visit the other manufacturers and to take a
jaunt through the countryside. As I drove away from the town I
knew that either I had found my entrepreneurial group or perhaps
they had found me.

Moving slowly toward the river and feeling very conspicuous in
Gagnon's car, I knew what I wanted to see first. Although I hope
that no one ever goes out of his way for the sole purpose of a
glimpse of Gold's Saint-Pascal, I very much wanted to see Miner's
Saint-Denis. The coincidence of this community being so near
was exciting and offered an ideal baseline for the study of rapid
social change from the traditional agricultural life of the thirties
to the mixed industrial and dairy farming economy of the seventies.

By dusk, overwhelmed by a cold, my head spinning from
exhaustion, I stopped for soup in a small Kamouraska *casse-
croûte*. The tiger-skin plastic seats and blaring jukebox quickly
removed me from the reverie about earlier days. A few boisterous
members of the local Black Spreaders motorcycle gang helped
clarify the situation.

The next evening I travelled with several of the most successful
of Saint-Pascal's merchants to a regional development bank meeting
in Rivière-du-Loup. Once in the car, business stories were swapped
and someone proposed a strategy for benefitting from the new
regional financial resource. Sitting quietly in the back seat and
feeling very insignificant, I considered the prospect of a year in
Saint-Pascal.

Insiders and Outsiders

Fieldwork began in June, when we took a hotel room and looked
around for a field headquarters. A week later I signed a lease on a
small basement apartment in what was then Saint-Pascal's only
suburban apartment block. I was ready to do research, although
the Pascaliens I had met earlier and anybody else I wanted to see,
were away on vacation. Even those who were around town hardly

came knocking at our door. It was not long before Rosaire Gagnon gave us a quick tour of the countryside and invited us to his home. Shortly afterward, his cousin, Maltais the television dealer, took me golfing in Rivière-du-Loup. Not a very exciting way to begin but we were determined to set up an everyday routine: we selected a grocer, tried the butchers, purchased a bed and some canvas folding chairs from Maltais and visited our neighbours and our landlord.

It was one of the neighbours who first involved me in the social relations between townsmen and the business community. Unemployed Paul Letellier and his common-law wife were, like everyone else in the building, strangers to Saint-Pascal who took the only housing available to them. It did not take long for Letellier to discover that "English" next door had nothing better to do than type. He decided to take me in hand and fill me in on his illustrious career and on his unfortunate experiences working first for Gagnon and then for Maltais. There was a bit of Major Hoople in Paul. Between fishing trips, beer drinking and sunbathing he was constantly coming over to spin tales about the power of the provincial deputy, the low wages in the factories and collusion between almost everyone. I could not get rid of him! Then one evening at the landlord's cottage, I learned that the Letelliers had never paid their rent. Later, a visit to the furniture dealer came up with the story that Letellier had the habit of swearing at customers while permanently dismantling their television sets on their living room floor.

A more helpful neighbour than "Major" Paul was Michel Cloutier, a provincial government employment officer from Quebec City who moved in upstairs with his wife, a secretary at the C.E.G.E.P. — the next service centre to the west of Saint-Pascal. Through Cloutier I obtained a list of businesses in the county with more than three employees and information on the relatively high employment in the town of Saint-Pascal. Taking side trips through the highland countryside we talked of unemployment and depression in the agricultural villages and an administrative and commercial boom in La Pocatière where the large locally-owned snowmobile plant had just been bought up by an American firm.[4]

By the end of July, fewer people would ask me, "Do you live here?", or "What do you plan to do in Saint-Pascal?" Building on

Cloutier's list, I had completed a survey of the businesses and institutions in the community. Other leads came from chats with the postmaster, the hotelkeeper, the grocer and any other townspeople who would strike up conversations during the daily rounds through the town. Gradually a street-by-street survey filled my notebooks. Keeping in mind the constant talk of phenomenal successes, I recorded every commercial operation that hung a shingle, had premises, a commercial vehicle or an acknowledged existence.

Meanwhile, like the other strangers in our building, our day-to-day life went smoothly as Pascaliens adapted themselves to our presence. Townspeople were talking to us, but these conversations seemed to be trivial and superficial. We had filled the role of the outsiders who had come to Saint-Pascal with industrial and bureaucratic expansion. This was no way of uncovering the relationships between our hosts. Optimistically I turned to the interview schedule which I had carefully prepared before my arrival hoping to get beneath the masks of toleration.

From a total of 84 enterprises, ranging in size from a hotdog stand in a school bus hulk to the largest factories, I selected a sample of 44 business families. (see Appendix A) Using earlier contacts such as Rosaire Gagnon and several others selected from my survey who I thought would be cooperative, I pretested the interview and made some last minute changes. I was still apprehensive. Would a structured interview only turn the welcome — the veneer of *tout le monde se connaît* (everyone knows each other) into antagonism and estrangement?

In a first visit I explained to each business manager my interest in the economic base and community life of a growing Quebec town. I promised confidentiality (most of the names in this volume are pseudonyms), but few were ready to share private information with a stranger. Wherever possible, questions became conversation, and were not necessarily presented in a sequential order or during the same visit. If someone wished to tell me about the early history of the town, the behaviour of a competitor, a philosophy of French-English relations or a reflection on the landing of the astronauts on the moon, I listened and noted or recorded everything, occasionally steering the conversation back to my chosen topic. The strategy was to open myself to continuing social relationships. I soon realized that relentless interviewing was not a primary goal.

There were no refusals, although two of the 44 people I had selected successfully avoided me for three months. When we were better acquainted through his activity in associations, one of these men approached me to arrange the interview. He and a number of other persons were well-briefed as to my intentions, either through rumour or through explicit third party requests for cooperation from those who had taken an interest in the project. On several occasions people stopped to ask me when it would be their turn for a visit. I did not want to tell anyone that they had not made my sample. They too were interviewed.

As the interviews proceeded some clear differences emerged between family-oriented enterprisers and about a dozen men in their thirties, including Rosaire Gagnon, who had built the new factories and regional entrepôts for consumer goods. As I coded several hundred pages of interview notes, I found that those who were responsible for the operation of the new businesses belonged to the same voluntary associations and expressed similar view-points on the future of their town. An exciting finding was that the new entrepreneurs had once been active in an unusually successful local chapter of the Rural Catholic Youth Movement.

In another way, the interviews were discouraging and I often regretted that I had ever begun them. They were no more than bottled slices of staged behaviour, usually without very much depth. Already my interest had been diverted to those families who were more cooperative than others, and I repeatedly in-vited myself back for long discussions in their living rooms and offices. These meetings served to interrelate the cast of the local scenario and interpret or validate information that others had given me without further elaboration. (For example, "Yes. I was once a Richelieu member, but I quit when my business needed all of my time".)

By September an empty apartment across from my own was occupied by Yves Turcot who was then teaching political science at the C.E.G.E.P. in La Pocatière. Turcot became my sounding board and dinner companion for the rest of the year. Contact with his uncle, a teaching brother in the secondary school, was to help introduce me to school teachers. These contacts were furthered when Brother Antoine, the newly arrived principal of the school, took the last available apartment in our building. My access to local networks was expanding rapidly.

In October, I was telephoned by a man whom I had not yet met and invited to be a guest speaker at the next Club Richelieu dinner. The meeting was a turning point in my study. It was a small gathering of twelve businessmen (including every major manufacturer in town), three teachers and two guests. I felt very much the outsider when I rose to address the Richelieu. Fortunately I had chosen to be humorous and inviting rather than overly informative. No one laughed, but the evening worked out better than I had hoped. Following good Richelieu procedure, Rosaire Gagnon rose to thank me for my talk and appeal for cooperation with my research. Feeling somewhat elated I followed the dinner friends from the table to the bar, which was the stage for yet another performance by the manufacturers who discussed business experiences and market conditions in a smaller and less formal setting. I left at about nine to hunt up Turcot.

"Yves, I think I've seen the entrepreneurial group in action." I don't know if anyone else would have been as intoxicated by so mundane an evening. Turcot certainly was not, when several weeks later, it was his turn to speak as a newcomer, and defend his separatist convictions to an unrelenting and unconverted Richelieu gathering.

I continued attending some Club Richelieu meetings throughout the fall and was invited to other groups such as the Centre Social, the Chevalier de Colomb and finally the Industrial Society for a public session about a potential snowmobile plant. Negotiations with the potential manufacturer were carried out in privacy by the Industrial Society executive. (No anthropologists invited.) Late October was full of rumours about political manipulation to prevent the new plant from using scarce or low-cost skilled labour. The gossip was fanned by the prospect of a municipal election three weeks later.

In January I turned to the problem of observing a half day of production in each factory so as to corroborate the owner's descriptions with my own observations of workdays selected at random. A more detailed study of each industry would have required observations over a longer period of time. Hence, apart from factory employment lists and the occasional meeting in the hotel bar or at a volleyball match, I had little contact with Saint-Pascal's workers. I had chosen my constituency with all its limitations in social distance to others and in the availability of my own time. Any short term study would inevitably be a relatively one-sided product (cf. Hughes, 1963). Saint-Pascal, an industrial town of 2300 souls was too complex for one man to study in one year.

The wintry streets of the town were like plowed skating rinks and highway travel was often difficult. Fortunately I could think of no other time when I would rather be in Saint-Pascal. Even with the passing of a small farm economy with its sleighs, snowed-in roads, and festive *veillées* on the *rangs*, winter remains the most socially intense season in Saint-Pascal. In the private lives of parishioners this is a time for visiting, snowmobile parties in the backwoods, and long private discussions. In their public lives the Pascaliens attend what seemed to be an endless round of club meetings and parish-wide gatherings.

Throughout that fall of interviewing businessmen and visiting community leaders, a somewhat fuzzy image of the traditional aspects of parish life steadily filtered into my field notes, calling for synthesis and clarification. Conspicuously absent from my first research reports was a section on the role of the curé and of religion in general. Occasionally I would pick up Miner's Saint-Denis where the curé is portrayed as the dominant civic and religious leader of the parish and where "religious behaviour and thought dominate all life" (Miner, 1939:100). "That is the way it was a generation ago in Saint-Pascal", more than one person told me. However, while Miner was able to affirm that "life in Saint-Denis is a flow of traditional behaviour", (*Ibid.*:91) the daily rituals of an ascetic Catholicism had been replaced, in Saint-Pascal, by the rituals of modernization — the routine of white-collar work, and the order and procedure of associations. This process of substitution was still incomplete; traditionalists, including the aging Curé Pelletier, looked askance at the changes in liturgy, the secularization of the schools and the erosion of mysticism and ritual from popular religious practice.

To strengthen some of the bonds of *communitas* within his parish, Curé Pelletier instituted an annual parish supper, one occasion on which his "extended family" could renew their identity through speeches, singing and commensalism. Of course I was pleased to attend the parish supper, but I had not yet had any private discussions with the curé. As my journal for that night attests, I was somewhat shaken by my meeting with the old

15

gentleman in the pre-dinner reception line:

> The curé came over to greet me and once again asked me what I was
> up to in the parish. We agreed that we ought to meet soon for a
> private talk. He complained about being overworked and advised me
> to make an appointment to see him. He was most concerned about
> having missed me in his *annual visit* to homes in the parish.
>
> What religion did I profess? (He found out rather quickly.) He then
> wanted to know what such a religion is all about. How could it even
> be a religion? "I . . . don't believe it . . . !" He shook his head in
> doubt. "How can you not see the truth of the gospel? Do you not
> want to be saved?" (etc.)
>
> I had dreaded such an encounter for six months. But when I told
> one of my regular informants about it, he laughed and added that
> the curé is quite obsessed with missionary zeal. "Fortunately he is a
> good deal less conservative than any of his predecessors."

When I finally saw the curé once again after the dinner, he tried
to remember my religion, and identified me as a Protestant. I was
still somewhat pensive when, an hour later, I attended a crowded
public talk by the wool miller, Louis Georges Landry, at the regular
meeting of the Centre d'Accueil ('Welcome Centre').[5] The subject
was the future of Saint-Pascal as a viable community. Predictably
all the manufacturers were present. The regular visitors of the
Centre d'Accueil were a silent but interested audience dispersed
in the back of the room. The mood was one of anger and even
desperation. The role of the curé slipped out of my mind. Rosaire
Gagnon exhorted the crowd:

> We are missing a spirit of entrepreneurship! People like Bouchard of
> Sainte-Anne — when he made his first snowmobiles he had no
> *financial* reason to go into business . . . . The youth between twenty
> and thirty are leaving. We need their ideas and projects.

Then everyone seemed to be talking at once. Louis-Georges
Landry pronounced that education might be "An industry to end
all others . . . ", and horticulturist Fleury made an impassioned
but unheeded plea for regional and cooperative planning. Seized
by the excitement of the moment, tire-maker Henri Fortier rose
to thank his neighbour Landry. "As the Jews in Montreal, we
should act better late than never." He continued with the success
story of the Steinbergs of Montreal. Then Northern Italy. "Last
summer I was in Northern Italy. That is also a poor region, but it
is industrialized! If we take risks here, we will be in rosy shape by
1980."

16

Information poured in from these meetings at a faster rate than I could record in my field notes. Every leader kept a file of documentary materials on current and past initiatives in community development. Submissions, petitions, parish census reports, surveys and electoral lists were easily available. Few public documents were destroyed. A recent history of the town and an age and occupational profile of its people were available from a variety of these unobtrusive sources. Life history material provided individual dimension to social changes in the county, although constant visits to the same informants were very obtrusive and visible (despite my efforts at times to be discreet) and became the butt of gossip. The phone in my Gagnon Street apartment rang constantly. Across the hall, Yves Turcot claimed to be astonished at my involvement in local social networks. I had assisted the Chambre de Commerce in designing their tourism plan, translated dozens of documents, photographed a sales catalogue, accompanied a merchant on a buying trip to New Jersey and tried to provide a number of townspeople (at their insistence) with feedback on their own abilities without comprising my own objectivity. Yves was probably right when on the eve of the provincial election he referred to me as an expert in village gossip (*"ragoût"*).

The 1970 spring election was perhaps one of the most significant political contests in recent Quebec history. The two traditional political parties, Liberal and Union Nationale, found themselves faced with two new opponents in the Parti Québécois and the provincial Créditistes. Two candidates were locals and Saint-Pascal was caught in a fierce partisan fever.

My first political involvement was being confided in by some of the Liberal organizers and then attending Union Nationale organizational meetings. The Créditistes had open meetings as well, but their candidate, the former lieutenant of the Union Nationale incumbent, defected to the Créditistes toward the end of the campaign and did much of his organizing in the villages and the *rangs*. It was at this moment that Yves Turcot decided to accept the job of official organizer for the Parti Québécois and the candidate, an agronomist from La Pocatière, came to dinner.

As I followed the thundering rhetoric of the rallies and the calculations of party organizers, I drifted further and further away from the entrepreneurial group that had absorbed my energies since my arrival. Significantly, the manufacturers and some of the large retailers stayed out of the bitter recriminations of the campaign. Their social activities continued, while others increased their social distance from neighbours and acquaintances of the wrong political colour.

In this way, while still living in Saint-Pascal, I had already made my first bow out of the fieldwork situation. The morning after the Liberal victory celebration in the school gymnasium (where three political parties once had hopes of holding a fête), I prepared to leave the town, fresh with the memory of the victors arguing over division of the spoils the night before. After checking out with the postmaster I encountered one of the manufacturers walking into the post office. Looking into the hopelessly overloaded VW he rhetorically asked, "Leaving already? . . . Will you be back?"

I did return several times. Twice, to make a film which served as a report on my research to the townspeople (Gold, 1972); and once to study the reaction to a fire which destroyed Rosaire Gagnon's tannery — and to offer the film as a way of inspiring a capacity audience with confidence in reconstruction. Not un-expectedly a good deal has happened since my departure. The teachers are better organized and some of them programme for community cable television. The tannery has been rebuilt with the help of a million dollar loan and subsidy. The candy factory has quadrupled in size, and a fire ravaged Landry's wool mill. Some people (Henri Fortier) passed away, or moved away. The new economic elite has made numerous compromises with leaders in other social strata and, more recently, with government and with large urban corporations.

The circulation of elites and leadership described in the follow-ing chapters continues. The innovative capitalists who turned a farm centre into a factory town are only one occupational stratum to have consolidated local support in their attempt to reorganize their community in accordance with new values.

Chapter Two provides a socio-demographic background to these changes and a physical sketch of Saint-Pascal and its hinterland. Chapter Three adds a history of each major leadership change to accompany the long term transformation of the regional economic system from mercantilism to capitalism and the redefinition of community-nation relationships. With this historical canvas as a background, Chapter Four delves into the economic organization of town life, particularly of small businesses as the bedrock of Saint-Pascal's economy. A more personal description of what characterizes the entrepreneurial group is taken up again in the chapter on common interest associations (Five). Then in Chapter Six, business, associations, community and leadership are related to politics and political behaviour. In the concluding chapter, the entrepreneurial group, cast in its economic social and political context is reevaluated in the light of several alternatives for implementing social change.

Saint-Pascal: Dramatis Personae[6]

Rosaire Gagnon — tanner and clothing manufacturer; organizer of Saint-Pascal's "leather complex".

Henri Fortier — manufacturer of recapped tires and operator of a chain of tire shops.

Louis-Georges Landry — wool yarn manufacturer with a mail order business and clothing store.

Jacques Maltais — furniture and appliance dealer; operator of the community television system.

Turcotte — investor and silent family partner in farm wagon factory.

Castonguay — trucker, ex-deputy in Quebec and ex-Mayor of Saint-Pascal.

Fleury — horticulturist, distributor and manufacturer of dried flowers.

Curé Pelletier — parish priest.

Hubert Leclerc — School administrator and secondary school teacher.

Alphonse Beaudet — Former parish priest and founder of a classical college for girls.

Footnotes

[1] Anthropological studies on elites in Quebec are virtually non-existent although Hughes (1943) comes closest in his methodology. The tendency in the social sciences, particularly in sociology, has been to study elites through their ideologies (cf. Bélanger, 1974; Cook, 1967; Dumont *et al* 1971-1974; Falardeau, 1960; Rioux, 1973 [1968]).

[2] The dangers of tautology in economic analogies are difficult to avoid. See Davis (1973).

[3] This debate was circumvented with the application of materialist models of peasantry in fieldwork situations (for example, Breton, 1973). The applicability of the peasant model to twentieth-century Quebec is still, in my mind, an unresolved issue.

[4] This factory was later sold to an American firm and then bought up by French-Canadian managed Bombardier who expanded it into the largest factory in the county.

[5] Le Centre d'Accueil — a crisis and social centre for townsmen with a drinking problem.

[6] Except for Beaudet (*) the above names are pseudonyms. For the most part the names recur throughout the book. In several cases, the persons discussed chose their own pseudonym.

Chapter Two
Saint-Pascal: One Spire Among Many

Bel endroit, Saint-Pascal, par sa croupe onduleuse,
Ses côteaux, ses vallons, sa route sinueuse!
C'est la Suisse ou l'Auvergne avec leurs gais chalets,
Leurs monts, leurs près en pente et leurs jardins coquets.
Et pourtant le touriste, à travers ce village,
Passe sans arrêter et descend au rivage.

(J.M. LeMoine, 1872:319)

Written over a century ago, LeMoine's verse portrays Saint-Pascal as an inland community, easily overlooked by an outsider travelling to the riverside resort of Kamouraska. His verse also suggests the perpetual dilemma of the small town in a competition for recognition and reputation within the nation and within its own hinterland. The outcome of Saint-Pascal's competition with other communities has been tempered by economic and geographic factors that have favoured some industries over others and indirectly, some social strata over others. Yet the course of the town's history is not atypical of that taken by other Quebec communities, and in a much more general way, the history of Saint-Pascal is a microcosm of two centuries of change in rural Quebec.

The Physical Setting

The parish of Saint-Pascal is in the Lower Saint Lawrence region, a long strip of Eastern Quebec which runs from the city of Matane in the northeast to the lower reaches of Bellechase in the southwest. An overriding feature of the Lower Saint Lawrence is a landscape sculptured by eroded mountains and glacial activity of the venerable north-south Appalachian chain. Over time, erosion has broken the mountain range into two distinctive physical zones (see Figure 2:1): the *lowlands*, flat and fertile lowland terraces which border the Saint Lawrence and lead into a series of plateaux which gently rise toward the higher ground of the highlands, a broad, hilly peneplain, 1300 to 2000 feet above sea level. These two features of the terrain, the *lowlands* and the *highlands*, correspond almost exactly to the two demographic regions of old and recent settlement (Blanchard, 1935:119). Saint-Pascal lies at the inland limit of the lowlands, its narrow southern perimeter of settlement making the steep jump to the high plain. To the north, steep quartzite croppings rise above the fertile soil of the flat terraces, shielding the town from inspection by riverside motorists.

The Saint-Lawrence and other watercourses have been important factors in the economic history of Kamouraska County. This great waterway is saline the length of the county and residents often refer to its wide expanse as "the sea". Despite a promising maritime past, rocky beaches (*battures*), a coastal freeze-up and shallow water have meant that Saint-Pascal's coastal neighbours are of little maritime importance. Of far greater economic significance are the numerous rivers and streams that run through the forest and fields of the interior. Some of these waterways flow as much as 43 miles parallel to the alignments of rocks along the Saint-Lawrence before making their rapid descents across the lowland plateaux and into the estuary.

These cataracts were important in the development of small service industries. In Saint-Pascal, waterfalls on the Ruisseau des Perles and on the Kamouraska River have long powered tradesmen's mills, and in nearby Saint-Pacôme, the Rivière Ouelle once powered a sizeable sawmill operated by the anglophone Power family. With the availability of cheap hydroelectric power after 1930, these watercourses lost their power-generating importance, which was never substantial due to a variable seasonal flow of water and the absence of significant drops in water level (Blanchard, 1935:172). More important in the present context is the potential that Saint-Pascal's rivers provide for the removal of the acidic wastes of industries and the sewage of an expanding urban population, a use of resources which has led to factionalism, litigation and intervillage disputes.

While water resources have been an important geographical factor in Kamouraska County's history, climate has been another key variable. The severe climate of the Lower Saint Lawrence region has had an important effect on the cycle of human activities. Winter is long, from November to the end of April,

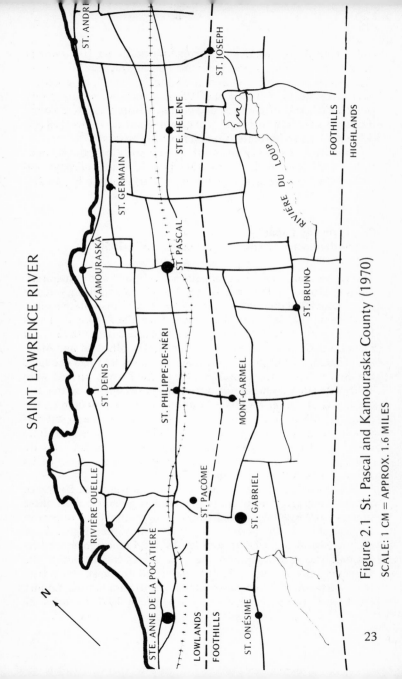

SAINT LAWRENCE RIVER

Figure 2.1 St. Pascal and Kamouraska County (1970)

SCALE: 1 CM = APPROX. 1.6 MILES

23

and a cold humid wind blows from the northeast (the *nordet*) keeping spring temperatures lower than in the Quebec City region. The severity of winter closed the roads to anything except a *carriole* or sleigh, and until the 1950s, farmers waited for plows to signal the end of another long winter. Before the Intercolonial Railroad was built through the Lower Saint Lawrence (1858), only sleigh trains prevented complete winter isolation.

The major features of the north-central portion of the Kamouraska landscape (lowlands, plateaux, rivers, roads, railways and settlements) are brought together in the large map in Figure 2:1.

People on the Land:
The Settlement of Kamouraska County 1674-1850

The Lower Saint Lawrence was sparsely populated by migratory hunting groups at the time of the French colonization, but the native peoples of this region have left little more than place-names.

Kamouraska, for example, derives from the Algonquin terms for "there are reeds by the water". Parish registers (from 1692-1727) mention baptisms and burials of Montagnais, Mic Mac and Malecites (Paradis, 1948:2). The Algonquin cultures that had occupied the South Shore for centuries before the French arrived were either relocated elsewhere or were quickly decimated by the new occupants of the region. Blanchard thus refers to a vacuum on the open frontier of settlement: "The white man was able to settle at will along the banks of the estuary " (1935:138 trans.), an effort that Curé Paradis describes as a baptism of a pagan land by courageous French colonists who brought God's mass to its waiting shores (Paradis, 1948:11).

Nonetheless European settlement of the Lower Saint Lawrence was considerably more controlled and regimented than these sources suggest. This is well illustrated in the four European applications of the Algonquin place name: the seigneury of Kamouraska, a feudal fief awarded by the French governor; the Catholic parish of Kamouraska that was later erected within the seigneury; the village of Saint-Louis de[1] Kamouraska that later blossomed around the parish church; and Kamouraska County the French regime in Quebec, and which in 1970 included 27 coastal and inland communities, many of which were carved out of the original parish by the reeds. Schematically the four Kamouraskas (village, parish, seigneury and county) are physical spaces of increasing size, each smaller space being enclosed by the next larger one. In practice the name was extended outward as the county was settled.

The Seigneury of Kamouraska dates back to 1674 when Frontenac awarded a domain to Olivier Morel, Seigneur of La Durantaye, and a captain in the Carignan Regiment. Morel did not develop his new fief, but sold his rights to a man who would encourage settlement, Charles Aubert de La Chesnaye, Seigneur of Rivière-du-Loup. The new seigneur had the land surveyed by the *arpenteur* Le Rouge, and riverside settlement began in the 1690s. At this time, the few dozen families who inhabited the seigneury awaited the arrival of a curé (1709) and a full complement of seigneurial services. It was not until the last years of New France that Kamouraska had its first resident seigneur — Pascal Jacques Taché — who built a seigneurial manor and a water powered mill. Assuming their seigneurial prerogatives, the Taché family collected rents (*cens*) for lands farmed within their seigneury and for the use of the harnessed energy of their watercourses.

The first settlers were peasant farmers, *habitant* migrants from the Ile d'Orléans, Beaupré and Beaumont who reached Kamouraska in 1711. By the end of the French Régime (1763), ten thousand Europeans had settled on the lowlands of the Saint Lawrence's south shore. Their farms and villages formed a long thin line from Beaumont in the west to Kamouraska which was, at the time of the Conquest, the eastern frontier of agricultural New France. These settlers cleared and burned the lowland forests. They planted cereal crops, practising a form of intensive agriculture as land was thought to be in nearly unlimited supply. Emigration and the fission of communities was encouraged by the preferred practice of allowing only one son, generally "chosen from about the middle of the sequence of children" to inherit his father's patrimony (Miner, 1939:79). Inevitably, a high birth rate coupled with immigration from the west forced the riverside parishes to reach culturally-imposed population limits. By the late eighteenth century some land-seeking Kamouraskiens were migrating inland to the rocky piedmont, establishing a second, and later a third tier of settlement.

The resulting grid of riverside settlements is an important legacy of the economic social realities of the seigneurial regime. The *rang* system (row system) as it came to be called, is best associated with the relative positions of man and river (Desfontaine, 1964). The Saint Lawrence was the main line of communication in New France and, as riverside land was valuable, the seigneurial domains did not extend as far along a well-defined waterfront as they did inland to an ill-defined frontier.

A long ribbon of farms stretched along the shoreline and the homes of the *habitant* settlers were close to each other, extending far into the interior. As settlement was directed inland, parallel rows or *rangs* of farms were established. Each successive *rang* follows the geometric pattern of the first *rang* and a *route* follows each *rang* in its course parallel to the river. Another road (chemin) connects the interior *rangs* with the main riverside route (the first *rang*).

Rang neighbours live within talking, marrying and politicking distance of one another. It was the *rang*, not the parish or village that formed the earliest and most basic social unit of rural Quebec. *Rang* dwellers united to support the parish that was closest them. This became difficult with the extension of settlement into the interior and created factionalism within the parishes over the division of resources. However, church expansion in the period after the Conquest was unrivalled by any developments under French colonial rule when civil authorities and the lucrative fur trade confined and even discouraged the type or unbridled agricultural settlement that was taking place in the more populated British colony in New England.

With the removal of civil barriers to the extension of the parish system, the burgeoning parish of Kamouraska, 5800 strong in 1813, was destined to a series of fissions that created new parishes. Thus when the third and fourth *rangs* of the parish of Kamouraska, already heavily settled in 1831 by 1904 habitants (Barnard, 1961: 98), petitioned Mgr. Panet in February of 1826 to set up their own parish (Rapport de 1934:349), the Bishop granted their request after a brief inquiry by Curé Viau of Rivière Ouelle. The canonic erection of the new parish of Saint-Pascal (or Saint-Paschal, in the spelling of that era) was declared on June 7th, 1827 and another little community was given its *clocher* (steeple) and launched as a distinctive and united civil-religious entity. This unity is captured by a cleric who gives a physical description of the parish over a century later:

> A chapel was built in the middle of the third *rang* which, at this point, must make a double twist to avoid a rock to the east and a great rocky ridge to the south. The village thus grew up next to the church on the "Z" formed by the road . . . You have to gò south on to the high rocky ledge beyond which are the fourth and fifth *rangs*. From there, all of the territory of Saint-Pascal appears in a panorama: the roads, the fields and the hillocks in relief, the homes which can no longer hide in the valleys, bouquets of trees climbing the slopes, and the mountains which protect the town without isolating it from the rest of the world. In this material parish, there is the religious and civil parish, the groups of the living who have succeeded their fathers and who do not wish to degenerate . . .
>
> (C.N.D., 1947a: XXI-II)

Directly behind the church and on available spaces along its sides, are the graves of the early inhabitants of the parish. The dead remained close to the living until lack of space motivated parishioners to open a second cemetery further west of the church. Towering above the ceremonial centre is the silver steeple, a symbol of the life space of the parish.

The parish has always included both the village and the farmland around it and was long a religious, political and educational entity. The curé, a spiritual and temporal leader, resides next to the church in his sprawling wood and later brick *presbytère*. Streets and buildings surrounding the church are named after early curés and the town's influential families, including the mayor's family. The stately grey buildings, of what was until recently Curé Beaudet's classical college and convent for girls, stretch eastward from the church and join groomed farmlands, themselves once part of the economic unit of the convent.

After the founding of the parish of Saint-Pascal in 1827, the parish of Kamouraska was left with only the first and second *rangs* of its original boundaries. Saint-Pascal, left with ample land in the interior, was whittled down to size by the founding of six neighbouring parishes between 1833 and 1893,[2] leaving only a few miles of farms in the third, fourth and fifth *rangs* of settlement and maintaining the parish population at around 2000. The resulting three tiers of settlement — riverine, plateau and highland — created a grid of argentine steeples which pierce the sky over the

27

arable lands between "the sea" and the Appalachian foothills (see Figure 2.2).

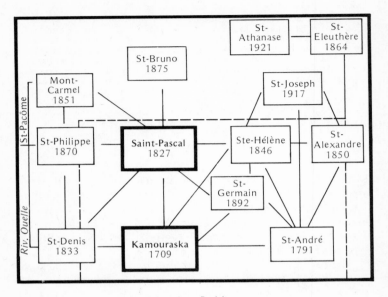

Figure 2.2   Kamouraska and Daughter Parishes
Dotted line defines the Seigneury of Kamouraska

Inland Frontiers or New England Mills?
Population Trends before 1918

Most of the present day parishes of Kamouraska County were already settled by 1871 and the frontier of settlement was to the south, on the inhospitable highland terrain of the Laurentian shield. The County's population reached a peak (22,181 in 1881) and steadily dropped until after World War I. The decline until the end of the nineteenth century may be directly attributed to emigration to other regions of Quebec and to New England. At this time, those who defined national ideologies in Quebec were committed to agrarian ideologies which proclaimed that "the fields belonged to the French Canadians" (Listeur, 1970). The social movement that accompanied the ideology — *colonisation* — continued to encourage the establishment of French-Canadian farming communities in both unsettled and occupied regions of Quebec and Canada. But there was already a shortage of good land on the south shore. One of Saint-Pascal's first curés, the Abbé Nicolas-Tolentin Hébert, led a historically important *colonisation* drive to settle the country around Lac Saint-Jean on the north shore of the Saint-Lawrence. Others moved to the rocky hill country to the south and over the border to New England; but the population continued to increase.

Large families were domestic units of production that were disengaged from the market economy and provided a continuity of labour throughout most of the later adult life of a farm couple. High birth rates were also encouraged by nineteenth century clergy as a *revanche des berceaux* (revenge of the cradle) against the English. This ideological position of elites provides an additional explanation for the prolonged period of unusually high birth rates in Eastern Quebec. The lowland frontier parishes had a birth-rate of 49.5 per thousand fertile women in 1790 that remained high (46.4 per thousand) in a more settled year, 1871 (Blanchard, 1935:146). Given the previously-mentioned inheritance practices, a continual population surplus was available both to colonize daughter settlements and for emigration. The balance between high birthrates and emigration was a precarious one. By 1891, emigration had reduced the population of both Saint-Pascal and neighbouring parishes by nine percent from the 1871 census levels. Clearly the Lower Saint Lawrence and Kamouraska County could not provide an agrarian vocation for all of its inhabitants within the limits of an unchanged technology and production system (cf. Miner, 1939:148). The towns provided few alternatives, although until after World War One the highlands grew at a faster rate than the coastal lowlands.

The industrialization of neighbouring New England resulted in a major population outlet for the inhabitants of Eastern Quebec. The geographer Raoul Blanchard (1935:191) has estimated that between 1850 and 1914 approximately 500,000 Québécois migrated to New England. He contends that these migrations changed the material culture of the farmer and enabled him to emerge from cycles of debt. Throughout his work on Eastern Quebec, Blanchard carefully distinguishes the old fertile lowland

29

parished from their less prosperous highland kin, the inland frontier being the most affected by migration to the United States. Miner (1939:41-42) observes that migration was temporary for many of the inhabitants of the older and soil-rich lowland parish of Saint-Denis, where "around forty adult parishioners spent a few years working in New England, but even this gave them little that was novel enough to live in their memories".

Despite this image of stability, much of the emigration to New England was permanent. There is hardly a family in Saint-Pascal which does not have relatives in Nashua (*Nashway* in local dialect), Manchester, Rhode Island or Maine. In some *rangs*, four or more families left in a single year. This diaspora shows up in Figure 2.3 as the parish of Saint-Pascal and its area of influence continue to lose population, although at a reduced rate, until the First World War. Meanwhile, in Saint-Pascal, Curé Beaudet had opened a classical college for girls; electric power came to Eastern Quebec; and the logging industry, both French Canadian and English Canadian, became firmly established on a number of interior rivers. The new industry provided winter work for farmers almost everywhere in Kamouraska county. With the expansion of its general stores and workshops Saint-Pascal became a service centre — strategically located on the railroad line from Quebec to the Maritime provinces. The village of Kamouraska, with no classical college, no railroad and no forested frontier, withered in economic importance. On the eve of the Great War, it lost its status as county seat to a more promising Saint-Pascal.

Emigration to New England slowed down after the First War and migrants from Quebec's rural areas began to fill the province's cities. Hughes (1938) hypothesized that the continuation of the rural parish system and of the family farm depended on the capacity of the cities to absorb surplus rural population. This seemed to be a reasonable prediction for its time, for in the post-depression years it was still possible to think of the family farm as a viable economic alternative. Hughes could be supported by other observers. Léon Gérin (1897, 1938) had noted earlier that the family-farm economy was unstable in a market society and in Saint-Denis de Kamouraska Miner found the number of landless wage labourers (*journaliers*) had been steadily increasing (1939: 253). Both Hughes and Miner recognized an imbalance in an equilibrated system; French-Canadian social institutions and dominant ideologies supported an ideal of a rural society, but the presence of landless labourers with few economic alternatives threatened the egalitarian base of the rural parish and laid the foundation for the emergence of a class system.

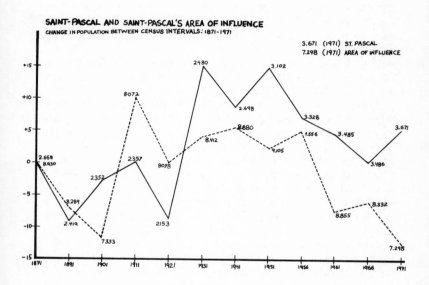

SAINT-PASCAL AND SAINT-PASCAL'S AREA OF INFLUENCE
CHANGE IN POPULATION BETWEEN CENSUS INTERVALS: 1871-1971

3.671 (1971) ST. PASCAL
7.298 (1971) AREA OF INFLUENCE

1881 not included since Saint-Pascal here includes the unorganized highland cantons of Woodbridge and Painchaud (non-seigneurial lands distributed by the English). 1881 shows a general rise in population for all parishes including the lowlands that lost population and later decayed. Not included in these calculations from 1901 on, is the village of Andréville, the population of which constantly averages about 550. The effect of its exclusion minimizes the 1911 increase for the area of influence.

31

What neither Hughes nor Miner could predict was that the rural-urban balance, held in check throughout the depression years, would tip toward the depopulation of rural areas. The exodus from the farms was to benefit both the large cities and local service centres. Saint-Pascal, like other farm service centres of the Lower Saint Lawrence expanded commercially with the opening of several new general stores, a cooperative feed mill and a butter-making plant. The eastern portion of the village swelled with an influx of landless day labourers — the *journaliers* when not employed in one of the scant service jobs in town, relied on winter wood-cutting in the highland forests or as far afield as the St.-Maurice and Abitibi regions. Road building and construction projects provided some summer work.

For the first time since 1871 Saint-Pascal's population began to increase (see Figure 2.3). Between 1920 and 1930 it experienced a population increase of 13.2 percent. The depression years mark the beginning of a twenty year expansion of Saint-Pascal's population while its hinterland registered only marginal gains.

This gradual growth of Saint-Pascal that began before World War II led to increasing occupational differentiation within what had for over a century been a single civil and religious unit, a parish community. Merchants and labourers were called upon to support the modernization of a village: the expansion of its school system and the creation of municipal laws to generate taxes for the provision of water sewage and other services. Meanwhile many farmers remained entrenched in their *rangs*, the fortunate heirs of their family farm. This dualism within the parish — egalitarian production-orientated small farmers and increasingly stratified consumption-orientated merchants, artisans and labourers — nurtured changes in leadership that favoured the middle-class elite of *notables* in the village,while a dwindling farm population became socially isolated from rapidly changing village institutions.

Even the youngest Pascaliens were affected. During the week, farm children walked to the *écoles du rang*, one-room school houses on their own *rang*, rarely more than a mile from home, while village children attended a "model" school located near the church at the centre of the village. Sunday catechism classes provided one of the few occasions for all of the parish children to meet; but the rural children did not fare well with the village children and fighting sometimes broke out between the two groups.

Parents were often no more sympathetic to each other. Villager and farmer still met in the large stone church to celebrate Sunday mass as a unified parish. But the civil-religious synthesis of the parish was irrevocably ended when farmers were unwilling to pay for the new village services, and the local political process was stalemated. In 1939, at the request of the villagers, the parish was divided into two municipalities (Village and Paroisse). Like virtually every other service centre in Eastern Quebec, the Village of Saint-Pascal became an oasis of town life governed by one set of rules and a lifestyle that was similar to other service centres in the Lower Saint Lawrence. It was surrounded by the new munici- pality of the Paroisse, which is a legal fiction — not a community, but a coalition of farmers living in three separate and distinct *rangs*. Their church, their agricultural society and its exposition grounds, and their commercial suppliers were still centred in the village.

In the depression years the general merchants became important as parish leaders, and as their ties with urban suppliers multiplied, Saint-Pascal was no longer linked to national social networks only through the good offices of the curé and those professionals who alternated in political office. With the rise of the Union Nationale in the mid-thirties, Saint-Pascal's petit bourgeoisie of merchants and other small tradesmen had a strong voice in Quebec City. Their new affluence and power in Kamouraska County was partially due to the commercialization of agriculture and a gradual shift from domestic production to the consumption of store-bought goods. In the village, those who would first feel the effects of this technological transformation were associated with the local distri- bution system of the era of semi-subsistence production. Artisans who served the farmer — the millers, the blacksmiths, the wheel- wrights, the tanner and harness-maker, and the butter-maker, were all faced with a declining demand for their services.

With the accelerated commercialization of agricultural produc- tion during World War II, tractors began to replace horses and the large horse market on the parish limits gave way in importance to agricultural implement dealers in the village. Fortunately, in 1949 Horace Miner decided to make a brief return visit to neighbouring Saint-Denis where he noted important technological changes. Saint-Denis was also becoming dependent on Saint-Pascal where merchants' exhibits at county fairs offered a wider range of con- sumer goods and farm machinery (Miner, 1939:257-8).

> All the other changes in material culture also represent a loss in self-sufficiency. Such increasing dependence upon the outside is but the local view of the growing interdependence of the parts of a larger social whole.

However Miner concludes that "The economic shift took place with little alteration in the old pattern of production. High prices, subsidies and family allowances poured cash into the parish. The principal production change was the increase in the number of milk cows and hogs" (*Ibid.*:267)[4].

The agricultural boom of the war years also meant prosperity for the growing village. Even though forestry was still the only large non-agricultural industry in the region, the population of the Village of Saint-Pascal increased by an unprecedented 15 percent from 1941 to 1951. The surrounding hamlets and farms were barely able to hold their own with an increase of 2.5 per cent over the same period. Throughout the forties the birthrate dropped as Quebec began to fall in line with national birth-rate trends. The heaviest losers were the rural areas, although the entire county was affected by a continuous out-migration of youth that continues as this book is being written.

Thus, the Fifties were a period of severe depletion, as farmers in the interior or on marginal lands abandoned their patrimonies to move to Saint-Pascal, La Pocatière or one of Quebec's urban centres. Kamouraska County as a whole increased in population by only 1.7 percent from 1950 to 1960 in the face of a calamitous demographic exodus which involved almost one in every five people in the region (see Table 2.1).

The demographic picture for Saint-Pascal is not nearly as discouraging. The parish experienced a higher birth rate and a positive overall rate of migration. As a result, Saint-Pascal was over a quarter larger on the eve of the sixties — mostly due to the centralization of mercantile services and the proliferation of small specialized commerce. The merchants were by this time firmly established as the village elite, but the artisans had less to gain from commercial and technological changes. As for industry, the few social scientists to visit Saint-Pascal around 1960 were not at all aware of any industrialization on the horizon.[5]

Nevertheless the fifties was a period of important, if less visible change in Saint-Pascal. Rosaire Gagnon was working in the local power company office or with the Rural Catholic Youth in

Montreal rather than in the Gagnon family's small tannery. Henri Fortier gave up running the convent farm and bought out a small tire-retreading shop. He too found himself involved in the youth movement with Rosaire Gagnon. Louis-Georges Landry, older and with less formal education than either Fortier or Gagnon, was working in his father's wool mill and was involved in the organization of a fledgling Centre Social, but was not in Rural Catholic Youth although its members actively supported the new Centre. Important friendships were being welded out of common organizational energies, and some of these friendships managed to cross the rigid barriers of age and peer groups.

Table 2.1

Kamouraska County and Town of Saint-Pascal
Migration and Natural Increase 1951-1966
as a Percentage of the Population

	Net Natural Increase	Real Increase	Net Migration
	in percentages		
1951-1960			
Town of Saint-Pascal	23.5	27.35	3.85
Kamouraska County	19.8	1.7	−18.1
1961-1965			
Town of Saint-Pascal	7.7	3.4	− 4.3
Kamouraska County	6.2	−2.0	− 8.2
1966-1970			
Town of Saint-Pascal	5.4	13.4	8.0
Kamouraska County	4.4	−1.3	− 5.7

Source — Vital Statistics Yearbooks, Statistics Canada.

Although migrants were trickling into Saint-Pascal, the population of the Village gained perceptively only from 1961 to 1966

(Figure 2.4). The population of Saint-Pascal's Paroisse declined in absolute terms for the first time since the 1940s and the county as a whole suffered a net loss due to emigration (Table 2.1). Between 1950 and 1960 the exodus was heaviest in the twenty to forty-year-old group (males and females) with the group between twenty-five and twenty-nine losing nearly half its number over the ten year period.[6]

Relative Growth of the Village and *Paroisse* of Saint-Pascal: 1941-1971

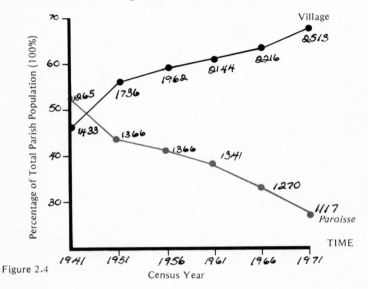

Figure 2.4

Village vs. Paroisse

The population statistics of the early sixties cannot tell us about Fortier's expansion of his retreading shop into a small factory. Gagnon's purchase and reorganization of his father's leather shop and Landry's redefining of the goals of his father's wool mill. For despite these industrial starts in a time of economic boom, the fledgling factories had not yet begun their large-scale recruitment of labour and skilled managers, workers or technicians. In the early Sixties, there was a gap between the early rush of the modernization and the industrialization that had come to Eastern Kamouraska County as it had to many but not all areas of Quebec.[7] The effects of these changes on demography and social organization were still embryonic.

Table 2.2

Number of Households in Saint-Pascal and
Average Household Size: 1951-1971

Year	Households	Percentage Increase from Previous Census	Average Household Size
1951	350		4.8
1956	393	11.2	4.8
1961	440	12.0	4.5
1966	482	9.6	4.3
1971	620	28.6	3.9

Source — Census of Canada.

The major expansion of the factories, aided by generous subsidies from the Federal and Provincial governments, did not come until 1966, when the Village offïcially became a town. By 1971, the number of households had increased by 28.6 percent over 1966 (see Table 2.2: Household size drops to 3.9). The outflow of youth between fifteen and thirty was reduced significantly from the previous decade. The town continued to grow at the expense of its hinterland. With a surge of in-migration the real increase in population over the five year period is an unprecedented 13.4 per cent, while the county as a whole, including its two industrializing service centres, had experienced a net loss of 1.3 percent. Kamouraska, an agricultural county in the eyes of government planners, had experienced a seemingly-sudden industrialization. Federal-provincial plans for regional development that were to have included the county with the development plan for all Eastern Quebec,[8] had to be precipitously changed to emphasize and legitimize an *ad hoc* industrialization and urbanization that was occurring in *every* service centre in the entire Grand Portage region that extends north to Rivière-du-Loup and east to Cabano.

Saint-Pascal and other service centres in this region had, by 1971, experienced an equally important shift. There was a realignment of the class structure by the replacement of the old middle class of merchants and professionals by a new middle class of industrialists and administrators who had been sent in to manage the services that were centralized in Saint-Pascal. This new strata was quick to establish its own voluntary associations, setting up an identity for itself. Through mechanisms of social control it kept its members faithful to their new status and developed means of recruiting potential members and support from allied groups. Gagnon, Fortier and their allies such as Landry became the core of an entrepreneurial group, a new economic elite that reached out to participate in the social networks and values of a national new middle class.

Meanwhile industrialization had created a large stratum of workers. By 1969, eighty percent of working townspeople were involved in commerce or in manufacturing and approximately forty percent of this work force was drawn to the town from surrounding farms and villages.[9] The countryside became an appendage of the town as men and women turned from agriculture to shop work.

In all, the combined labour force of the town's factories had increased from several dozen men in 1960 to approximately four hundred in 1969. They produced over five million dollars a year in leather, tires, candy, wool, wagons, pork, butter and horticultural products.

Before the growth of the industries the only white collar or professional persons in Saint-Pascal were a doctor, a dentist, a notary, three priests and a changing group of nuns. The construction of a regional secondary school in Saint-Pascal (1958) marked the beginning of an influx of lay and clerical teachers — over 125 of them by 1970 when one in five families in the town were in some way connected with the burgeoning school system.[10] There was a numerically smaller but equally important increase in white collar workers both in industry and in new government offices such as the regional Highway Department garage, the Provincial Police detachment (*Sûreté du Québec*), a health department office (*Unité Sanitaire*), the town clerk, the county registry office, secretaries, accountants and a sizeable staff of clerks in the bank and *Caisse Populaire* (credit union). There were also the financial and bureaucratic professionals who come with modernization — the bank manager, accountants, insurance brokers — everything one might expect to find in a town that had industries and a range of regional governmental services. To add to the growing "main street" atmosphere of the old village, both the provincial deputy to the Quebec National Assembly and the Federal Member of Parliament maintained their homes and private offices in Saint-Pascal.

Saint-Pascal as an Industrial Town

Becoming a central place and the redefining of the occupational structure have had the effect of irrevocably altering the physical unity of the old parish that was so deliberately crafted around features of church, farms, river and mountains. Even the sacred centre of the parish has undergone rapid transformation since 1966. The convent is now an expanding regional secondary school and a sizeable old people's home has been built by local contractors next to the older grey buildings once occupied by nuns and their select group of students. The one-room *écoles du rang* are now closed, and so is the old village "model" school.[11] A new regional elementary school, built behind the church, already has a temporary addition which is almost as large as the school itself. Twice daily on school days a fleet of privately operated buses motors in students from farms and villages as far away as fifteen miles. Another drastic change to the village centre is a gleaming brick and glass bank which local businessmen have constructed directly opposite the front door of the tin-roofed Québecois church. West of the bank is a rocky prominence around which are built the stylish office-homes of the few parish professionals, the dentist, doctor and notary (see Figure 2.5).

We have seen that the village centre grew around a "Z" turn of the third *rang*. The third *rang* later became a major provincial highway and is now an access road to the four-lane Trans-Canada Highway. Its paved thoroughfare is bordered by a number of small groceries, general stores, auto and implement dealers, and several government offices. Close to the heart of the town are the three remaining general stores. Most of the older family enterprises are close to the post office, the one place in town which someone from every family and business visits on a weekday.

Several of the residential *quartiers* have an identity of their own. The best known of these neighbourhoods, 'Tit New York[12],

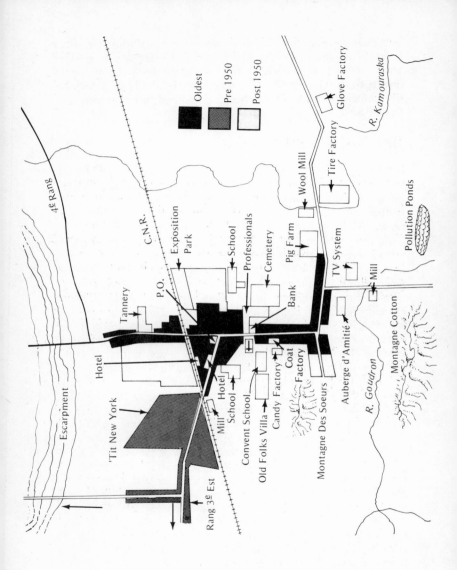

Figure 2.5   Ville St.-Pascal *Kamouraska* (1970)

is a collection of brightly-painted frame houses on a gentle hill leading eastward from a railroad crossing which intersects the main highway. This *quartier* has been considered a workingman's neighbourhood and many of its residents migrated to Saint-Pascal as employment opportunities increased. Immediately to the west, and north of the CNR tracks is a new subdivision of ample urban-style bungalows which have been built since 1960 for local trades-men and manufacturers. South of the tracks, on the extreme west of the town lies another, larger suburban-style subdivision that includes three multi-unit or low-rise apartment buildings put up by the entrepreneurial builder of the bank to house newcomers and newlyweds. All of these buildings have created an urabn agglomeration surrounding the thin older core of the parish. They house the owners and managers of the factories and stores, skilled workers and tradesmen, teachers and white collar employ-ees. Taken together, they give the observer the impression of recent, haphazard and unexpected growth. The placement of industry confirms this observation.

Industry is everywhere in Saint-Pascal and yet at the time of my fieldwork it was concentrated in no single location. Only the towering cooperative feed mill is on the railway line. As for the other industries, someone jokingly suggested at a public meeting that the best way of finding them is by their odour. Until destroyed by fire in 1971, the original Gagnon tannery, which then employed about 200 workers, operated out of the founder's home to which his grandson, Rosaire Gagnon, had attached sheds for the commercial tanning and finishing of leather. With expan-sion, supplying water to the tannery and removing acidic wastes became a serious problem. Ultimately, sewage from the town and the tannery was funnelled into four, large treatment ponds off the Kamouraska River on the north edge of the town at considerable economic and political expense to the town. Another volume of chemical wastes was flushed almost directly into the Kamouraska River by a small and relatively unmechanized tannery that Gagnon's older brother with nine co-workers run out of a small shed east of 'Tit New York .

Near the centre of town is the oldest industry, the Turcotte wagon shop, recognizeable by its sprawling mustard colour wooden sheds and uniform sepia brick buildings put up by its own labourers during slack periods. Founded in 1857 and modernized in 1946, this family enterprise has a stable work force of 20 employees who turn out relatively small quantities of farm wagons and medium-weight metal goods.

Near the wagon shop, nestled behind the church and the convent school, is a small candy factory, transformed from a family-operated bakery. Another landmark in the north of Saint-Pascal is the community television antenna built by furniture-dealer Maltais in 1965 on the rocky summit of the Montagne à Cotton, where legend claims, a Benedictine hermit once lived.[13] At the mountain's base, close to the new four-lane highway, is the neon-fringed Friendship Inn (Auberge de l'Amitié), a cooperative project of businessmen and the local Industrial Society.

West of the mountain, at the town limits, is a large commercial pig farm whose owners also run a feed mill to grind the grain for 14,000 pigs, another problem for the overworked municipal sewage system.

Just outside the town limits, in the Municipality of the Paroisse, Louis-Georges Landry's mill has adapted a small production of yarn to a thriving mail order business. A neighbouring wool mill was not successful in its attempt to adapt to the changing market requirements and after a ruinous bankruptcy in the 1950s its buildings were taken over by an equally unsuccessful canning plant. When Henri Fortier's tire retreading factory outgrew the confines of his service station, it became the third and only successful occupant. Between 1962 and 1970, Fortier's tire factory and Gagnon's tannery became two of the most important industries in the entire Lower Saint Lawrence jointly employing over 300 people and indirectly providing jobs for many others in mercantile and service trades. Castonguay's trucking firm grew steadily from 1931. In the early 1960s he centralized the firm's operations and truck fleet in Montreal, leaving only a shed and freight yards near the agricultural exposition grounds. The presence of his firm and private office, together with his role as mayor and provincial deputy was nevertheless invaluable to most of the new industries for providing dependable, regularly-scheduled transportation links to urban markets, and even more so to Fortier's tire factory as a large local outlet for retread tires. Throughout the postwar period Castonguay was an important local employer when there were few regional alternatives other than cutting wood in the highlands.

If this relatively modest but rapid growth of economic activity in small and remote Saint-Pascal strikes the reader as unusual, it has appeared all the more incredible and even tenuous to commercial travellers from Montreal and Quebec City. That Saint-Pascal should *modernize* can be explained on a macro-level. In all of Quebec, the period between 1960 and 1966 was one of unprecedented state-centralized social development especially in the field of education. This does not explain why, in the same period, Saint-Pascal and many other similar communities have *industrialized under local capitalist initiative* when some towns have declined in prosperity, have been industrialized by multinational outsiders, or have launched cooperative industries with less success.

It is my contention that the evidence for some kind of critical mass that brought about the changes of the sixties will not flow easily out of this brief review of demographic and economic change. The centralization of services in Saint-Pascal and the emergence of indigenous industry are, however, related to a circulation of personnel in the power structure of the county and the entry of new institutional forms and values. As standard bearers of a new order, Rosaire Gagnon and Henri Fortier relied on legitimization by an older order. Theirs was not the first such attempt at change. A grasp of the social history of changing leadership over 150 years places the population movements and production changes into the context of the control of dominant groups, of the bases of their power and, ultimately, of their eventual demise. The interplay between the national and regional social systems here becomes critical. It could be said that certain national changes such as industrial capitalism would *eventually* have come to *every* town and region of Quebec. But as the next chapter illustrates, the path of development, *no matter what its chosen objective may be,* is a highly contested one. The losers are not clearly replaced and do not suddenly yield all of their power and legitimacy. As Pareto's foxes endlessly discover, victory has its own social costs.

Footnotes

[1] The name of a patron saint (for example, *Saint-Louis* de Kamouraska) or the descriptive suffix that identifies a community (for example, Saint-Denis *de-la-Boutellerie*) is dropped in common usage. Some place names do not change — Saint-Jean-Port-Joli; others have no official descriptive suffix — Saint-Pascal, although one may unofficially be added — Saint-Pascal *de Kamouraska.*

[2] The political struggles creating new parishes in Kamouraska should be researched from the point of view of the economic expansion of the county and competition for scarce resources by competing factions.

[3] Saint-Pascal's area of influence: communities that support Saint-Pascal politically in "obtaining" things from government (see Chapter Six). They use Saint-Pascal's regional schools and shops (Mount-Carmel, Saint-Philippe, Saint-Denis, Kamouraska, Saint-Bruno, Saint-Germain, Sainte-Hélène, Saint-Joseph, Saint-André).

[4] The best description of the status of the family farm in Kamouraska after 1945 is Marc-Adélard Tremblay's detailed survey of a large sample of farms throughout the county (Tremblay, 1950).

[5] Here I rely on private communications from Hubert Guindon, Marc-Adélard Tremblay and Gérard Lapointe (1960) in his sociological study of the Diocese of Sainte-Anne de la Pocatière.

[6] Population Loss of Five Age Cohorts, Kamouraska County: 1941-1971

		1951		1961		1971
Age Group	Size	As percentages of 1941	Size	As percentages of 1951	Size	As percentages of 1961
15-19	2695	85.6	2931	85.0	3150	90.1
20-24	2249	69.1	1789	60.6	2340	66.9
25-29	1844	60.5	1445	53.6	1765	60.2
30-34	1687	70.5	1542	68.6	1285	71.8
35-39	1453	78.7	1557	84.5	1215	84.1

[7] All areas of Quebec, especially Eastern Quebec, were not equally affected by this expansionary period. Much of the Gaspé and the highland parishes of Kamouraska remained little changed from the previous century except for the centralization and superficial modernization that was earlier described for Saint-Pascal before 1960.

[8] The plan for the development of Eastern Quebec as set forth by the B.A.E.Q. and subsequently revised to include more than the "rationalization" of traditional sectors.

[9] Compiled from factory employment records.

[10] Compiled from municipal voting lists for 1970 that list age, address and occupation of all adults aged twenty-one and over.

[11] The model village schools were constructed by the Duplessis administration and complemented a renewed programme for the building of one–room *écoles du rang* placed on the rows of farms that fan out from the village.

[12] A member of a merchant family told me that this *quartier* looks very

much like a city to a child looking at the hill over the railroad tracks at night through a frosty window. However I doubt that this is the origin of the place name.

[13] Paradis, quoting F.X. Garneau (1882:197-8), notes that Georges-François Poulet, a Benedictine monk, took refuge in a tree house in this area until a long winter of heavy snows drove him out under the pretext that his cabin had burned. He was then entertained by numerous religious institutions and by important families until a letter from Europe reached the governor denouncing the monk as a Jansenist heretic who was wanted by the superior of the monastery from which he had secretly escaped. He would not repent and was excommunicated and exiled from Canada. The legend of the hermit lived on — a tale of missing sheep, a *bon-vivant* who treated visitors to champagne and who lived from theft and bootlegging until M. le Curé succeeded in making him leave. Some even attribute the cross on the mountain top to the work of the hermit (Paradis, 1948:344-45 from M. Dérome, Réminiscences et portraits, *Le Foyer Canadien*, 1866).

Chapter Three
Seigneurs, Notables and Industrialists:
Changing Leadership in Saint-Pascal
from 1800 to 1970

An important insight gained from the study of Saint-Pascal is that, like ocean waves[1], small town elites in Quebec have been internally-unified microcosms moving through the changing demands of different eras; and just as the crest provides both direction and finality to the wave, the circulation of personnel within an elite and the changes in its external alliances and controllable resources will eventually lead to its downfall. It follows that there are problems in comparing Quebec's industrialized and bureaucratized present with an agrarian and frontier past. The discontinuities between two eras too easily fog over the underlying similarities. To put it plainly, there is no equilibrium that we can construct as prototypical of the "normal" state of Saint-Pascal's social structure or of that of rural Quebec. Any single moment in time would be as illusory as the frozen frame of a film.

This chapter is a series of frozen frames taken at different points in time and then spliced together to build a unified model of changing leadership. Four leadership groups stand out as the most influential elites in Saint-Pascal's history : the seigneurs of the Taché family and their associates in the liberal professions; the curés, leaders of the late nineteenth century; and the professionals and local *notables* who supported them; a mercantile bourgeoisie whose eminence marks the first half of the twentieth centuryqand the small-scale industrialists such as Gagnon and Fortier, who led the new economic elite of the sixties. Each group has encountered opposition from other groups who vied for the same legitimacy and the support of other social strata. Regarded with the advantage of hindsight, there is also an alternation between nation-orientated community elites and those whose status is rooted only in the parish or at best only in the Lower Saint Lawrence region. The first of these elites to be considered, the seigneurs, were part of a national elite whose precarious position in a colonial and colonized society led them to use their resources to occupy the professions, the only lucrative niche left open to them. Thus, the Tachés, seigneurs of Kamouraska, left their legacy not as feudal lords, but as lawyers, notaries, members of parliament, bishops or prime ministers.[2]

Seigneurs and Censitaires[3]

The first resident seigneur of Kamouraska was Pascal Jacques Taché, the son of a French trader ruined by the Seven Years' War, who acquired his estate through an intricate chain of gifts and inheritances that followed the first seigneurial concession (see Figure 3.1). While one branch of his family became eminent in national life, a second branch was more important as a regional gentry; but all of the Tachés long regarded the seigneury of Kamouraska as their "little kingdom" where they were the brokers between the local peasantry and the nation.

Philippe-Aubert de Gaspé, whose family enjoyed a similar status in the up-river seigneury and parish of Saint-Jean-Port-Joli, reminisces about the paternalistic tie between Pascal Taché and his censitaires — the *habitants* of Kamouraska:

> In my youth I knew all the seigneurs in the Quebec area and a large number of those from elsewhere in the province of Lower Canada and I can affirm that they were almost all the same toward their censitaires . . .
> . . . It seems that I have always known M. and Mme Taché. My young friend Paschal, so amiable and charming, enjoyed a familiarity with the habitants of the kind that could conceivably cause annoyance for him . . . but . . . they never failed to provide the respect that they thought was due to the young seigneur.
> I often accompanied Madame Taché, with her son, in the frequent visits that she paid to the poor and to the sick of the seigneury who welcomed her like a charitable deity. Besides the abundant alms that she distributed to poor families . . . she reigned as a sovereign in her seigneury by the very dear bonds of love and gratitude.
> When Madame Taché left church . . . the habitants who were prepared to depart, stopped their horses and a long line of coaches immediately fell into step with hers, following her until the beginning of the avenue that leads to the seigneurial manor . . .
> (De Gaspé, 1866:531-3)

Pascal Taché and his family maintained most of the traditional seigneurial rights.

> At church the seigneur occupied his own raised and padded pew facing the altar. At the Manor house, the *cens* and the *rentes* were

Figure 3.1

The Seigneurs of Kamouraska and the First Four Generations of the Taché Family in Canada

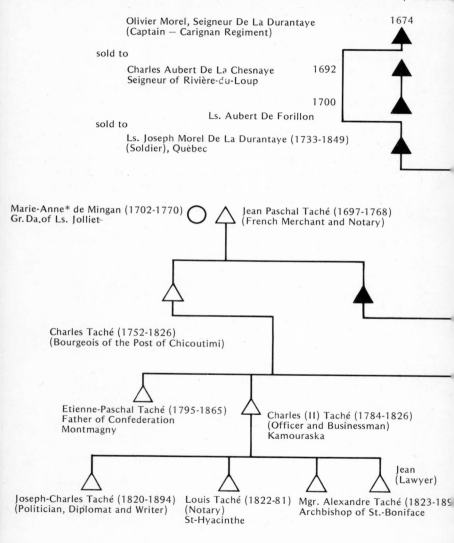

Olivier Morel, Seigneur De La Durantaye
(Captain — Carignan Regiment)   1674

sold to

Charles Aubert De La Chesnaye   1692
Seigneur of Rivière-du-Loup

1700

Ls. Aubert De Forillon

sold to

Ls. Joseph Morel De La Durantaye (1733-1849)
(Soldier), Québec

Marie-Anne* de Mingan (1702-1770)   Jean Paschal Taché (1697-1768)
Gr. Da. of Ls. Jolliet   (French Merchant and Notary)

Charles Taché (1752-1826)
(Bourgeois of the Post of Chicoutimi)

Etienne-Paschal Taché (1795-1865)   Charles (II) Taché (1784-1826)
Father of Confederation   (Officer and Businessman)
Montmagny   Kamouraska

Jean
(Lawyer)

Joseph-Charles Taché (1820-1894)   Louis Taché (1822-81)   Mgr. Alexandre Taché (1823-189
(Politician, Diplomat and Writer)   (Notary)   Archbishop of St.-Boniface
                                     St-Hyacinthe

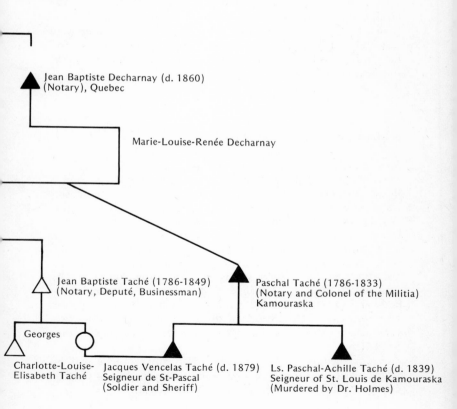

▲
● = inherited or acquired part of all of the Seigneury of Kamouraska and/or Saint-Pascal.

Sources

Bossé, 1971:18; Paradis, 1948:153-164)

given to Henri Hiché
(Merchant and Notary)

Jean Baptiste Decharnay (d. 1860)
(Notary), Quebec

Marie-Louise-Renée Decharnay

Jean Baptiste Taché (1786-1849)
(Notary, Deputé, Businessman)

Paschal Taché (1786-1833)
(Notary and Colonel of the Militia)
Kamouraska

Georges

Charlotte-Louise-
Elisabeth Taché

Jacques Vencelas Taché (d. 1879)
Seigneur de St-Pascal
(Soldier and Sheriff)

Ls. Paschal-Achille Taché (d. 1839)
Seigneur of St. Louis de Kamouraska
(Murdered by Dr. Holmes)

49

still brought to him on Saint-Martin's Day with the same accompaniment of loquacious *censitaires* and squawking capons. Many other long standing privileges such as the communal mill, the corvée and the right to hunt and to fish, continued as they always had. From his manor the seigneur still exercised a very paternal surveillance over his 'serfs'.   (Bossé, 1971:69)

Yet, despite these rights, no habitant on the South Shore paid more than 12 shillings in annual rents and there was little to prevent the "tenant" from leaving or from lashing back a verbal tirade at his feudal landlord if he were overtaken on a roadway.
                                                                      (De Gaspé, *op. cit.*:534-5)

The importance of the seigneurial elite must thus be found elsewhere. The Taché family trained in the traditional liberal professions and active in the post-conquest colonial regime, actively promoted the interests of the Village of Kamouraska with the support of other lawyers, notaries and clerics, some of whom were from seigneurial families. Their local power was based more on their influence and prestige than on their incomplete control of the means of production.

Seigneurs, Professionals and Curés

The erudite group of politicians, notaries and wealthy merchants that gathered in Curé Jacques Varin's large parlour would discuss the intellectual and worldly questions of the day or administer justice when the circuit court met in the county seat (Bossé, 1971: 16). Others would come from the Quebec region and the entire Lower Saint Lawrence to take in the reknowned salt air of Kamouraska (LeMoine, 1871:318) and rest in one of Kamouraska's comfortable inns. As the writer Arthur Buies recalled, in Kamouraska there was "a legion of young educated people, more worldly than most *canadiens* of their era, liberal as hell, absolutely the body and spirit that is needed for the big election campaign next year" (Paradis, 1948:186). Omnipresent at these gatherings were the Tachés and the Seigneur-merchant Chapais from neighbouring Saint-Denis.

From the early 1800s to the 1830s Pascal Taché and his seigneurial team (my term) vigorously campaigned for a classical college. As the surveyor Joseph Bouchette records:

However, disappointment came in 1827 when Monseigneur Panet
rejected the application on the grounds that the parish could not
support a college. The new school was ultimately awarded (1829)
to rival Sainte-Anne de la Pocatière, the seat of the regional diocese, a parish which was scheduled for service by the planned
Intercolonial railroad (*Ibid.*:195-96).

Obviously, new institutions were not available to every parish
in the region, and from the nineteenth century until the 1970s
there has been considerable competition among local communities
for the scarce resources distributed by government, the church and
private industry. Furthermore, each technological development
has had major social consequences. The new railroad, for example,
opened new tourist centres[4] and threatened the well-established
seasonal business in Kamouraska. Rail lines also contributed to
the growth of inland parishes, adding to the original number of
competitors seeking new institutional resources.

Kamouraska was also under internal pressures to fission into
several smaller parishes as the interior settlement continued. First
came Saint-Pascal's (1827) separation which was eventually accepted by both habitant and seigneur. Pascal Taché divided his
seigneury between his two sons, one of whom (Jacques Vencelas
Taché), inherited that part of his father's domain which embraced
the new parish of Saint-Pascal. The new seigneur of Saint-Pascal
then built a small manor house on the third *rang*, but only rarely
did he leave the comfort of Kamouraska.

Only four years later, in 1831, the Chapais family was instrumental in getting the Bishop's permission for a further division
of Kamouraska to found the parish of Saint-Denis. Local loyalties
ran against the plans of the urban clergy, and parishioners in Kamouraska unsuccessfully petitioned against further fission on the
grounds that this "would necessitate a loss of revenue to the
fabrique". There were also "more sacred considerations" involved
in the relocation of the parish church and cemetery (Barnard,
1961a:113).

Neither partition could detract from Kamouraska's final moment of glory — the acquisition of a permanent district superior

court. In 1851, the three doctors, three notaries and several important merchants successfully banded together with the seigneurs and exerted pressure on Lord Elgin, the Governor General of Canada, to confirm Kamouraska as the site for a regional courthouse. Jean-Baptiste Taché gave over his manor to provide appropriate quarters and a cohort of lawyers, judges, notaries and sheriffs arrived to staff the court and a county registration office (Paradis, 1948:183-6). But Kamouraska was no longer at the centre of the region's development. The seaside village quickly witnessed the collapse of its new institutions and the displacement of its elite of professionals and merchants. The influence of the local clergy, however, did not wane as can be seen from developments in Saint-Pascal.

By 1851, popular sentiment in this new parish had been turned against the privileges of the seigneurial system and the church tithe (dîme) by the Liberal, Luc Letellier, who had defeated the Conservative, Jean-Charles Chapais of Saint-Denis, in the first election of 1851. Confronted with this strong opposition, Curé Hébert of Saint-Pascal appealed to his superiors for assistance; they, in turn, worked through the parish curés of the diocese to ensure that the 'radical' Letellier would be defeated in the second election of 1851.[5] The electoral contest of 1851 is a convincing example of the strong local power of the church in the mid nineteenth century.

It was Curé Routhier, the parish priest of Kamouraska, and not the Tachés and their 'team', who in 1850, founded a small commercial academy. The ambitious Routhier also built a convent and set out on a search for distinguished occupants. His quest was realized by his successor Curé Hébert (formerly of Saint-Pascal) who, as President of the School Commission, obtained the services of the prestigious Congregation of Notre Dame of Montreal. The convent was an important addition to the parish, but in itself offered no guarantee of future prosperity as it had to rely on an uncertain economic future. The parish had already lost half of its population through the various fissions, and the railroad was headed toward Saint-Pascal. Rival centres now had an equal claim to Kamouraska's institutional resources — including its mobile national-orientated elite. In the meantime the attack on seigneurial prerogatives was gaining momentum.

The Tachés and their allies bitterly opposed the 1854 abolition of seigneurial rights. Jean-Charles Taché, writer and deputy for Rimouski, made a strong plea to retain some of the traditional privileges while seeking to identify the advantages and separate them from the abuses of the system. But not even a convention of seigneurs in Rimouski could prevent the commutation of most seigneurial rights, leaving only the saleable and vestigial right of token rents (Bossé, 1971). Before these legal steps were taken, some Taché land rights had already been sold by Ivanhoe Taché, Seigneur of Kamouraska, to raise money for his rising personal debts with a finance company. In an appropriate comment on the end of the seigneurial era in Kamouraska, Curé Paradis concludes that: "We are thus not surprised to see the seigneur play a disappearing role. He had to have a profession or a business in order to live" (1948:152). In Kamouraska this was law or for some, business, and there were better opportunities elsewhere.

First to disappear was the commercial academy. Disenchanted with their new quarters the teaching brothers left in 1857. Then in 1884, despite an impassioned plea in Parliament by Jean-Charles Chapais of Saint-Denis, the District Court of Kamouraska was moved to burgeoning Fraserville (Rivière-du-Loup). Subsequent losses were to benefit Saint-Pascal, where an innovative parish priest Alphonse Beaudet, had gathered the support of local notables in a campaign to establish a classical college for girls. Between 1860 and 1918 Kamouraska's elite had moved to Quebec and to other regional centres such as more fortunate Fraserville. By 1948, no doctor, lawyer or notary had a base in Kamouraska. "The village of Kamouraska never recovered from this amputation. After 80 years, its fine court house still stands, a witness to the glory of its past" (Barnard, 1961b:181).

In the leadership vacuum created by the departure of the seigneurial team, clerical leadership assumed a more important role. Inland parishes such as Saint-Pascal were favoured by the railroad and by the strong moral leadership of their curés that extended to virtually every aspect of parish life. As Father Paradis tells us, even before the misfortune of Kamouraska's seigneurial team, one of the first parish priests of Saint-Pascal took a direct hand in a church-sponsored colonization movement into untilled lands.

During his twelve years as curé of Saint-Pascal, M. Hébert built the *presbytère* and the present church which replaces M. Varin's modest wooden chapel. In 1849 he became the principal organizer of the Société de Colonisation de l'Islet et de Kamouraska; he was the guiding spirit, to the point that the society was designated *Monsieur Hébert's Society.* In this way he organized a team of forty-four men, chosen from the parishes of Saint-Pascal, Saint-Denis and Kamouraska and went off to found a colony (Hébertville), opening this rich territory to civilization.   (Paradis, 1948:223)

The aspirations of men like Hébert were supported by the merchants, craftsmen and farmers of Saint-Pascal. Perhaps existing resources could be distributed to their benefit as well? This new railway stop had few of the institutions that post-conquest elites defined as prestigious and depended, when financially able, on the classical college in Sainte-Anne de la Pocatière to gain entry to the priesthood or to the professions. Isolated from national elite networks and competitive with other parishes, Saint-Pascal's local *notables* were willing to encourage church-sponsored development plans that would increase the regional and national status of their community.

"I am Your Right Arm . . ." —
The Moral Leadership of Chanoine Beaudet

Given their relative parochialism, it was only natural for Saint-Pascal's *notables* to be curious about the arrival of a new and well-known curé, who had been an active promoter of classes in domestic economy when he was curé of Saint-Philomène-de-Fortierville. Alphonse Beaudet found Saint-Pascal to be an established parish with its own way of doing things. His seven predecessors had set up parish schools, a good church and a presbytère with a comfortable dependence. Faced with this stranger, parishioners asked each other, "who he was; what he would do; what would he keep and what would he change?" (C.N.D., 1947a: 15). The role of the curé was understood to pervade every aspect of parish life and Beaudet's biographers emphasize that he undertook his mandate with no hesitation: "I am curé and nothing which involves the flesh and life of my parishioners is a stranger to me" (C.N.D., 1947a:13).

The new priest was omnipresent, warning his parishioners of dangers that could undermine their community. Thus, the curé's offensive of 1897 was directed against three taverns which he had discovered within his new parish.[6] Appalled by the moral negligence of some of his parishioners, the good priest turned to the pulpit and used informal pressure to redress the situation.

His efforts at moral persuasion were not immediately successful. The tavern-keepers, strangers to the parish, circulated a petition in favour of drinking places which was signed by a majority of parishioners; furthermore, the taverns became a campaign issue in a municipal election. This was a type of local level contest that is rarely brought to an open confrontation and the situation challenged the leadership of the curé and his supporters. But in Beaudet's day, the prestige and political immunity of the curé proved more effective than the ballot box in resolving an escalating dispute.

Addressing his parishioners *en chaire* (from the pulpit), Beaudet thundered:

> It seems that everybody wants it! I am going to prove to you that this is false. Those who are for a tavern, stay seated; those who are against, stand!" With the exception of four or five, all of the parish stood, and those who remained seated did not dare to venture back to the taverns. The curé, single-handed, was able to chase away the strangers and keep in line the people from home.
>
> (C.N.D., 1947a:19)

Even without his pulpit, the curé always had the reserve resource of the confessional, a private and powerful means of social control which was promoted regularly.

This moral influence of the curé did not constitute a one-way flow of services. Beaudet reciprocated as an entrepreneur within the parish. He organized *corvée* labour to build a system of municipal roads, plant trees and improve existing buildings, especially the parish church. He was a prime mover in the improvement of municipal water systems and in bringing electricity to the village. Of all his projects, the most important for Saint-Pascal was the construction and staffing of a classical college for girls.

Curé Beaudet began this enterprise with an inventory of available educational resources. He decided to replace the French nuns teaching in village schools with members of a prestigious Canadian order since French Canadian nuns, familiar with the behaviour of good families, could implement the curé's goals of:

> . . . training women of superior accomplishments, good masters of
> the home who are capable of excelling in the kitchen as did the
> seigneuresses of long ago, in the salon with as much grace and spirit
> as the ladies of the grand century, and above all as enlightened
> Christians, worthy in their duty. There is no doubt that this is not a
> dream of launching the *canadienne* woman on the dangerous road of
> the suffragettes. All the same we wish to awaken her. This land
> ought to interest her. She should know to applaud when a candidate
> of great worth is elected. And when a candidate is elected by accla-
> mation, even in Saint-Pascal, it is necessary, as a good patriot, that
> she bless heaven and strongly sing out her content.
>
> (C.N.D., 1947a:70-71)

Between these objectives of the enterprising curé and realization
of the objectives lay a complex network of political relationships.
The *dramatis personae* of his campaign were the sisters of the
Congrégation de Notre Dame (C.N.D.), who refused his request
several times, the Minister of Agriculture, who quickly granted a
subsidy, and the local school commission and private benefactors
and supporters, each with his own arrangement with M. le Curé.

The first requests for support were rejected by several orders
of nuns, especially the C.N.D., but the refusals did not stop Beaudet
from writing and visiting mother superiors, bishops and ministers
to impress influential people of the legitimacy of his enterprise.
Once financial support was obtained from the provincial Department of Agriculture, he built the school, hoping that the new
building and considerable newspaper publicity in Quebec would
sway the nuns of Notre Dame to reconsider his offer. Fortunately
for the curé, he had an aunt within the order who listened to his
appeal. He reminded his aunt that offices and industry had dis-
placed young women from their real vocation in the family so
that mothers alone could no longer complete a girl's education
and it was domestic labour that benefitted society by keeping men
on the land. This, Beaudet insisted, is what the intellectual class
were crying for. It could only be done by French-Canadian nuns;
four, to begin (C.N.D., 1947a:34).

The curé's petitions succeeded in bringing the Congregation
into a round of successful negotiations. The nuns asked for a
contract guaranteeing the permanence of their stay and control
over ministerial subsidies, school commission grants and donations.
An agreement drawn up by the curé and a team of merchant and
farmer *notables* promised land which belonged to the *fabrique* and
permanently loaned the roadways around the new convent. In

return, the sisters would manage a girl's school, teach and direct the schools of the village and the parish, and care for Mme Goudreau, a benefactor of the new convent. Contract in hand, Beaudet returned to report to a parish assembly on the details of the new project.

While the opening of the convent in 1905 is a unique event in the parish history, the political process of getting a new school is familiar to present day community leaders. There is also a similarity to the strategies of the seigneurs of Kamouraska and their support-ing team of professionals. In both instances local and extra-local support were mustered to get things from the wider society. A clear difference between Beaudet and the professionals is in the composition of the team of supporters and their relationship with their leaders. In one case, an urban-orientated professional elite sought resources in a field where it was quite well-connected. The seigneurs played the role of *primus inter pares* and not that of broker or of intermediary local supporters. In the second case, it is clear that while the curé and few others were well-connected with urban institutions, most of the merchants, tradesmen and wealthy farmers who supported him were far more parochial in orientation than the professionals who worked in the court of justice in Kam-ouraska. Curé Beaudet marks a phase in Saint-Pascal's history when the elite of the parish was turned inward and relied on a number of intermediaries such as the curé and the elected deputies in Ottawa and Quebec, to act as brokers in obtaining desirable things from the larger society.

The full story of the growth and eventual demise of the Institut Chanoine Beaudet[7] need not delay our analysis of the role of its priest-principal as a moral and civic leader in Saint-Pascal. Each change that Beaudet introduced brought about a demand for other additions and innovations and the presence of the school was the major cause of most changes. The capacity of the rudimentary waste-disposal system was insufficient to serve the new school's resident population of 125. Raw sewage flowed through open ditches and the curé faced a law suit from indignant farmers. While the *Conseil Municipal* remained silent, Curé Beaudet de-ployed his moral influence against those who would choose "the most humble of persons in order to attack all of them" (C.N.D., 1947b:9-11). In a letter, Beaudet enclosed $11.01 in damages, a gesture motivated by "the love of peace", and promised to ask the

Conseil to establish a sewer system. The completion of these public works however, would take some time.[8] The curé warned a farmer that a law suit would be a dishonorable act:

> I therefore plead with you not to complicate things *as I am your right arm in helping you meet your ends.* You know as I do, that trials are the life of lawyers; this should tell you much and bring you to reflect . . . If I want to help you, despite your compromising proceedings, I want to continue to love you (as I love all my parishioners), and I want to prove to you that I am not slighting you, nor will I slight you even if you would take me to court
>
> Your curé
Alphonse Beaudet
(C.N.D., 1947a:12, emphasis mine)

In this case, as in many others, the transaction between the curé and his parishioners was a moral one dependent on the spiritual authority of the parish priest, and was concluded privately in the confines of his quarters in the *presbytère.* With strong moral pressure in favour of arbitration, few local disputes were settled by recourse to outside legal institutions.

Until the 1950s, clerical leaders maintained the support of their mercantile and farmer *notables.* It was this leadership team that petitioned for institutions and services such as a fresh water supply and electric power for the village. The fresh water was supplied by three private enterprises operated by local investors, but the problem of acquiring electricity was not as easily resolved.

After the first world war, A.R. Desjardins, an industrialist of nearby Saint-André, began to promote Kamouraska Electrique Ltée., a company which sought $100,000 to develop a 345 horsepower waterfall near Sainte-Hélène, ten miles east of Saint-Pascal. Curé Beaudet expressed great interest in the plan and sought funding from the Congrégation de Notre Dame in Montreal who roundly replied that religious orders had no business in promoting industry! Only with the strong support of his backers was the curé able to sustain his campaign. He again appealed to the Montreal nuns and this time received their backing (by a long-distance telephone call). Ultimately, the curé's efforts were thwarted as the new electric company was not financially viable. When electricity did come in 1927 it was sponsored by outsiders with Anglo-Canadian capital.

Though he was not always successful, parishioners still respected their curé's ability to obtain good things for their parish: "Everywhere he was known as the initiator . . . It was known that something undertaken by him was already something done . . . " (C.N.D., 1947b:4-5). Parishioners recall that it was Alphonse Beaudet who in 1917 obtained the order-in-council which transferred the county seat (*chef lieu*) from the village of Kamouraska to Saint-Pascal. Also noticeable to the Kamouraskiens was the departure of the C.N.D. nuns from Kamouraska, while that order was in full bloom in Saint-Pascal. Such acts could only expand the curé's local base of support and identify his own projects with a strong parochialism.

While the curé promoted the interests of the parish, he also cultivated the federal and provincial deputies for their support. Endless dinners and banquets were held at his school and politicians and clerics were placed in the school's book of honour. The visitors were received in honour and in return, supported the new school. An example is Georges Bouchard, the federal member of parliament whose frequent visits reinforced his image as a campaigner for rural handicrafts and farm improvements. Even after Beaudet stepped down as curé in 1917, he continued to be influential in government-parish ties until his death in 1936.

The parish curé remained a basic hinge in the relationship of the parish and the wider society. His personal network included government, clergy and parishioners. As secular and clerical authority networks interlocked especially in the realm of education, the operation of parish schools required the support of both the political and the church hierarchy. The bishops and the Congrégation de Notre Dame were his links with the church hierarchy and the deputies, provincial and federal, were his ties with government.

Thus, in a broad sense, the rapid institutional growth of Saint-Pascal in the early twentieth century was marked by continuous clerical leadership. The curé's needs were cared for by the parish who annually chose a prestigious parishioner to be one of the three *marquilliers* who governed the church *fabrique* that takes care of the administrative and financial affairs of the parish. The *fabrique's* funds came from the fees for religious obligation (masses, church pews). The tithe (la dîme) supported the curé. Until the 1950s, when cash payments became the norm, some farmers paid their dîme with one of every twenty-six minots of grain. All of the clerics in Saint-Pascal — the curé, his vicar, and the nuns and priests of the girls' college, benefitted from substantial farmlands, gardens and orchards that encircled the grey stone school that dominates the land behind the church.

It is important to note, however, that while the clergy were leaders in Saint-Pascal, they also were only one component of the regional elite that developed in Saint-Pascal. The *notables* of the parish (as they were called) abided by their curé's decisions as a team in matters that concerned the welfare of their parish. The son of the owners of one of the largest general stores emphasizes this support in his description of the founding of Saint-Pascal's parish credit union, the Caisse Populaire:

> On the 20th of December 1934 in a recruitment drive sponsored by Curé Langlais . . . 62 parishioners signed their membership in the movement . . . To assure the vitality and the development of this founding work, the founding members thought first of putting it under the *tutelage of serious men*, capable of assuring its good management. Elections were held and the suffrage favoured citizens who were *well known and highly esteemed*, four of whom became mayors of the village.   (Michaud, 1950, emphasis my own)

Michaud's account raises a number of questions about the "serious" and "esteemed" men who backed Curé Langlais. Of particular interest is their relationship with other parishioners and persons in their immediate area of influence. This leads to a study of the occupational and class structure in the era that preceded Saint-Pascal's industrialization. Also, we return to Horace Miner's field-work, as Saint-Denis is representative of the hamlets and farm parishes that surrounded Saint-Pascal when its *notables* launched their Caisse Populaire.

Class and Status in an Agrarian Era

Saint-Denis in the mid-thirties had a relatively egalitarian class structure with a large group of small farmers, whose status differences were based on wealth rather than on perceived class differences. The landless day labourers, the *journaliers*, formed a second social group that was rapidly increasing in size during the depression years, and thus menacing what has been referred to as an egalitarian parish community. The few village tradesmen are also included in this "landless" group that had less overall status than the farmers (Miner, 1939:250-1).

The smallest group, an elite that included the postmaster,

the senator from the Chapais family, and the curé and his relatives, remained aloof from local social networks. In Miner's words these were:

> ... persons who are socially so far removed from the society of the parish that they cannot carry on personal social contacts with other parishioners. If they do attempt it, there is a distinct feeling of strain or lack of ease ... These persons do not owe their positions to anything within the immediate society. Their position is due to contacts which they have had with the world outside the parish, from which sphere they have gained recognition far higher than anything the parish can give ...

> It would be *quite possible* for the son of a family below the lines (farmer, journalier, tradesman) to go away to college and receive the necessary recognition. Any professional man would probably enter this class.
> (*Ibid.*:250-1)

My field data from Saint-Pascal does not support the existence of so strong a gap between the *notables*, the farmers and the *journaliers*. In the service centre the *notables* were what an outsider could call a rural middle-class and do not seem to have had a clear counterpart in Saint-Denis. In an occupationally heterogeneous milieu, non-landed social groups had greater opportunities for local and regional social mobility than in a small hamlet. Merchants, tradesmen and wealthy farmers were able to form recognizable social strata as the *notables* of the parish. Externally orientated villagers could not all be placed into a single social category. Even though a very few parishioners were aloof from local networks, the service centre had a more complex and hierarchical status system based on occupational groups and, to a certain degree, wealth. Time has blurred the existence of factions and cliques. But even without the advantage of a detailed parish history, certain distinctions among the gentry are well remembered and are still influential when it comes to prestige and influence. In all, there were four strata of *notables: gros cultivateurs* (big farmers), artisans, merchants and members of the liberal professions.

Big and Little Farmers

Important economic differences among farmers have long been embedded in a folk taxonomy of status. There were two major categories of farmers, *gros cultivateurs* (big farmers) and *petits cultivateurs* (little farmers) and, as Miner suggests, wealth was the basis of the distinction. The *gros cultivateurs* were more prosperous and displayed this prosperity in their life style. They participated in the voluntary associations, political offices and leadership of the village. The *gros cultivateur* could use his earnings and assets to send some of his children to a classical college, a mobility route to the prestigious liberal professions. And on retirement, the big farmer could leave his farm to a younger son and take a house in the village, becoming a *rentier* and entering the everyday life of the parish centre.

In the past status differences did not sever inter-group sociability, but there were status prescriptions in social relationships such as marriage choices. A townsman remembers the difficulties he experienced when he courted the daughter of a *gros cultivateur* who was a graduate of Chanoine Beaudet's domestic college.

> *Gros cultivateurs* were the dominant agricultural class. For the *petit cultivateur*, who was establishing himself to be able to pull the devil by the tail for the rest of his life, it was quite difficult to look for the daughter of a *gros cultivateur*, a girl who had a dowry, for example, a cow, a horse, or $200-$300 in cash.
>
> In my wife's family, I was hardly welcome. My wife's father was an authoritarian *bonhomme*, who dominated everyone. It stands to reason that he thought he could dominate his daughter's relationships. Even though I was brought up by his brother (my uncle) who was as good a farmer as he is, they decided that I had quit the Pelletier family and took me for a little *va-nu-pieds* (ragamuffin). They told me that I was just three or four hairs below the nose of a small valise. I was worthless. Finally, her relatives intervened and told her, "You cannot marry that guy; he cannot support you; he has nothing under his feet."

As this example suggests, wealth differences cross-cut the rural parish, but although relationships in the *rangs* were not always egalitarian, they were not a basis for well-defined class differences.

The *gros cultivateurs* once took a role of central importance in the voluntary associations of the village. Together with the merchants, they directed the County Agricultural Society, the Cooperative Movement, the Caisse Populaire, the Saint-Jean Baptiste Society and the Municipal Council. Farmers and villagers had common interests as long as their parish was an agricultural centre. As the importance of prosperous farmers diminished, merchants and artisans made up the group of influential parish *notables* — the "esteemed and serious men" who supported new national associations that reflected their class interests: the Caisse Populaire, the Chevaliers de Colomb, the Chambre de Commerce and Maurice Duplessis' then promising political party, the Union Nationale. The curé remained influential in both sacred and secular domains, but special interest groups were potential compromises to the unity of the village under his counsel.

Merchants

There were four families of general store merchants in Saint-Pascal. Two were *bleu* (conservatives) and two were *rouge* (liberals). They operated the largest enterprises in the village, stores that maintained up to a dozen employees and carried a complete line of merchandise from flour to stoves. The merchants extended credit throughout the region and took an active role in politics. By local standards, they were powerful and influential. Their daughters had their own knitting and card-playing circles, and a regular series of social evenings (*veillées*) often continued into the early hours of the morning. These families are sometimes referred to as the "royal families" of the parish and their fortunes were linked in marital alliances.

Artisans

Only the wealthiest of artisans had the status of a village *notable*. In practice, this included the butter-maker, the tanner, the wagon-maker and several of the millers and wood merchants. The status of these craftsmen has been more locally-based than that of a merchant and little higher than that of a prosperous farmer. The fabrication of farm goods implied work with one's hands, a proposition that was antithetical to the activities of Quebec's traditional professional elite. The status of these tradesmen was thus the most insecure of the village *notables*, although it was their sons, and not the sons of merchants or professionals, who *remained in the parish* to become the industrialists of the 1960s. Merchants and professionals were better connected with the cities and, along with the more prosperous artisans and farmers could afford to provide their sons with a *cours classique* and training in one of the liberal professions. Despite the urban connections that came with a general store or a law practice, these proved to be not nearly as good a base for economic transformation as a workshop with an established clientele. However, few artisans in Saint-Pascal had access to industrial capital, expertise or markets for manufactured goods. After the last world war, the wagon-making Turcottes, a family with some experience in regional marketing and in dealing with outside suppliers, expanded their workshop and purchased the machinery to manufacture metal wagons. Their shop prospered but did not expand and the town remained an agricultural service centre until the 1960s.

The professionals formed a fourth category of *notables*, only there were precious few of them. Saint-Pascal has always had a notary, an agronomist, a veterinarian and a doctor or two, as well as a handful of resident clergy, but never did this village approach the diocesan centre of Sainte-Anne de la Pocatière or the railroad hub of Rivière-du-Loup as a centre for the liberal professions. What few professionals there were in the parish can be placed in the same category as Miner's externally orientated elite. They were part of a national upper class and were somewhat marginal to parish life where the effective elite were the merchants, tradesmen and farmer *notables*, and the most important professional, the curé. Members of the professions were brokers between national French Canadian culture and the parish and region.

The Notables

Those families who were not active in the professions or in national networks depended on a number of social criteria other than wealth to validate their local status. Of specific importance to parish notables were a broad religious participation (long synonymous with civic participation), a classical education, and kinship or alliance with large local families that had enjoyed a privileged position during the years of Saint-Pascal's importance as a mercantile centre. These traditional standards of worth which were the normative scaffolding of an agrarian leadership are still quite important in an industrial context, even though they compete with more secular evaluations (see Chapter Six).

Religious Participation

Religious participation and support of the curé were always *sine qua non* as basic pillars of familial worth and thereby of status. Furthermore, while the outward show of religiosity in French-Canadian towns is not necessarily correlated to spiritual enlightenment (Moreux, 1970), regular attendance at mass is still a prerequisite of high status in the community.

Catholicism remains the only religious option in Saint-Pascal. All of the government-subsidized schools, a primary school and two regional secondary schools, are organized under a Catholic school board and religion is taught several times a week. However, aside from church attendance, prestigious social participation is no longer equated with participation in church activities or in Catholic and nationalistic associations such as the Société Saint-Jean Baptiste. Until the 1960s, those who frequented mass regularly, and who supported social activities condoned by the curé, were people who "made a great demonstration" of their faith, people to be looked up to even if their economic success had not been complete.

By 1970, exclusive activity in Catholic organizations and a heavy involvement in church activities was considered a very "traditional" way of behaving and was sometimes the object of mild jokes — but never to the face of the person being chided. Women are more active than are men in church associations, but there are many more opportunities for men to participate in secular associations. Wealthy families are expected to make substantial contributions to church needs, and the names of the most generous donors are conspicuously displayed in bronze at the back of the church. Chronological study of this plaque shows the changing occupations of parish leaders: general merchants, contractors and then manufacturers.

For many, religious participation may only involve catechism in the schools, attendance at the weekly mass and an annual confession. The mass is no longer the major form of supra-familial association. This does not mean that the parish and the priest are irrelevant in Saint-Pascal. The religious integration of the parish is not seriously questioned, but religious practice outside Saint-Pascal and new forms of assembly within the town de-emphasize religious life as a cultural focus in favour of more secular pursuits.

Since 1950, Saint-Pascal has modified its religious practices following the changes of Vatican II and its implications for the Catholic Church in Quebec. The traditional *grande messe* on

Sunday has been supplemented with additional morning and afternoon masses and, since 1970, by a Saturday evening mass. The mass is now sung in French, and parishioners participate directly in the service by reading an Epistle. The interior of the church has been transformed by removing the altar rail and by moving the tabernacle from the altar to the *autel* on the wings of the *nef*. Against the strong objections of some Pascaliens, the elaborate carved woodwork on the front of the church has been replaced by a simple and well-lit facade which contrasts markedly with the carved Gothic spaces of the back of the church. Outside, a commemorative centennial statue of the Madonna has been topped with a red neon halo.

The secularization of the physical space of the church is paralleled by the decreased importance of the moral leadership of the curé. On several important occasions since 1968, laymen have made public appeals during the Sunday mass, a role that has long been reserved for the curé who spoke *en chaire* from the top of a winding staircase or from the inspiring altitude of the choir loft.

Until recently, church pews were auctioned off once a year and the centre aisle was the station of the parish *notables*. Even though the sale of pews has ended, some townfolk claim that "pretentious" people still tend to sit by the centre aisle. Weddings, funerals, and special masses have always been times for class display. On ceremonial occasions, the fur coats and fine dress of the *notables* once set them apart from other parishioners. On religious holidays such as *Dimanche des Rameaux* (Palm Sunday), the *notables* would lead a procession, carrying costly palm fronds while less prestigious Pascaliens carried local tree branches. The annual Saint-Jean Baptiste parade was an occasion for the *notables* to tour the parish arrayed in all their finery and riding in their best buggies. Differences in dress have now disappeared; the fine clothes of the old elite are more universally available. In more recent Palm Sunday processions, some members of old *notable* families have carried a local branch to emphasize their strong ties with parish tradition, while other Pascaliens can easily purchase a palm frond.

The calendar of religious processions and parish-wide celebrations (*fêtes*) has all but disappeared. May 16th, the *fête* for the patron saint, Saint-Pascal, is now only a mention during the two daily services. At one time the Pascaliens held a special mass for the occasion. Such modifications of ritual reflect the deeper social transformations within the parish where the functions of religious organizations have been expanded and taken over by secular associations such as the Centre Sociale and the Club Richelieu. Parish allegiances nevertheless remain strong, renewed annually by celebrations such as the Carnaval at Mardi Gras, the curé's annual parish supper, the June 24th patriotic dinner of the Société Saint-Jean Baptiste and by numerous inter-community sporting events. The parish loyalties which these events bring out are a form of local sentiment with both a secular and a sacred base, and the curé is always invited to speak on such occasions. In recent years the curé has provided special masses for smaller organizations: such as on the 25th anniversary of the Chevaliers de Colomb, or as the culmination of a day of snowmobiling by the Club Richelieu.

Until the 1950s, the parish *crieur* announced events of importance outside the church after Sunday mass. Then the curé began to edit a weekly *Bulletin* printed by an outside company that serviced hundreds of other parishes. The covers are covered with the calling cards of some of the church's most vocal public advocates: politicians, the Chevaliers, the Société Saint-Jean Baptiste, the Union Catholique des Cultivateurs, the Caisse Populaire, Chrétiens d'aujourd'hui, the Institut Chanoine Beaudet (now a secondary school), the Fraternity of the Tiers-Ordre franciscain (a mission-oriented group), out-of-town doctors who maintain an office in Saint-Pascal, insurance brokers, contractors, the funeral parlour, several merchants and the Turcotte wagon factory. The new industries, the Club Richelieu and other, newer associations are conspicuously absent! The *Bulletin* announces the masses for the week, memorial masses, weddings, births and funerals, church and community festive events and the annual parish census. In a community where religion penetrated everyday life — religious training at school, the rosary (*chapelet*) as a family prayer in the evening, the omnipresent crucifixes over doors and even favourite swear words which refer to the ritual objects of the mass — the legitimacy provided by religious observance could not rapidly disappear.

A family with some of its close kin in religious orders receives special additional prestige. A Pascalien considers these factors in an evaluation of another parishioner.

There is a little of the elite in the Plante family — there are about five priests. Although it is less important these days, the more priests in the family, the greater the social standing given its members. Nuns count for less as this is more ordinary. We have a few nuns in our family.

The prestige is even greater if the relative is a missionary or a member of the church hierarchy. Missionary activities are still boldly announced in the regional newspaper and promoted by the curé from the pulpit and in his *Bulletin*. While having a priest in the family remains honourific, Quebec's seminaries have virtually ceased producing priests, and other professions are now far more prestigious. There is now more talk about families who have produced industrialists, professors, actresses and politicians. Until the creation of Quebec's C.E.G.E.P. system[9] in the late sixties, entry into most white collar occupations demanded a degree from a classical college.

Classical Education

A classical training with a heavy emphasis on Latin, Greek and religion was, until 1958, the only post-primary education available to the Pascalien youth other than agricultural college or vocational school. Throughout French Canada, the rigorous training of a residential college guaranteed certain social standing and access to the liberal professions — often compensating for a lack of other economic opportunities. Graduates of the classical colleges in La Pocatière (boys) and Saint-Pascal (girls) draw more respect than the *primaires* — those who have only attended elementary school. "Giving" a son or daughter to the calling of God was even more honorific, but those whose children went on for higher degrees in the professions or even in the arts also commanded great respect. The curé has always provided a seminary training for those youth who have promise as future priests and some students have used this training as an entry into non-traditional forms of education, as the classical college was the gateway into both traditional and modern professions.

Women who have graduated from Saint-Pascal's classical college, the Institut Chanoine Beaudet, have a prestigious place in the community. Together they form the Amicale de Notre Dame de Foyer, a social club for the alumni of the convent school. Many of these women are known as *grandes dames*. They have held the positions of leadership in the few women's social clubs such as the Fermières, the Association of Catholic Parents, the Femmes Chrétiennes (Christian Women) and in school-related interest groups. There are several cases of women whose social status is superior to that of their husbands. In many families, the wife is better educated than the husband, reflecting the greater availability of private education for women and the economic necessity which often pushed men into the labour market at a younger age. In business families, few of the men have a classical training, but almost all of their wives have a diploma from Saint-Pascal's Institut Chanoine Beaudet, and many have taught in a one-room *école du rang* for several years before their marriage.

Training in business, such as a commercial course at the classical college in La Pocatière or even a degree from Montreal's École des Hautes Études Commerciales, has been over regarded, in the past, as a less desirable type of education. Unlike law or medicine, business management was not seen as a profession — not something that was noteworthy about a man. It is significant that most of Saint-Pascal's new manufacturers have no more than a commercial or an agricultural diploma or some technical training. As the sons of artisans and farmers, they had less of a chance to make their way into the liberal professions. When industrialization eventually led to a critical shortage of technical expertise in Saint-Pascal specialists were imported from larger centres. The serious lack of local technical expertise may be one reason for a slavish respect often accorded to outside-educated experts both knowledgeable and incompetent. However, outsiders no matter what expertise they offer, are not considered to be Pascaliens unless they have spent most of their lives in Saint-Pascal.

Locals and Outsiders

Birth as a basis of social status can be more of a hindrance to outsiders than a disadvantage to locals, and social prestige or even social acceptance is difficult to achieve for townsmen who were not born or raised in Saint-Pascal. This is especially so for women because of the high social status accorded graduates of the local classical college. Some outsiders claim that even after ten years in Saint-Pascal they are not accepted. While important, marriage to an insider is no guarantee that a "stranger" will be accepted, especially if he or she is not native to the region or comes from a large city. The outsider — businessman, bureaucrat or the occasional anthropologist — must relate to a circumscribed series of kin and friendship networks in which rules of behaviour and boundaries of membership have been established over 150 years.

The older established *notable* families of the village are thought to have more prestige than undistinguished farm families and the families of day or wage labourers. These "royal families" have intermarried extensively and have transmitted property and money from one generation to another. While members of one of these families may not be as wealthy as some business people, their staid wooden homes and lifestyle which costs relatively little to maintain and the long standing legitimacy of their status in the community make their family as prestigious as that of another living comfortably on recently acquired wealth.

In the face of major social changes everywhere in postwar Quebec, Saint-Pascal's elite of *notables* could hardly retain control over important community-nation relationships. With large movements of people in and out of the region and the continual integration of the small service centre into national networks, new organizational forms filtered into the community at a rapid rate. The particularistic nature of some social movements directed toward specific age groups, occupations and social strata did not favour their being taken over by the *notables*. A few interest groups that emerged in the forties and fifties did in fact question the existing social order. In Saint-Pascal it was the artisans' sons who sought to regain ground that their families were losing after the gradual erosion of their status as a result of commercial expansion and the mechanization of farm services.

The Jeunesse Rurale: Village-Nation Networks

In the early fifties several artisans' sons took over the local leadership of the Montreal-based Jeunesse Rurale Catholique (or the "Jacistes" as they were called). As was the case with many other branches of Quebec's post-depression Catholic Action Movements (Dumont, 1963), the Jeunesse Rurale failed to attract a large following within its chosen rural audience. Their national charter laid out sweeping objectives.[10]

> The J.R.C. does not only address itself to the sons and daughters of the *cultivateur*. It is a movement of a class or a profession. The movement must show in relief the qualities of the rural soul and try to kindle among J.R.C. members pride in belonging to a rural milieu.

Villagers made up over half of the local membership of about one hundred men and women ranging in age from sixteen to twenty-five. The movement's loosely structured parish-level organization afforded its aspiring artisan leaders a wide latitude for ideological redefinition of the charter and a possibility of structured vertical contacts with a group of reformers whose national activities were *in opposition* to dominant agrarian ideologies.

At the base of the Jeunesse Rurale was the parish club which, using Jaciste terminology, formed the "cord" in which individuals were the "threads" of a parish team. The cords of the parishes were united to form a second tier of organization at the level of the diocese. Local clubs such as that of Saint-Pascal were divided into several teams, each having a director who also served on the parish executive. The directors rotated teams annually "to develop leadership". The local president also served on the diocesan level which had a similar organizational structure representing all of the clubs in the diocese. The national level served as a "bridge among the dioceses" and Saint-Pascal invariably had several representatives working at both the diocesan and the national level.

Locally, Jaciste activity began with bi-weekly meetings ("sowings") where common ideas could be exchanged and "group training" started. Affiliation with the Jeunesse followed a "committment of good will" and an experience in group study. In practice, this was a spinning-off process whereby one recruiter would make speeches in the *rangs*, seeking others who would later do the same.

The Jaciste emphasis on teamwork (*travail d'équipe*) was an innovation in Saint-Pascal imposed by the very structure of the organization. The study groups quickly turned from moral concerns to a serious analysis of social and economic problems. This was a considerable jump from the lofty national ideology of creating "an army of apostles . . . which will lift up the masses as yeast in dough . . . a youth conscious of its Christian and rural responsibilities".

Members described their collective preoccupation with the industrialization and development of their region as "a move away

71

from the individualism of our fathers . . . a movement that was avant-garde even to some of the clergy". One member thought that it was amusing that a letter from the club president should have contained a prayer for the well-being of the members.

The practices of the movement held some resemblance to the rigours of ascetic Protestantism in its demands for sacrifice and commitment. Worldly pleasures were discouraged and drinking and social mixing between the sexes were considered to be distracting and antithetical to the goals of the movement. At one time, members donated a day of their salaries, but more than that every member gave, in the words of a former leader, "a gift that could not always be seen to have immediate results. Above all, the cost was of themselves, not so much in money."

Ascetic Catholicism was not new to Quebec. It was worldly action which was the fundamental change proposed by the Saint-Pascal Jaciste. This was not a cooperative venture, however; individuals initially relied on their own limited means to begin the economic transformation of the community. While many women in the movement went on to be nuns, the men developed a community of interest which they fed back into the small enterprises were inheriting or thinking of developing. One graying leader recalls that the Jeunesse Rurale was "a school for entrepreneurs . . . an *école difficile*" where a man learned that "he must always forget his security". Jaciste activities gave members a self-confidence bordering on a feeling of superiority over other parishioners whose "ambitions are limited". This confidence was rooted both in ideological factors and in the social structure of the movement which opened up networks into a wider society.

These nation-directed networks may account for the unusual success of the Jacistes in Saint-Pascal. Regional and provincial study sessions were well attended by leaders of the Saint-Pascal club, who took advantage of these opportunities to meet innovative participants in all Catholic youth movements that contributed to social ferment in Quebec during the early fifties. Thus they came to know and to identify themselves with the wider circle of leaders[11] who had the "immediate objective of making Quebec into a modern state, as opposed to the state of Quebec which we know as traditional" (Lamarche, 1966:55). This leadership is still remembered in Saint-Pascal, 15 years after the initial contacts, and is one of many indications (cf. Trudeau, 1949; Rioux, 1973

72

[1968]) that the "quiet revolution" of the sixties has its roots in the social action of the Duplessis era.

More important for later development in Saint-Pascal was the contact with other youth of the Lower Saint Lawrence and Eastern Quebec, men whose names are not national legends but who make up an important community of interest. The number of contacts made depended on the extent of participation. Jacistes in the national organization were able to leave their regional boundaries and travel throughout Eastern and Western Canada. For Rosaire Gagnon and for Henri Fortier, these conferences fostered an awareness of potential outside markets and civil service contacts that outlived the ill-fated Jaciste movement.

For these leaders, the Jeunesse Rurale became their own local social movement which expanded at a time when their leadership had great charismatic appeal. When they left the movement and joined other associations, the Jacistes of Saint-Pascal were no more significant as a formal voluntary organization than they were elsewhere, and it was not long before they ceased to exist on the local level. Former Jacistes offer a number of reasons for the movement's demise. One explanation is that too many local youths had emigrated from the parish leaving few leaders to continue Jaciste activities. This seems to be an after the fact rationalization since strong leadership continued in other activities especially in politics and in recreation. Furthermore, emigration of youth from the parish was declining. A more appealing local explanation is that the Jacistes found themselves to be operating "with outmoded goals, not adapted to a new generation". A third interpretation incorporates both of the above insiders' explanations with an outsider's analysis of social process in Saint-Pascal.

The formal analysis of the shell of an association provides only superficial treatment of institutional change. Men who shape policy in one organization can just as well take over and redefine another structure, especially if established associations are not giving their needs the expression they desire. When the members are close in age as well as in purpose, this mobility may be generational, the response of an age-set moving to a new set of circumstances in their life cycle. The Jaciste group moved from the J.R.C. into other clubs such as Club Richelieu, Saint-Pascal's Industrial Society, and Management Club, associations more adapted to their needs as a group of businessmen. This shift did not occur overnight since until the early 1960s the Jaciste leaders were occupied with establishing their own enterprises and as yet were not seen as eligible for membership in the village men's clubs. Even with their other commitments, many former Jacistes participated briefly in the Jeunesse Libérale (Young Liberals) when Jean Lesage and the Liberal Party upset the conservative post-Duplessis Union Nationale regime and undertook a far-reaching series of socio-economic reforms. It is in this period that the age set of Jaciste leaders redefined themselves as *industriels* (industrialists) and *dirigeants d'entreprise* (managers), expanding the size of their group and the scope of their common interests.

Organizational Strata of the Industrial Town

The Entrepreneurial Group[12]

What became the entrepreneurial group is not at all a group of businessmen or of industrialists in the strict sense of the term. Some manufacturers and merchants are excluded either on generational grounds or because of personality conflicts; others who are school administrators and insurance salesmen are key members. Those who are incorporated into this coalition of several dozen administrators and businessmen identify their colleagues as part of the "C.D.E. group" (after the regional Management Club — Le Centre des Dirigeants d'Entreprise), the "group of *industriels*" and the "group of Richelieu friends" (those who are active members of Club Richelieu). A local branch of a national French-Canadian men's service club, the Club Richelieu is also the group's widest arena for contracting local friendships and legitimating their identity. Here, the transactions within the entrepreneurial group are ritualized and extended to local allies. The Richelieu is thus the outer skin of the onion which is Saint-Pascal's new bourgeoisie. Inside the onion are several organizational layers — walls within walls — within which circulates economic, social and political information available to the leaders of the entrepreneurial group and, in a more modified form, to the followers.

Leaders and followers are close in age — between 35 and 40 years old in 1969 — and they participate actively in the same common interest associations. Significantly, of seventeen persons who are listed as *active* in Table 3.1, fourteen acquired control of their businesses between 1960 and 1970 and the remaining three began in business after 1957. The *inactive* group is substantially older and only nine of 26 in this group began their businesses (or took control of an enterprise) in the eventful 1960s. The wave of new firms and managers that came after 1960 did not repeat itself in the last part of the decade. Only four of these traders were under thirty in 1969; none of these was involved in manufacturing! Fewer young people were going into business and fewer still were starting new enterprises.

Table 3.1

Participation in Three Associations as a Function of Age

Participation in the J.R.C./C.D.E. or S.I.P. Executive	Decade Entered into Present Enterprise						Total
	Pre-1950 Age in 1969	1951-1960 Age in 1969		1961-1970 Age in 1969			
	49-60	40-49	50-60	20-29	30-40	41+	
Active	0	3	0	3	10	1	17
Inactive	7	7	3	1	1	7	26
Total: all ages	7	10	3	4	11	8	43

Key: J.R.C. = Jeunesse Rurale Catholique (Rural Catholic Youth)
      S.I.P. = Industrial Society of Saint-Pascal
      C.D.E. = Centre des Dirigeants d'Entreprise(ManagementClub)

Expansion of the group involved some recruiting of newcomers and age mates who had not been Jacistes — sons of artisan *notables* or Richelieu members. Expansion also involved the casting off of earlier adherents who no longer shared common interests or those who were members of a club before members of the entrepreneurial group became involved in it. Thus, the group grew more demanding in its admission criteria as its members prospered and aged. Younger businessmen and the growing group of white collar workers have been inactive in these elite councils and more directed toward sports and leisure activities organized by the Centre Social.

The expansion of the Jaciste group, its identity changes and overlapping common interest associations can be followed in Table 3.2, which demonstrates the layering of interest group participation and the merging of interests at the leadership level. The former youth club leaders, most of whom are manufacturers, are the core of the Management (C.D.E.) group (1967-70), of the Industrial Society (1968-70) and of the Club Richelieu (1969-70). Most are also contributors and policy makers for a regional development cooperative that provides its members with expansion capital.

Table 3.2

Relative Participation of Forty-two Saint-Pascal Businessmen in Four Associations

| Member of | Membership in Other Clubs | | | |
	C.D.E.	S.I.P.	Richelieu (after 1965)	Total
Jeunesse Rurale — J.R.C. (1950)	9	8	8	9
Manager's Club — C.D.E. (1967-70)		13	13	15
Industrial Society — S.I.P. (1968-70)			13	13
Richelieu Club				
(a) 1965-1970			18	18
(b) 1960-1965 (only)				7
No participation				14

As the overlapping memberships suggest, the entrepreneurial group (or team) is more of a fluid coalition or quasi-group than a formal structure. Informality facilitates flexibility in decision-making as well as considerable anonymity and secrecy in intragroup transactions — all this in a community where it is often said that "everyone knows each other". However, the amorphous nature of the entrepreneurial group also acts as a brake on rapid and concerted action even when the community as a whole may be threatened. Surface unanimity is almost always apparent. The entrepreneurial group has all the features of a coalition in that it is a collage of individual interests and alliances, any one of which may forestall decision-making. They are dependent on the continual support of other occupational groups some of which have come to share a different vision of what development means for Saint-Pascal.

The entrepreneurial group as such, *cannot* be identified by their life styles which are similar to those of other middle-class groups of the region. They have broken the Quebec custom of placing their home over or next to a store or factory and live in the new suburban-style *quartiers* of the town where they own substantial but not extravagant middle-class homes. Neither automobiles nor dress styles distinguish these men from teachers, other merchants or some white collar workers. Envy and intense competition for business success are complemented by levelling mechanisms that affect material style of life. The same cannot be said for the more heterogeneous category of merchants and skilled independent tradesmen.

Merchants and Tradesmen

The postwar expansion of retail trade swelled the ranks of store owners and contractors who operate small scale businesses, some of whom employ up to half a dozen assistants. A few general comments should help to place this group for succeeding chapters. Perhaps most important is our finding that some sixty families of merchant-artisans are not recognized within the community as a coalition or as a corporate group, nor do they recognize themselves as having a group identity. There are also considerable distinctions in wealth and in material style of life among small businessmen. These socio-economic variations lead to different choices in sociability and in political affiliation. In general, few parishioners in this category are leaders of voluntary associations or belong to Club Richelieu. Many are active in provincial politics, especially at election time.[13]

Merchants and tradesmen are strongly dependent on a local market and the goodwill of their community. Furthermore, their businesses are almost all family enterprises in which the fortunes of their kin are interlocked with the fate of their business and each employee represents a "packet of clients". By contrast, the *industriels* are moving away from the family business, and the markets of the manufacturers in the entrepreneurial group are predominately extra-local. Well organized and influential on all levels of political action, they are more of a local power class than the merchants and tradesmen, who are not organized as an occupational group.

White Collar Workers

White collar workers and teachers live in the same new residential quarters of Saint-Pascal and their homes are difficult to tell apart. However, the resemblance between the two groups ends with their material style of life, as their loyalties are quite separated. While the teachers are a product of the expansion of Quebec's rural educational system, the white collar workers spring from the growth of industry and government services; each attracts a different kind of salaried worker.

One kind of office manager works for the chartered bank, the Provincial Police, the Provincial Health Service, the Roads Department and the Manpower office. These officials recognize that their stay in Saint-Pascal is temporary and subject to orders from central offices in Quebec City. Examples of their impermanence came during the time of my stay when two bank officials, including the manager, were transferred. Also, after a provincial election, the Quebec Government employment office was closed completely. In this case, there was no notice given; the movers arrived even before the placement officer was informed of the closing and his transfer. In general, this kind of "visiting" civil servant rarely participates in local associations unless he occupies a top echelon post. Two exceptions are the chief of the Provincial Police detachment and the bank manager, whose participation in community events is encouraged (for example, in the Club Richelieu). The manager of the bank has been incorporated into the entrepreneurial group, and so was his predecessor, who later returned to be a partner in Gagnon's tannery. The bank executive is a gatekeeper to sources of needed capital and a resource for financial skills and expertise; as such, he has little difficulty relating to the *industriels.*

A second type of white collar worker is employed in industry and small business. These clerical workers still have no group identity other than a general attachment to the interests of their employers. They do participate in parish organizations, and by the time my fieldwork was complete, their involvement had stopped just short of the top leadership positions. Most active in politics and social life are the factory administrators in middle-level positions such as accountants and department managers. These personnel identify themselves with the entrepreneurial group and a few have been asked to join Club Richelieu. Those who occupy lower-level positions, clerks, bookkeepers, foremen and salesmen, are active in less prestigious clubs such as the Chevaliers (Knights of Columbus), sports activities and the Carnaval committee of the Centre Social sports organization. A group of white collar workers will occasionally get together to have a beer (*prendre un coup*) and watch the Saturday night hockey game.

The white collar workers are more active in associations than the industrial workers. However, those at the bottom of the white collar and merchant group hardly participate at all. Warner found the same situation in the midwestern town of Jonesville where participation reaches a minimum among an alienated lower middle class, "subordinated by the rest of the community" (Warner, 1949:143). In both Saint-Pascal and Jonesville, the white collar and merchant groups show some of the most striking cases of upward mobility. In Saint-Pascal a group of young administrators with some shared friendships became active in the Centre Social and in the Jeune Chambre de Commerce until it became inactive. One respondent classified this group as *les hommes en voie*. These "men on their way" are not overtly satisfied with the Richelieu group just as the Richelieu members are not yet desirous of their fellowship. They are doing things which they see as more useful by adapting new institutional forms to their needs. They define themselves in relation to the dominant *industriels* and as such they have no corporate identity and their common interest associations are unstable.

The boundary between *les hommes en voie* and the *industriels* is not impenetrable, but is one of those discontinuities in a social system which requires the correct rites of passage for admission into a new peer group. This does not mean that the *industriels* do not have serious doubts about whether the social milieu they

79

have created will be acceptable to the generation now completing secondary school and university. This last question reflects on the ability of rural areas to sustain capitalist industrial development, and a full discussion must wait until the final chapter.

The largest number of white collar jobs and the highest paid sector is not in industry, but in the school system. Here a collectivity has formed that is both independent of, and competitive with, the entrepreneurial group.

Teachers and School Administrators

Education in Saint-Pascal has become an industry which has created jobs for 120 teachers, of whom 95 are laymen. All told, one-fifth of the municipal voters are in some way connected with the school system.[14] Such a sizeable a group of well-paid and educated workers is foreign to the social institutions of the region. Considered to be intruders, teachers and school administrators have gained only gradual acceptance in the institutions of the town.

The first teachers to participate in politics and social clubs were the school administrators. Other teachers have become active in sports clubs and in the Chevaliers de Colomb, although until 1970 their community participation had been limited largely to regular social gatherings with other teachers. The teachers have a sociability advantage over the businessmen in that they see each other frequently in the school common rooms. They do not feel obligated to patronize Saint-Pascal, and often purchase automobiles, appliances and building materials outside the parish. If anything, their social activities are somewhat circumspect as many parishioners believe that anyone who teaches their children should not be seen in the hotels or out drinking late at night. With the notable exception of some school administrators, teachers have not been involved in the same mutual obligation network that motivates the behaviour of other townsmen. This segregation of the teachers has been complete enough for the Pascaliens to identify them as a "group apart", and only rarely are they included in the friendship choices of businessmen. Similarly, the only public contacts I have seen between teachers and the community is at Parent-Teacher meetings, at organized sporting events or at parish functions during Carnaval. In the early seventies teacher participation in the activities of the Centre Social increased dramatically. Several teachers took responsibility for all the programming of a new community channel on the cable television system setting up an improvised studio in the secondary school basement. This extended their influence beyond the classroom and has generated a greater awareness among all townsmen of associational activities and community problems. It would be incorrect to say that the teachers control the new television system if only because it is owned by a merchant in the entrepreneurial group.

In the case of elections and in everyday activities, teachers often have relied on school administrators as brokers in their transactions with parish institutions. School directors and their clerical staff together control one of the town's most significant economic resources and, unlike the teachers, they are active in almost all of Saint-Pascal's voluntary associations, including those the *industriels* have chosen to participate in. They frequently visit each other and some administrators belong to the same fishing club.

As I will explain in Chapter Five, an alliance between the *industriels* and school administrators facilitated the downfall of the old *notables* from positions of power and prestige in the community. This union was an expedient one, but it was also quite temporary, as considerable mistrust exists between the two groups. In organizations where school administrators and businessmen were in regular contact the contest became an open one. Some businessmen pronounced that the educational plant was an "industry to end all other industries"! Some teachers ceased supporting the political status quo and in 1969 sought (unsuccessfully) to topple the municipal administration when the school administrator, Hubert Leclerc, ran for mayor. In 1973, the postmaster and president of the school commission was elected mayor by acclamation as his candidacy was acceptable to both sides.

While Quebec teachers are a militant force on the national level,[15] their local strength is less marked in a community which is distant from metropolitan centres. The educational "team" controls the operation of schools, but is entirely dependent on politicians and outside civil servants for economic resources. The schools ultimately depend on school taxes and to a lesser extent, on their relationship with the religious establishment; the administrators need both the pragmatic and the moral support of the community. They are not able to widen the base of their social and political activities without becoming vulnerable to confrontation. Several school administrators have made efforts to enter the arena of provincial politics in Saint-Pascal and other towns of the Lower Saint Lawrence. Yet in 1970, no particular party was selected for coordinating a teacher coalition, although an increasing number of local teachers are active in the separatist Parti Québécois. If Saint-Pascal continues to follow national trends, the teachers will probably continue to consolidate their efforts politically on all levels of government, forming an alliance with those who have facilitated the industrialization of the town, the factory and service workers.

Blue Collar Workers

In 1970, Saint-Pascal's workers had few organizational activities and virtually no collective identity. This lack of unity in the expanding group of labourers in the town is a result partly of the dispersion of much of the working force in surrounding parishes. A few workers had begun to participate in adult sports leagues organized by the Centre Social and others joined a baseball team sponsored by Henri Fortier's tire factory. A small chapter of the Jeunesse Ouvrière Catholique (Young Catholic Workers) had been organized, but had recruited no more than a small membership. The factories organized occasional social events; however, these were not a regular form of social activity and even the parties are avoided by many workers. A labour union which was completing negotiations with the tire factory had not yet played a role as an after-hours social club (see Chapter Four: Unions). The entrance of organized labour reinforced the collective identity of Fortier's workers by straining the strong paternalism between owner and workers. After a disastrous fire in Gagnon's tannery in 1972 which threatened 275 workers with unemployment, the crisis and its aftermath brought forward potential leaders from the ranks of the tannery work force.

Isolates

A Pascalien's perception of the social group of his neighbour is very much a function of participation in common interest associations and in friendship networks. However, many people are difficult to place and fall into an "isolate" category. A number of townsmen have few ties with associations and few, if any, intimate friends. Part of the image of non-participation is illusory because involvement in associations may have dropped in a person's elder years. It is also possible that control of many of the town's associations by the young industrialists temporarily reduced the range of associations and left some people without effective organizational attachments. Other Pascaliens confine their social activities to their own kinfolk and a few participate solely in regional and national networks (usually related to their occupational roles) which have no base in Saint-Pascal. These townsmen, and they are not many, are the traditional externally-oriented elite mentioned earlier. Sometimes referred to as *millionaires* or *monétaires*, their association with locals is mainly for special economic or political purposes, and they act as brokers for those who are without external influence.

Summary: Regional Elites in Eastern Kamouraska County

Four regional elites have been discussed with an emphasis on the teams that formed their core, their objectives and means of transacting with their leaders, what they were able to control and how they lost that control. The clergy provided the transition from the seigneurial team of which they were a part, and a potential competitor for scarce resources. The merchants provide the transition from the second elite to the third — a very subtle and smooth shift that was conditioned by social movements on a national level and even more so by the change from a production-based economy to a consumption-based economy among the client farm population. The fourth transition is more subtle on the local level than on the national level, but it involves a value change that is more profound than that of any of the preceding shifts. The traditional mercantile base of the region is rejected in favour of industrial capitalism and a new type of class system. But this revolution is certainly by now a secondary one, and nineteenth century laissez-faire capitalism is not the model that the new manufacturers could efficiently adopt in seeking a niche in the national economy. Even the local milieu with its developing white

Table 3.3 Regional Elites in Eastern Kamouraska County: 1800-1974

	Economic Base	Network	Regional Corporations (dominant)	Opposition
I 1800-1854[a] Seigneurs and Kamouraska Court Officials	seigneurial rents; taxes and vertical payments to gentry	national	Court: families	clergy (once part of the same group
II 1855-1934[b] Curé(s) - professionals - merchants artisans - gros cultivateurs	agricultural service centre; vertical payments to gentry	regional	Cercle Agricole; Saint-Jean Baptiste Society; Société de Colonisation; L'Union Catholique des Cultivateurs; Fermières and parish-based associations	partisan: internal factions of Liberals and Conservatives (Liberals dominant)
III 1935-1960[c] Merchants - artisans - Curé	mercantilism and centralization based on agriculture	regional - provincial	La Chambre de Commerce; Chevaliers de Colomb; L'Union Nationale; La Caisse Populaire (some occupational differentiation)	partisan: Union Nationale dominant
IV 1960-1974 Entrepreneurial Group - white collar and teacher allies[d]	small scale capitalist manufacturing with state subsidies; regional school system and transfer payments; farm services	regional - national	Club Richelieu (national and secular) connected associations (C.D.E.)	teachers[e]

a. The abolition of seigneurial rights, the subsequent arrival of the railroad in Saint-Pascal and closing of the courthouse seem to mark the end of this era.
b. The rise of the Union Nationale and the start of the war mark the beginning of an era of mercantile leadership.
c. The fall of the Union Nationale in Quebec City and the organization of manufacturing and secular service clubs in Saint-Pascal clearly mark the beginning of a new town leadership.
d. Until about 1969.
e. After 1969, but excludes some school administrators who communicated with both groups.

collar bureaucracies is not a favourable environment for the un-challenged dominance of a capitalist class.

It is important to note that none of these leadership changes were absolute. In every case the group that lost its regional power was aware of and collaborated with its opponents to maintain its own position of dominance. Even after that position had slipped the incumbant teams retained a great deal of power and prestige.

Nowhere are these discontinuities more visible than in the economic system of Eastern Quebec where traditional family enterprise and bureaucratic industrial firms compete in the same market. As the next chapter illustrates, this discontinuity in Saint-Pascal often exists in the midst of a single enterprise.

Footnotes

[1] This systems analogy is taken from Sir Stafford Beer's Massey Lectures (1973), *Designing Freedom*, as carried by the Canadian Broadcasting Corporation's *Ideas*.

[2] The Taché family was heavily committed to the political and religious mainstream of nineteenth–century French Canada. Etienne Taché served as the last prime minister of Lower Canada, and his nephew, Monseigneur Alexandre Taché was the first archbishop and promoter of settlement in Saint-Boniface, Manitoba. Pascal Jacques Taché, notary and first resident seigneur of Kamouraska, was elected deputy of Cromwalis (Kamouraska) to the Chambre d'Assemblée.

[3] This account of nineteenth–century Kamouraska is largely taken from Curé Alexandre Paradis' parish history (1948).

[4] Such as Gros Cacouna near Rivière-du-Loup where the French elite of Quebec have built large rambling summer homes.

[5] Luc Letellier, a renowned political figure in nineteenth-century Quebec, was also a member of the anti-clerical Institut Canadien. The Church's reaction against the liberals in Lower Canada after the 1837 rebellion, has been interpreted in terms of its increasing entrenchment and the simultaneous rise of an "ideology of conservation" which prevailed in French Canada for the next century (Rioux, 1973 (1968)).

[6] Temperance crusades were long a favourite target of Kamouraska curés. Barnard (1961a:232-3) and Miner (1939:15) report on the Black Cross Movement which diffused throughout the region under the vigorous leadership of Curé Quertier of Saint-Denis. Father Charles Chiniquy, a legendary advocate of temperance and former curé of Kamouraska had been an active crusader in Saint-Pascal where he created a scandal after it was discovered that Chiniquy attempted to seduce Curé Hébert's housegirl (Trudel, 1955:67).

[7] See biography of Chanoine Beaudet (C.N.D., 1947a, 1947b).

[8] Remedial action did not come quickly, for the construction of a well for sewage had to wait over twelve years, and a complete sewage system took forty years to be constructed.

[9] The C.E.G.E.P.'s (Collèges d'enseignement général et professionel) set up after the Parent Commission's report on educational reform in Quebec, are non-confessional colleges that are tuition free to secondary school graduates. They have largely replaced the *collège classique* although a majority of students still take a two year arts (general) option with the hope of continuing in university rather than the specialized ("professional") options that lead to specific careers.

[10] From the papers in the personal file of a Jaciste leader.

[11] Included in this group are Claude Ryan, editor of *Le Devoir*, Gérard Pelletier, Jean Marchand and Norman Toupin who were once active in the Catholic action youth movements of the post-war period.

[12] I have maintained the use of "group" from Chapter One since coalitions of entrepreneurs have been referred to this way in the social science literature (for example, Geertz, 1962). "Group" is also the emic or folk term used by the businessmen to refer to themselves. However, the word "team" is probably preferable in a comparative sense, especially in this chapter (see Bailey, 1969) and Goffman, 1971 (1959):83ff).

[13] Small contractors are the most active local level party leaders and they have the most to gain from partisan politics (see Chapter Six). More than half of the small tradesmen were Liberals (then in opposition), but as if to underline their separation from the entrepreneurial group, they supported a different candidate in the 1970 Liberal nominations (he won the nomination and the election).

[14] Compiled from municipal voters lists (1969) and from interviews with school administrators.

[15] The nationalist Quebec teacher's union (C.E.Q.) is a strong lobby and an important outside agency of social change.

Chapter Four
The Town Economy

Writing in the early forties, Everett Hughes observed that "on the economic side, French-Canadian city culture has become stabilized about an earlier phase of capitalism (Hughes, 1943:210). Somewhat later Norman Taylor (1964:294) added his assessment of the French sector of Quebec's economy as essentially eighteenth century capitalism. The Taylor thesis is that French-Canadian manufacturers siphoned off capital to meet civil, family or religious obligations, "thereby expressing the emphasis on security inherent in the French-Canadian outlook and the resistance to business growth" (*Ibid.*:285). These conclusions raise important interpretative questions about the economic activities of Pascaliens and in particular of the entrepreneurial group. Have they been as reluctant as those Eastern Quebec businessmen whom Francine Dansereau (1967) studied to accept capital from outside sources or to make risky allocations of their scarce resources? Has an individualistic control of local economy been maintained through self-financing?

To begin an answer to these questions we must turn to the relative occupational mobility of those who run the local economy and compare the careers of the sons of merchants, artisans, farmers and white collar workers. There are significant differences in education, available family capital and intermediate work experience. Looking backward at local leadership we have already seen that money did not necessarily breed more money, especially within the local elite. There has been some mobility at the top, even though there is good evidence of severe restrictions to intergenerational mobility at the bottom among farmers and industrial workers (Rocher and de Jocas, 1957). The old *notable* class is overrepresented among Saint-Pascal merchants and manufacturers, but not the merchant and professional families who dominated regional elites over the previous century. To understand this about-turn within the national middle classes (the regional elite) and the unusual mobility of some members of the working class, I will turn from occupational mobility to the sources of investment capital and the family enterprise. Investment and the degree of kin involvement are found to be parts of a developmental cycle which some enterprises have gone through by reallocating their resources, and which others have avoided. Both "progress" (as the first type perceives its own development) and "stability" (as the second type rationalizes its retrenchment or decline) have social costs and advantages that emerge in the discussion of associations and group affiliation in Chapter Five.

As the general store merchants and self-employed shop owners were the most prestigious businessmen before 1960, their children should have had the shortest route to follow to stay in the world of commerce. This is particularly so for the shopkeepers, where an established business can keep running in family hands with a minimum of skilled training or changes to its traditional mercantile organization.

Merchant Fathers and Merchant Sons

As recently as 1955, the general store was Saint-Pascal's principal type of retail commerce. The merchant and his sons sold most anything from groceries, hardware and clothing to construction materials, radios and furniture. In 1970, three of four family stores remained, and two of these have narrowed their inventories to include mainly groceries and hardware. Established businesses such as these have had a stable and assured clientele — an enormous advantage to an inheriting son or daughter. Eight businessmen in the Saint-Pascal sample were born into merchant families; their fathers were either prestigious general store owners (four cases), or operators of more specialized enterprises such as an undertaker (who was also a general merchant), a jeweller (who had begun as a farmer and logger), and a garage owner.

Retail specialty shops are quite recent. Saint-Pascal had no drugstore until 1954 when a pharmacist came from Quebec City and offered some competition to the doctor's dispensary. Until 1945 general stores were the only local source of cloth and garments, although there were always some women who worked as seamstresses. For at least 50 years Jewish peddlers have visited the farmhouses and villages of the Lower Saint Lawrence annually with vans full of clothing to be sold with individualized credit arrangements.

Figure 4.1

Paths Toward Business Ownership:
Father is a Merchant

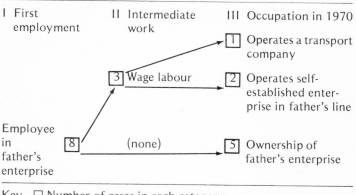

I First employment	II Intermediate work	III Occupation in 1970

Key □ Number of cases in each category
    → Direction of occupational career

In the 1960's, the shutters began to close on the old *notables* who ran the cornucopia-like frame stores as the parish centre. With competition from chain stores in nearby cities and from new stores within Saint-Pascal, their businesses could only continue in a somewhat truncated form. Nevertheless, as the flow chart above (Figure 4.1) indicates, most businessmen who are merchants' sons have chosen to remain merchants. All of them began their careers working for their families, and five out of eight were selected to take over the store on their father's retirement. The three men who were not chosen as inheriting sons worked as wage labourers for a brief period and then invested the money they had earned to begin a new business. None of these three is the son of a formerly prosperous general store owner. Along with two others who inherited a specialized retail trade they experienced, during the 1960s, a sudden expansion in the sellers market for services and luxury goods. In comparison, those who inherited the established general stores experienced dwindling clientele and a corresponding loss of status in the community.

The pattern of inheritance among the merchants' sons is similar to the one Miner (1939:79) describes for the family farm. One son, perhaps two, can be supported by the family enterprise, but the others either leave or continue as employees. On the retirement of the father an inheritance agreement is drawn up by a notary giving the business to the inheriting sons who in return are required to provide for the needs of their aging parents. As is often the case with sons who have been selected to inherit a farm, there may develop considerable tension between the father and his heirs (Verdon, 1973:100).

Higher education was reserved for those sons who would not take over the business. For the others, such a luxury was usually considered to be unnecessary; a few years at the college classique provided adequate instruction. Otherwise all of the merchants' sons "learned the ropes" from their fathers with little outside technical or specialized training. Three merchants' sons are *primaires* — with no more than primary school behind them; five others have attended a classical college, two of whom took a perfunctory and perfunctory commercial course. The most successful man in this group, Mayor Castonguay, has only a ninth-grade education. He left his father's general store in 1931 to begin his transport company which, by 1970, was the largest trucking firm in Eastern Quebec. For years he lived frugally in a flat near the church, putting his money into trucks and investments.

With this very notable exception of the entrepreneurial Castonguay, the sons of general merchants inherited viable enterprises, but few have expanded their family fortunes. In 1970, they represented what remains of the mercantile *notables* of the agrarian service centre era in Saint-Pascal. In comparison, the specialized merchants are more upwardly mobile. They have depended less on the wealth or prestige of their families and more on capital and experience accumulated from intermediate jobs working for others. In pre-industrialized Saint-Pascal, only the skilled craftsmen could obtain shop and technical experience without leaving their family enterprise.

90

From Shop to Factory

With an increase in the scale of production and a corresponding reorganization of the techniques of manufacture and of distribution, an artisan's shop can be transformed into a small factory. The increased volume of production requires regional and then national markets and a sizeable *unskilled and semi-skilled labour* force to achieve profitability. In Saint-Pascal the first craft trades to be industrialized already serviced a regional population of farms and villages. Ten businessmen in our sample have fathers who were skilled craftsmen serving the hinterland of the county centre. Three of these artisans were *tanners*, two were *millers*, and there was one printer, *baker*, butcher, *wheel and wagon maker*, and *a builder*. All told, six of the artisans' sons have made the transition from craft to industry (those trades in italics), although no member of this group has wandered far from his family's specialization. The occupational histories of these men are plotted in Figure 4.2

Figure 4.2

Paths Toward Business Ownership:
Father is an Artisan

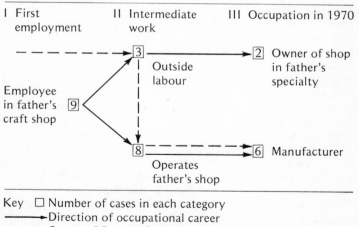

I First
employment

II Intermediate
work

III Occupation in 1970

Key □ Number of cases in each category
⟶ Direction of occupational career
- - -→ Career of Rosaire Gagnon, tanner

91

from their first employment, intermediate jobs and lastly, their occupations in 1970.

Most of the artisans' sons first worked in their fathers' shops. As is the case with the merchants, not every son was able or willing to inherit his father's enterprise. Two of the artisans' sons, faced with unprofitable and unpromising family enterprises, soon left for more remunerative work, accumulating capital to set up their own enterprises. One man who did not begin working with his father is Rosaire Gagnon (dotted line on Figure 4.2).

The Gagnon family had the means to send Rosaire to La Pocatière and Rimouski for a classical education, and in 1949 he returned to Saint-Pascal as an employee in the regional office of the then privately-owned Quebec Power Corporation. From 1949 to 1953 he was active in the Jeunesse Rurale Catholique, leaving Saint-Pascal to take a full-time directorship with the youth movement's Montreal office. Later, he moved on to an administrative job with a Montreal flour company. During all this time he perfected his English and had the opportunity to travel in Canada, the United States and Europe. By 1962, Gagnon returned permanently to Saint-Pascal, fully involved in the operation of his family enterprise, where he proceeded to deploy his father's capital and outside loans to mechanize his father's eight-man tannery. Other artisans' sons also reorganized their family workshops — converting a bakery into a candy factory while services such as a butcher shop and printing shop were mechanized and expanded to serve a regional clientele. The builder began to organize his equipment and men for large commercial and government contracts.

While the artisans' sons gained practical training which contributed to the town's growth, they are, with the exception of Rosaire Gagnon, less educated than others. Most (five) have no more than a primary school education. Only one man, a builder, has any technical education (carpentry). In both craft and merchant families, sons who were provided a ready-made work opportunity did not continue for a classical degree, and those who took the college commercial course rarely finished, turning to the family enterprise after a few years of schooling. For despite the financial success of a few craftsmen, the pre-industrial artisans of Saint-Pascal were at the bottom of the *notable* class, families whose status was locally validated and who rarely participated in national political life.

From Farm to Shop

The mobility path of farmers' sons encompasses the largest sampled group of business managers (15 or 34 percent) and occasionally has all the qualities of a French-Canadian Horatio Alger story. Most have had only a primary school education (13 or 86 percent); but significantly, two men, both of whom were active Jacistes, tire-maker Fortier and a horticulturist, were trained at the agricultural college in the nearby town of La Pocatière, where they were instructed in commercial agricultural production techniques. Their experience is not typical. Furthermore, education is but one indication of the restricted opportunities open to migrants from family farms who began with only minimal access to trade networks and could not easily obtain starting capital. Their occupational histories are longer and frequently more innovative than those of the sons of merchants and artisans (see Figure 4.3).

Figure 4.3

Paths Toward Ownership of a Business:
Father is a Farmer

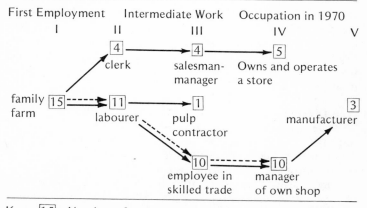

Key   15   Number of respondents at a given phase in their occupational careers

⟶   Direction of occupational career

- - - ⟶   Career of Henri Fortier, tire maker

In almost every case, the farmers' sons were not selected to inherit their family farm. But good jobs did not come quickly to the disinherited. With few exceptions, men in this group joined the thousands of others who migrated from Kamouraska to find work as far afield as Southern Ontario. This first job was inevitably as an unskilled labourer, a *journalier*, although several men managed to gain employment as clerks in local enterprises. Those who departed as *journaliers* were able to train themselves for skilled labour. They worked as apprentices until their financial status or a marriage ended in their return to Saint-Pascal to open a shop of their own in the same line of work — carpentry, plumbing, electricity or dry cleaning. Those who began as clerks opened their own stores in a similar type of commerce, taking up what they perceived as available niches in the town economy. Thus, a tractor salesman used his contacts to get a franchise for selling automobiles, and a general store clerk with experience in the farmer's cooperative opened the town's first supermarket as a franchise of the cooperative-affiliated chain. Fleury and Fortier, trained at the agricultural school, began their careers as horticulturists in Saint-Pascal. Fleury worked for the one local florist, and Fortier (the florist's brother) managed the C.N.D. nuns' farm that once ringed the eastern borders of Chanoine Beaudet's girl's school. After a few years experience as an employee, Fleury set up his own processing and contracting business on his father's farm. Fortier, eleven years older than Fleury, abandoned horticulture in 1951 to purchase the village's tire-retreading shop which in the late 1950's he developed into the town's largest industry (see dotted line in Figure 4.3). He is the most innovative and nation-oriented of his generation of farmers' sons who turned to commerce, but it still took him about ten years to acquire the capital that he needed for expansion.

While capital is in every case a problem, expertise in a skilled trade and practical knowledge in business management are equally, if not more, crucial. Thus while many farmers' sons migrated to urban centres, those who came back have had a decided advantage over more affluent age-mates from the village who never strayed far away from their parish or region. The contacts made in new jobs later became indispensable, especially in the construction trades where skilled workers rose to the position of foreman. They took on the responsibility of ordering building materials from supply houses in Montreal and Quebec, and in several cases performed some rudimentary accounting which they also learned from their out-of-town employers. These simple technical and managerial skills were a valuable resource in Saint-Pascal during the general period of economic expansion in the early 1960s.

Skilled tradesmen could benefit from a building boom to obtain lucrative contracts for new public works. For others, capital was obtained through alliances with kinsmen and other investors, and bank loans were more readily available. Significantly, two of the three farmers' sons who entered manufacturing have special technical skills that they could use to reorganize production. With his experience and specialized training Fleury adapted the facilities of his ancestral farm to the organization of a family-operated greenhouse and dried flower-processing business. Another farmer's son with intermediate experience in the servicing of sewing machines launched a work-glove factory in Saint-Pacôme. Semi-skilled female labour from the western reaches of the county were hired to sew work-gloves from the large volume of finished cow bellies that Rosaire Gagnon and his brother were tanning in Saint-Pascal. This is not to say that all farmers' sons with special skills were successful at reallocating the resources of their new trades. Several (a shoemaker, a dry cleaner and a miller), have constantly encountered financial difficulty, and have been supported only by the versatility of a small-scale trade complemented by other means of support such as wage labour or welfare payments.

While the craftsman's son could benefit from his family shop, the farmer's son had to obtain his own starting capital and training; however, the small group of five businessmen whose fathers were a teacher, an engineer, a yard foreman and a stationmaster had access to higher education and to some capital. They are also outsiders or descendants of outsiders who were relatively well-educated and of high status in Saint-Pascal. None of these men were obliged to begin working as day labourers. Their fathers had the means to provide them with a specialized training in business administration, electronics, pharmacy or photography, in addition to a classical training. The result of such security and careful training is a level of economic success that provides a security that is not conducive to taking of innovative risks.

Only one of these men launched a new industry, and this was as an agent for a furniture plant in neighbouring Saint-Philippe. However, he still holds down a full-time position as county registrar, and his furniture business began as a sideline of the wagon factory for which he had long been a salesman. Others in this category are prosperous, specialized merchants or administrators who are cautious in their search for economic security. They operate a family business. Their wives do the bookkeeping and participate in decision-making; their outside financing is limited to a credit margin at the bank and to mortgages; they are highly involved in community affairs and are the only businessmen who still regularly serve as *marguilliers* for the church. Also, contrary to what one might expect from socially-involved locals, they are not deeply involved in partisan politics. Their background and economic stability, together with a restrained approach to politicking, may lead them to be considered as "saints" (see Chapter Six), and they are the ones who are frequently asked to lead the school commission and sensitive municipal committees, or any association with a bi-partisan membership. The fact that their families are largely outside of Saint-Pascal means that they have few local kin and could potentially be regarded as neutrals in disputes where one large family is ranged against another.

From this brief review of intergenerational mobility within Saint-Pascal's business community it may be asserted that economic success has depended on a combination of strategies which incorporate both expertise and family connections. *Without exception, Saint-Pascal's industries are not the culmination of the reinvestment of inherited wealth* even though the possession of some family capital eliminates the number of intermediate steps which individuals must take to attain their objectives.

Marriage is another means of career mobility from which a few businessmen have benefitted. Occasionally a farmer's son has benefitted from the monetary assistance of his merchant father-in-law, but such interoccupational marriages that have brought financial advantages are rare in Saint-Pascal. Instead, merchant dynasties have married into other merchant and artisan families. These marriages are primarily along political lines. However, this is more a result of the pattern of interfamily sociability among merchants (Chapter Five) than any conscious attempt at political alliance.

When an outsider observes upward or downward mobility from a single point in time, neither should it be assumed that a business person's career has run its full course, nor that career objectives can be clearly stated. Furthermore, it is unlikely that the historical pattern of mobility can be used accurately to predict future growth. A case in point is Maltais, the television and furniture dealer and the son of a salaried clerk, who had explained to me in 1969 how television could become a local industry based around his community cable system. Several years later he was able to initiate rudimentary local programming with the assistance of teachers and members of the Centre Social. This and other expansionary plans require capital. Once an enterprise has reached a certain scale of operations, credit and financing can usually be obtained although sometimes only by incurring certain social costs.

Sources of Investment Capital

We have seen that new enterprises were not begun by the most wealthy families of professionals or by those already in possession of mercantile background. The launching of an enterprise has required other inputs. Such was the quandary faced by traders who sold or mortgaged their homes to raise starting capital. An example of a reallocation of assets — value foregone in one area for an uncertain return in another — is the case of the candy manufacturer who accepted five hundred dollars for his car to raise the money he needed for his first machine. A more common way of gathering starting capital is by borrowing a lump sum from a successful local entrepreneur who has risk capital for new ventures. Some have been able to get support from the Federal Government's Industrial Expansion Bank or from government subsidies offered to new enterprise in Eastern Quebec. Whatever the means, the beginning always needed an infusion of starting capital from a minimum of about one thousand dollars, to twenty thousand in the case of some industries. However, capital investment in Saint-Pascal's businesses is an ongoing process,since every reorganization of a physical plant, or change in the objectives of an enterprise generates new demands for money and for expertise.

A survey of the different capital inputs and major expansions of businesses turns up a rather limited range of alternative strategies of capital investment. Particularly interesting are the local financial institutions such as the money lender, the Caisse Populaire and the chartered bank — three institutions which have been important to Saint-Pascal in its growth from an agricultural service centre to an industrial town.

One source of crucial starting and expansion capital is "obligated friendships" — patron-client relationships made with local "millionaires", the silent investors whose wealth has financed some of the riskier ventures of younger businessmen. In some cases the return is nothing more than a financial one. There is a certain assurance or security in lending to those who are close at hand and whose businesses could be taken over if the borrower incurred heavy debts. But there are also pressures within the entrepreneurial group not to permit colleagues in innovative competition to be taken over by powerful patrons. This would jeopardize the semblance of equality within the business elite and possibly the autonomy of other enterprises through a concentration of economic and political power.

Thus when Jacques Turcotte, whose wife is considered to be a *grande dame* in Saint-Pascal, made a private loan to Rosaire Gagnon enabling him to purchase the leather in the hold of a sunken Liberian freighter, it was not long before all the "industrialists" knew the alleged details of the transaction. In conversations in the post office lobby and on any private occasion that arose, some concern was expressed over whether Turcotte had plans to take over the tannery. The story then circulated that Gagnon's shares in the tannery had been locked in a trunk as collateral. Several months later, Turcotte, together with industrialist Henri Fortier purchased an aging and financially shaky implement factory in nearby Saint-André.[1] Rumours flared about the outcome of these transactions. Both Fortier and Gagnon felt obliged to reassure people of the integrity and financial independence of their enterprises. Meanwhile the silent investor had placed his money before a not-so-candid camera. His own involvement in the local community, which had never been as great as his wife's, was now established and respected.

Other cases are closer to what Dansereau (1967) finds in her discussion of the developmental sequence of family businesses in Eastern Quebec in which economic mobility through loans and government contracts is a function of the partisan involvement of the client in provincial politics. In Saint-Pascal, political patrons are of importance mainly to small contractors who rely on road and construction contracts when their party is in power. In other cases clients will deal with those transport companies and suppliers to whom they owe political favours (see Chapter Six). To most businesses, local political patrons have rapidly become secondary to the building of networks which include bankers, accountants and top-ranking civil servants. The industrialization of the town has been accompanied by a shift away from private financing. Therefore, I will turn to the role of the two most important local financial institutions in Saint-Pascal's economy, the Caisse and the bank, and the Federal Department of Regional Economic Expansion.

The Caisse

In Chapter Three I introduced Saint-Pascal's Caisse Populaire as a credit union and savings bank that is a concrete representation of the economic nationalism which spread rapidly through the towns and parishes of Quebec, reaching Saint-Pascal in 1934. The idea caught on and "social shares" were purchased by thousands of parishioners who were strongly encouraged in church, in the classroom and at home to save with the Caisse. In return for this confidence, the Caisse offers low interest loans as well as life insurance and investment opportunities through its national programmes. In 1960 the Caisse was able to move out of a private home into its own bank-like facilities on the main street of town. In 35 years the original assets of $515.80 have grown to over a million dollars.

The organization of the Caisse is highly localized and quite stable. The directors and a credit and a surveillance committee are elected by the members. There have been only a few changes in officeholders over the past 20 years, and the *notables* of the parish have held virtually all of these posts uncontested. Public interest in the Caisse is not very great and the directors feel the need to promise attractive door prizes to promote attendance at the annual election meeting.

The extent to which the inhabitants of Québecois communities have involved themselves in a cooperative credit union with civic and religious approval underlines a fundamental institutional difference between French and English Canada. Still, the Caisse Populaire is not a chartered bank and cannot legally advance commercial credit to small businessmen despite the local and national support it received from Quebec. Forty-six percent of the businessmen I interviewed have built major commercial buildings with the help of the Caisse Populaire. This includes the largest retail enterprises, but not the industries, except when Caisse Populaire mortgages are made on the homes of manufacturers and then converted into risk capital. In many cases, home and business are in the same building and a loan from the Caisse may be used to renovate both.

The president of the Caisse, a retired farmer who lives in town, is aware of its special appeal to the average Pascalien:

> Some merchants and industries do their business with the Caisse — all except the largest industries. This is because the *Caisses Populaires were founded to help the little man.*

Small-scale merchants and the old families who run the general stores have an almost dogmatic preference for the Caisse:

> Both myself and my father have always preferred the Caisse Populaire over the Provincial Bank, where we do keep a nominal account. (Printer, 40, one employee.)

> I am a fellow who makes use of our Provincial Institutions! (Pharmacist, 53, one employee)

> Seeing that we are both shareholders and borrowers, it is natural that we should turn to them. (General merchant, 46, three employees.)

Others are not convinced that the Caisse is a very business-like place to bank, and reply that "banks are the only way". One man, a migrant from a rural parish, is insistent in his refusal to deal with the Caisse where he has to "tell too many stories to too many people". At the bank, he has only the manager to deal with.

The Bank

The Bank and the Caisse do co-exist however, with a strong degree of mutual understanding. The president of the Caisse has this clearly established:

> The Bank has not retarded our growth. There has always been an entente between the manager of the Bank and the manager of the Caisse. Mme Pelletier has been our manager since 1936!

The bank manager is more explicit on the financial division of labour:

> If they wish to come to our bank and borrow, I tell them to bring their money with them as well. But the bank still feels an *obligation to encourage the Caisse* — that's normal.

Legally, all except the smallest of tradesmen must rely on bank credit to pay for incoming shipments and to maintain their inventories. The increase in bank credit reflects the general increase in commercial activity. Credit extended to Gagnon's tannery and to Fortier's factory rose from several thousand dollars in 1964 to well over one hundred thousand dollars in 1969. On a typical business day, every important business person in town can be seen in the bank. All this is quite evident to everyone in town, for the private office of the bank manager faces the street, and his plate glass window is directly opposite the massive doors of the church.

During the church's years of liturgical reform, the bank in Saint-Pascal also experienced significant personnel and policy changes. In the fifties, the bank manager was well along in years and known as someone from whom it was impossible to get a loan should there be any risk involved. He stepped down in 1963 and was replaced by a banker of the same age and temperament as the entrepreneurial group. The new banker joined Club Richelieu and became an influential promoter of the new factories and stores. Four years later he was transferred and replaced by an equally ambitious 27-year-old manager. Credit margins were liberally raised and working capital became more readily available than ever before. With twelve full-time employees, the bank has become an integral part of the expanding county centre. Recent managers have kept monthly records of the economic health of most every business in the region, and because their record-keeping involves endless telephone calls and visits with businessmen, the manager acts as an information broker who is able to provide counsel on financial procedures and even market conditions. Saint-Pascal's several accountants play a similar role in information management and are also active within the councils of the entrepreneurial group. Both banker and accountant keep their knowledge of what is happening to themselves in situations in which their clients are actively trading confidences, such as at Club Richelieu meetings.

Even with the expansion of the bank there is a divergence of opinion on the availability of bank funding for expansionary projects. Successful Henri Fortier is a good example:

> Fifty per cent of the people are pessimistic about getting loans. There are no major complications in getting money. This is an old attitude which does not change, for in the past, people organized their finances by borrowing privately.

Aside from the optimists, and these are almost entirely in the entrepreneurial group, a considerable number of businessmen complain of exorbitant interest rates and a reluctant banker. These are intermediate enterprises with sales of between $75,000 and $400,000 a year. Their margin of credit at the bank is crucial and sometimes so are good relations with the banker. This group includes four contractors who emphasize that their livelihood depends on the ability of the bank to discount their contracts. For many small scale industrialists such as Fleury, lack of available funds means a lost business deal:

> All of my creditors have declared me persona non grata, except one, Robert (the bank manager). He knows all about these new schemes of mine and seems ready to offer his support again. Even so, he returned one check to an important seller. There are $400 worth of C.O.D.'s at the post office and neither the money for the expropriation nor the insurance claim on my warehouse have arrived. With all this, I must buy $150 worth of new stock every week. My margin of credit is not adequate . . . . this is the time when I must invest.

Fleury relies on the statement his accountant produces to bargain higher credit margin with the bank manager. He knew that government-supported expansion loans were available, but because of the risk to his livelihood, he was reluctant to apply for a government loan or expansion subsidy, or a loan from the regional industrial credit union to which he and others were contributing regular investments.

Operators of small retail enterprises with sales of under $50,000 a year refused even to consider loans (they may not be eligible for bank credit) and some shy away from mortgages. They express the view that borrowing is dangerous, and its value is negated by the high interest rates. Several have cut down on labour costs to prevent borrowing. As a craftsman put it, "The ideal thing is to have a surplus. Taking out loans is a loss for your business." The goal of the part-time desk manufacturer is to reduce stock, increase profits and, in doing so, build up his credit margin. To accomplish this, he is willing to expand slowly. Several other small manufacturers hesitate to invest in new machinery because of the threat to the security of their enterprises. The two brothers-in-law who manage the Turcotte wagon factory were the only managers who felt that they could run an industry without borrowing.

Solvency and Growth of the Enterprise

Capital has never been very easy for French Québecois to obtain; yet, there is also a division between cautious, risk-avoiding small businessmen and optimistic, risk-taking enterprisers — the majority of whom are included in the entrepreneurial group. This is not to say that the latter manage economically rational enterprises and that the other businessmen have created family enterprises in the spirit of Sombart's traditional businessman.

In practice, small businesses tend to experience a developmental cycle which cannot be separated from the life cycle of businessmen and the long term distribution of wealth and status within a single family. The addition of bureaucratic organizations in Saint-Pascal's businesses has not eliminated the importance of family control. At certain moments in the life of an expanding business, family management may be advantageous. However, there is a marked contrast between what the Pascaliens *call* a family enterprise (*entreprise familiale*) and some of the new factories and stores established in the sixties in which family control has been systematically reduced by the controlling family member. It is therefore worthwhile to begin a discussion of the organization of family businesses in Saint-Pascal with a description of the type of enterprise which has long characterized the Lower Saint Lawrence and French Canada.

The Family Enterprise: Sleeping on Both Ears

Both inside and outside their place of work townsmen make a strong distinction between kin and nonkin. I was often told that "You can't treat a *kinsman* as you would treat a *stranger*" or that "kinsmen are more reliable than strangers".

Only a dozen parish businesses do not incorporate kin into their organization. Invariably, one man or woman is recognized as the major owner or manager of the family concern. In some instances these firms were once totally staffed by family members, but a regular pattern of succession was not established and the aging owner is now left without heirs. In a few institutions, such as the chartered bank, bureaucratic practices are established outside of the town and the bank manager's relatives are not easily introduced as employees. On the other hand, kin who once managed a firm together, have decided to go their separate ways. This fission within the family is an essential part of the developmental cycle of a family business. Noninheriting children leave for other opportunities and inheriting children must work out the division of rights and responsibilities of management.[2] If they are unable to do so, the enterprise will split, often resulting in two businesses of the same type competing for a small and saturated market. The number of claimants to the enterprise is also reduced by daughters who marry men from outside Saint-Pascal and move away to their husband's community, and by those who leave for higher education and then settle elsewhere in Quebec.

Few businessmen in Saint-Pascal completely separate their business life from their home life. In twenty-two (47 percent) of the businesses I surveyed, the owner's residence is incorporated directly into his commercial building, and in another twelve cases, the family quarters are only a few doors away. Perhaps the most dramatic case of physical integration of residence and family firm is the Landry Wool Mill, where the family kitchen opens directly into the second storey of their factory. This has been the traditional residence pattern of small craftsmen, and explains why Henri Fortier surprised his neighbours when he decided not to move into the old residential quarters above his first tire retreading plant. Fortier could hardly disagree that kinship is an organizational principal in many of the town's enterprises, including his own.

A family enterprise begins with the participation of the owner's wife as bookkeeper, clerk and manager. While authority within the business has not been consistently measured, in numerous cases women were powerful inside decision-makers with an equal or dominant role in controlling the family firm. Business wives, however, do not represent the firm in public and they do not make business trips or belong to service clubs with other business women. Their participation in business affairs is added to their household responsibilities and to the raising of children who may be brought into the business as trustworthy and low-cost employees.

The second most common type of kin involvement is the incorporation of brothers and sisters into the enterprise as junior partners and trusted employees (sixteen cases or 27.5 percent). In two of these firms, the father who founded the enterprise continues to work with his sons as an associate; five other men employ their sons as prospective successors. Only eleven businessmen (25 percent), employ no kin at all in their enterprises.

This high degree of kin involvement in business does not mean that every manager of an enterprise in Saint-Pascal condones kinship involvement. While some conceive of kin as an irreplaceable asset in their business, others are quite vocal in their disapproval of the practice of hiring kin over non-kin. They are conscious of something amiss in having family members within their enterprises, and consider the *enterprise familiale* to be an illogical and irrational practice. Nonetheless, their behaviour contradicts their universalistic ideal. Frequently I encountered statements such as: "This is the worst thing you can do. Mind you, *I* have had no troubles!" or "We must all get away from the *entreprise familiale!*" What then are the advantages of family businesses, and are there any grounds on which businessmen specifically reject kinship ties in the administration of their businesses?

Only seven tradesmen insist that having kin in their businesses was an unqualified advantage. These replies were generally worded with clichés such as: "Kin are security for an enterprise. They take an interest in your business and you can trust them; they need less supervision and assistance." A small manufacturer is much more explicit:

> As to hiring relatives, my brother's kin are the most intimate with me and there is no danger of *chiâlage*. They often provide me service without pay and there is never any question of working hours. On my wife's side, however, hiring is more difficult and dangerous.

This security angle is emphasized in another conversation with the manager of a family industry:

> It is always easier to be partners with one's relatives. When you go on a trip, you can be certain that clients are well treated. *You can sleep on both of your ears.*

What one man thinks is good in kin participation, another thinks is detrimental to the flexibility and growth potential of his business. Most of my sample (73 percent) recognize negative aspects in working with kinsmen, and the majority (56 percent) were not conscious of advantages in a family business. Speaking from personal experience, they cite problems such as flexibility, the delegation of authority and competence:

It is perhaps safer to have members of your family working with you, but it is also a debatable thing. *They hang around like furniture in the middle of your business.* They are inflexible, and because they know that your reprimands don't matter, or that they are not to be considered as ordinary employees — it often creates serious problems.

Partnership between kin tends to work out in only a very few instances. The survivor of an unsuccessful partnership with his brother recognizes the main problem as envy and jealousy between wives who urged them to gain more advantages from their alliance. His brother (and ex-partner) concludes that "a four-way match is difficult to manage". Wives or no wives, few partnerships in Saint-Pascal have lasted for more than several years. Positive attitudes towards kin prevail only where family members are in a privileged and well-defined working relationship with the business manager rather than full partners (status equals), or as employees or paid labourers (the insecurity of bureaucratic universalism). Such privileged linkages may on the short term be a necessary insurance for the continuation of the firm.

Perhaps the overshadowing problem of the family business is succession, guaranteeing the life of the enterprise beyond the life of its owner or manager. Lack of a suitable heir leaves a family enterprise with serious succession problems. The rewards for expansion are inseparably related to the responsiveness and the capabilities of family members. An uncertain future may lead the family decision-makers to seek a precarious stability through non-expansionary business strategies which reduce risk and guarantee a steady short run return for their family and for their employees.

At least four of the town's small industries are low-risk family enterprises in which stability is shored up by an enduring and un-written contract between employer and labourer. The employer hires a worker (and if possible that person's kin) on a regular basis, without lay-offs or any significant fluctuations in salary. In the Turcotte farm-wagon factory, when there was nothing to be done in the plant, the twenty workers were deployed in building sheds, or in manufacturing small metal parts, and building or rebuilding machinery. Wages are set close to the minimum legal wage as set by government or the provincial parity committee. In special circumstances work is done without any extra renumeration. In return, the labourer must regularly put in up to a ten-hour day and Saturday morning. He sets the pace of his own work since there is no foreman other than occasional supervision by the shop owner and his kin who labour alongside their employees.

The owners express pride in their businesses as reliable places to work, rather as cornerstones for future expansion. More generally, they perceive of their companies as dead ends and limited opportunities and insist that they will guide their sons and daughters to higher levels of education to avoid "the obsolescence" they have attained. Since there is now a greater diversity of specialized regional employment and educational opportunities such as the C.E.G.E.P. collegiate courses in La Pocatière, many of the children of successful family industries are directed elsewhere while the least likely to succeed fall back on the family business. Admittedly it is difficult to generalize for all the family enterprises, since idiosyncratic goals and peculiaristic management practices can take many forms. Nevertheless, to place the family business in perspective, I will turn to the Landry wool mill, a successful small firm where kinship pervades both management and labour.

The Old Wool Mill

The frame structure of the old wool mill faces the paved roadway of the third *rang*. Next to this imposing wood structure that was once the Saint-Pascal seigneurial mill, a small waterfall, La Chute Landry, spills out toward the road. Once an important local resource, the mill was bought and sold several times before coming into the possession of the Landry family in the late nineteenth century.

In 1946, Louis-Georges Landry (47) began to purchase used machinery to mechanize the mill for yarn production. Financing came from a locally-raised private loan of $25,000. A clothing goods store was added to the front of the mill in 1948, while the Landry family continued to live on the second storey of the mill, dividing off their home from the factory with massive wooden doors. Landry made his last production change in 1954, when he purchased used machinery with a loan from the Industrial Expansion Bank.

When Landry's father ran the mill as a small shop, production was geared to the needs of farmers who raised sheep. Even after 1946, transactions with farmers did not involve a cash economy;

the Landry family gathered wool from farmers in the region and exchanged it, less a commission, for finished yarn.

> Then the *cultivateurs* let their sheep go! But we were tied to a particular system of transformation. Our trade fell, and then one year when we were ready to close the doors, we decided to produce for sale.

The farmers' product was rapidly replaced by imported Australian wool.

> At first we organized a system of trucks which covered the county, gathering wool. Then we decided to let the trucks go and take on salesmen who already had other lines. In this way, our wool sold as far east as Newfoundland.

The greatest transformation came in the 1960s when Landry began a mail order operation with the assistance of a Montreal advertising agency and the encouragement of friends in the entrepreneurial group. Sales rose at the rate of 23 percent per year, and the mill has been able to maintain production with a steady complement of 13 employees. An ad agency designed a company symbol of a spinning wheel and magazine advertising aimed at the needs of a home knitting market across Canada.

Organization of the Mill

The mill is entirely in the hands of the Landry family (see Figure 4.4). Louis-Georges Landry is president, his brother is vice-president,and his sister is secretary-treasurer. Several of the family's children work in the mill during vacations, and two full-time employees in their twenties assist in the mailing of wool shipments. Madame Landry and her sister-in-law work in the clothing store at the front of the mill. Although Landry initially wished otherwise, his eldest son has dropped out of C.E.G.E.P. and then worked for the family until an opening could be found for him in Henri Fortier's tire factory. Much of the factory work is organized by Louis-Georges' brother, who drives the company truck and handles supervisory problems in the factory. In the spring, an out-of-town employee makes the rounds of those farmers who still supply wool for the mill. This task has been his for years and he alone maintains all records of these transactions.

Figure 4.4

Kin Ties among Workers
The Landry Wool Mill

A. Production Workers

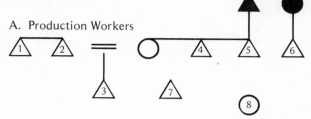

B. Managerial — Clerical Staff

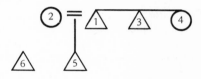

A. Operators	Years of Service	Age
1 Twister	12	34
2 Carder	22	45
3 Picker	1	26
4 Foreman	28	50
5 Threader	25	45
6 Spooler	—	45
7 Winder	1	24
8 Warehouse (Students)	1-3	18-21

B.

1-5 Landry Family
1   Louis-George   47
    (Manager)
6-7 Clerical Staff
▲● Connecting Kin

Seven workers operate the machines of the mill. All but one of the workers are related and most have been working for the Landry family since the mill was reorganized. (see Figure 4.4) Only one position, that of the winder (no. 7), has been occupied repeatedly by young workers unrelated to the others — it is a temporary job until other work is available in the mill or elsewhere. The work week of five days is 48 hours long. An hour is provided for lunch, when everyone goes home to eat and the 'foreman' takes over key machines.

The 'foreman' of the mill (No. 4) has no official title. He has been with the Landry family for 28 years, beginning at a dollar a day for a six-day week. Before that, he had done winter road work and summer farm labour. One of his important tasks is keeping the old machines in repair. Over the years he has experienced some loss of hearing as a result of the incessant thud of machinery.

There are no special production quotas other than what is needed to replenish the stockroom. The machines regulate the men and the amount of production depends on the repair of the machinery. No one knows exactly how long will be required to produce a lot of wool.

Capital Investment

Machines which are likely to break down are operated by the more experienced of this family of millworkers. The manufacturing process is labour-intensive. Many operations are performed manually, such as winding finished wool into skeins by wrapping strands of wool around a wooden spindle embedded into posts in the floor. As Landry explains: "There is a machine available for this, but it is not worth getting".

Landry believes that he has reached a production ceiling using his present plant. He would like to be able to diversify into the production of washable and mothproof wools which call for specialized machinery and competence; however, his existing machinery is inefficient and outmoded; the "mule" in the mill is one of three of its kind in Quebec and could well be replaced by a new spinning frame. But the cost is prohibitive and government subsidies are not readily available for new machinery which does not create new employment. Moreover, Landry is reluctant to buy more low-cost machinery: "We have been using the "American

110

System' in making wool, which does not give as nice a product; the Italians are specialists in making these kinds of machines. When I do buy, it will be something new instead of used and obsolete equipment."

Decision-Making and Expanding Markets

Once Rosaire Gagnon went to Toronto to sell leather to department store buyers and Louis-Georges Landry accompanied him with his woolen goods. The buyers found the price very reasonable and they took samples to test for quality, but they were not interested in his yarn until it could be attractively packaged. To meet the store's specifications, Landry needed to purchase a fifty-thousand-dollar packaging machine, yet he hesitates to risk all the security he has attained over the years with the purchase of such costly new machinery. If one of his sons were to decide after his education that he wants to work in the mill, then he would be more at ease in taking risks and making investments. "I have evolved the business rapidly with the times. Today it is a *business, not* a craft shop! The future will depend on my family. I am no longer as young as I once was, and time has passed very quickly." Without industrial expansion and with the limitations of mail order sales, the family firm moved to improve its regional market as a specialized retail outlet. The small store windows and the painted wood facade of the store were replaced with white brick framing an imposing display window, and a large plastic sign announcing the Landry "Boutique". (see photograph)

In 1974, a disastrous fire gutted the mill, sparing only the boutique and warehouse. The regional paper announced that the mill "will not resume operations without financial assistance from the various levels of government"(*le Saint-Laurent*, April 24, 1974). Faced with these alternatives and the promise of municipal assistance, Landry began negotiating for subsidies to allow him to build a factory in a new industrial park at the town limits.

In many ways the Landry mill exemplifies what some have referred to as the cultural moulding of French-Canadian enterprise (Taylor, 1964) in which family security dominates decision-making. In other aspects, especially in his approach to marketing, Landry is nontraditional. At 47, he is still able to be a peer of the entrepreneurial group. Although he was never a member of the Rural Catholic Youth, he has been influenced by the intimate friendships and by the innovative competition for business success within this group. In this respect, no manufacturer in Saint-Pascal has been able to remain aloof from the networks and coalitions of the *industriels*.

Transformation of the Family Enterprise

While kinship ties are dominant in small enterprises, families have not demonstrated the ability to rapidly and unilaterally expand a small firm without the help of outside expertise. The process by which the larger enterprises have expanded involves the gradual forcing out of some kinsmen from management and the universalization of employer-employee relationships. The dichotomy between kin and stranger becomes less important. The newcomer is the hired expert — the general manager who will be evaluated primarily on performance criteria.

Conflict arises when kin are expected to meet these same criteria of performance. This conflict is significant in the growth of Saint-Pascal where every large business began as a family venture and, over a period of years, kinsmen who did not fit into the enterprise were either bought out or forced into managerial roles that reflect their level of competence *en affaires*. However, family obligations versus business priorities is not the only role-conflict of the Québecois small-town businessman. Even when there are no kin ties to account for the employer must at times still differentiate the employer-employee relationship from other social relationships within the community. In a town where "everyone knows each other", friendship and community allegiances which are strong in club life and in politics easily spill over into business relationships. As pressures of kith and kin constantly influence the decision-maker, it is all the more remarkable how outside experts are introduced and integrated into the fabric of the enterprise. I will illustrate the transition from an organization that is interrelated with family interests to a more bureaucratic form of management drawing mainly on the example of Rosaire Gagnon's tannery and to a lesser extent, Henri Fortier's tire retreading factory. Then I will

112

place the newly expanded industries into perspective by comparing them with other commerce in the community.

The Old Tannery: The Expansion of a Family Enterprise

Three generations of the Gagnon family tanners have practised their craft in Saint-Pascal. The first was Joseph Gagnon, who purchased a small tannery in 1891 after he had learned his trade from an uncle in Saint-Onézime, a highland parish southwest of Saint-Pascal. His business was a service trade, producing for farmers in much the same way as the Turcotte wagon shop and the Landry Wool Mill. In 1925, his son, Paul-Émile Gagnon, joined the family firm which at that time had begun to produce harnesses and *robes de carriole* (sheepskin sleigh robes). Fifteen years later, Paul-Émile purchased his father's interest in the business and continued in much the same line of work. In the years following the Second World War, three of Paul-Émile's sons went to work in the tannery and a fourth son entered the priesthood. By 1958, the two eldest sons, Rosaire and Clément, formed a corporation with their father and purchased a small out-of-town glove factory from which they kept only the sewing machines and other equipment. During this entire period, the enterprise remained on the lower floor of Paul-Émile Gagnon's frame house on the main street of Saint-Pascal and, as I explained earlier, Rosaire Gagnon then was very much involved with his own career.

When Rosaire returned in 1962 to work full time in the tannery with Clément, the small shop had eight full-time employees producing $12,000 worth of leather a year. Eight years later, the tannery was supplemented by three sewing plants, and the combined operation employed over 200 workers, the basis of what Gagnon hoped would be a "leather complex". This rapid expansion required funds from diverse sources, including a series of partnerships, loans, and subsidies from government agencies.

The old family quarters continued to be used as company headquarters and as a retirement home for Paul-Émile and his wife. Sewing plants were set up in an adjoining shed, an old convent in Saint-Pacôme, abandoned *rang* schools, basements of Gagnon family homes and the homes of workers (through a putting-out arrangement). Several barns about the parish were given over to leather storage, while other farms have been vacated by factory workers who abandoned their land to work in the expanding tannery. The Gagnon tannery had outgrown the confines of its ancestral home all the while making an irreversible economic and social impact on its agricultural surroundings.

From Partnerships to Subsidies

Some funds for the initial development of the enterprise came from the Gagnon family capital. Subsequent loans were obtained from the Industrial Expansion Bank and the local chartered bank through a credit margin. At the same time, Gagnon had actively sought associates who would buy into the enterprise. His first partnership was with Clément, an expert tanner. The two brothers did not share the same values in running a business. Clément bought out of the partnership in 1965 and set up his own small tannery. Rosaire however continued to expand his tannery by adding glove factories to increase the demand for leather. This led to the joint venture with the sewing machine dealer-mechanic, that also did not last, leaving Gagnon with a need for both tanning and mechanical skills. These requirements for expertise were met through working agreements with local and out-of-town skilled craftsmen and management consultants (the latter supported by provincial government subsidies).

What the firm needed most was financial order — a comptroller and more capital. This required a person who was trustworthy and dependable. With the help of several industrialist colleagues, and in particular the regional golf network of his cousin, Maltais, Gagnon negotiated with Saint-Pascal's ex-banker, the man who had opened the bank to easier credit arrangements. The banker's old network was strong and the "bank" was brought back as partner and comptroller in the tannery. At the same time as Rosaire Gagnon obtained financial expertise, Henri Fortier hired his accountant from Rivière-du-Loup as Vice-President of his tire factory that had just moved into stylish new offices. Both newcomers were integrated into the entrepreneurial group, although their families, as nonnatives of Saint-Pascal, encountered a less spontaneous introduction to small-town life.

A more secure way of raising capital is to sell shares of the enterprise to long–time employees. This strategy was used by

Rosaire Gagnon with some success after his factory was destroyed by fire, and by the candy manufacturer, Tremblay, who joined with his mechanic and a trusted foreman to form a managerial team. On a token or symbolic basis, share buying characterizes the entrepreneurial group. Fortier bought a few thousand dollars worth from Gagnon and vice versa. Others have made similar arrangements, and these usually are private matters known only within the councils of the entrepreneurial group. Nevertheless, Gagnon and Fortier's major involvements with local silent investors (as discussed earlier) have been undertaken with great caution.

The expanding firm also needs social capital in the form of public legitimacy, and local political support on a regular basis especially in case of a catastrophe. Fortier has been the most prepared to undertake local social and political obligations; for example, he outfitted the town's baseball team and has contributed heavily to numerous local projects and was more overtly involved in the political support of his friends. Other businessmen reinforce their relationships with local *notables* through golf games and timely gifts. More important are donations of money and prizes during the winter Carnaval, and a public response to requests for assistance from schools and associations.

Investment propositions by outsiders are frequently turned down; businessmen consider this to be more risky than purely local transactions, where sentiment and shared rules of behaviour still operate and where others are intimately interested in survival. Outside investors have offered to purchase Fortier's tire factory and portions of Gagnon's leather operation. These offers are not kept secret and both men have made certain that their friends knew what had transpired. However, resistance to control does not mean that outside aid is never accepted, particularly when this leads to market advantage. Gagnon entered into specific agreements on such matters as the supply of linings and the manufacture of leather garments. Fortier owes much of his success to a franchise for the exclusive use of a cold retreading process and to infusions of capital and credit from suppliers. Another source of outside capital is the Industrial Expansion Bank which provides a secure loan as the Federal Government in particular has expressed little interest in taking over of small industry. The manufacturers are more apprehensive about grants-in-aid and loans from the Provincial Government to which they claim "strings are attached".

The scale of business in Saint-Pascal is directly related to how many civil servants the owner knows in Quebec and Ottawa. Townsmen who are outside the entrepreneurial group often assert that "our *grandes industries*" (large industries) would collapse without government subsidies. In practice, since 1968 federal regional development legislation has entitled the tannery and tire factory to liberal subsidies for the purchase of new machinery or for the construction of factories. Since then high-ranking provincial and federal civil servants frequently visit the larger factories. At least five manufacturers in Saint-Pascal have accepted government subsidies for the "retraining of their workers". Despite stories of inefficiency, wasted time, and blatant political patronage in the granting of industrial subsidies, in 1972 Saint-Pascal's manufacturers received nearly two million dollars in provincial government assistance alone. After fire destroyed the Gagnon tannery in 1971, a federal regional economic expansion grant provided most of the funds needed to rebuild a modern, well-equipped tannery. Subsidies, initially a minor factor in the growth of Saint-Pascal's industry, have now become a prop to small-scale capitalism in the Lower Saint Lawrence. Without them, it is doubtful whether the town or the region could sustain their new industrial growth. This has led the region and its government-supported industrial capitalism to a fundamental ideological shift toward state financial and technological dependency, the implications of which need not deter us until the concluding chapter.

The Supply of Labour

Manning Nash (1958:35ff) found that after industry was brought into isolated Cantel, the factories adapted to the cultural institutions of the Guatemalan Indian. However, Everett Hughes (1943) found a less than a harmonious adaptation to industrialization in his study of Cantonville. There French Canadians became the working class for Anglo-Canadian industrialists and their foremen, and the French-Canadian elite directed their sons toward the liberal professions, small businesses and politics. What of Saint-Pascal, where industrialization is indigenous and where the rapid and unplanned introduction of factories has had the effect of creating a new occupational group within the labour force? The new industrialists never imagined that they would be directing large factories.

Without exception they were as unprepared as their workers were for their new roles and for the uncertainties of the labour market.

The size of a labour market is shaped by the available population and the willingness of men to work (Bloom and Northrup, 1965:289ff). Cultural factors are therefore determinants of a labour supply as Rosaire Gagnon discovered when he looked for female labour in Saint-Pascal:

> The girls in the village do not want to work with their hands. They are a little educated here and for a girl to work in a factory, that isn't very chic. They want to be secretaries and office workers. In a village like Saint-Athanase, labour is more available.

In contrast, there is no shortage of local men who wish to work in the tannery or in the tire factory and all manufacturers have long waiting lists. If a man wants work quickly he needs a connection, a friend or a friend of a friend, a *tuyau* within the factory. The application process is informal and factory records are at their best imprecise, at their worst nonexistent. It is not surprising that in the small-scale labour market of Eastern Kamouraska, fifty-seven percent of Gagnon's female and male applicants have a friend or a relative working in his factories.

From 154 of these loosely-filed applications and from employment lists for the tannery (the only such file kept by any of the factories), some indicators can be found of the supply of labour for Saint-Pascal's industries in 1970. Firstly, given the shortage of male jobs,[3] nearly eighty percent of the tannery workers are from Saint-Pascal. A similar percentage of locals exists in the other factories. The tannery workers are mostly semi-skilled and relatively young; their average age is twenty-six and their average level of education is grade seven.

The example of the sewing plants reveals a reverse situation for the female labour force, and, in line with Gagnon's observations, 75 percent of the girls are from outside Saint-Pascal. This is almost completely semi-skilled and unskilled labour, and turnover of female workers is a major labour problem. After a girl is trained, she often leaves to be married and only a handful of married women work in any of the factories. Nonetheless female application forms outnumber male applications by five to one and none would be required to learn skills that could not be rapidly acquired from in-shop training.

In 1970, the labour supply in absolute terms did not greatly preoccupy the factory owners. In general, they had rather an imprecise idea of the regional labour market. They were aware of a critical shortage in skilled industrial trades. A far more pressing problem was labour-management relations — the problems of delegating authority, wages and labour unions.

New Managers and New Workers

Very few employer-employee relationships in the larger industries continue the unwritten contract of security of the small family enterprise. As with most changes in Saint-Pascal's economy, there are visible contradictions. In the Gagnon tannery several long-standing craftsmen remain with the firm and one still handcrafts sheepskin to make *robes de carriole* for automobiles. These employees refuse to take orders from young foremen and report directly to the owner-manager or to his younger brother. If it is an emergency, they want Gagnon's immediate attention no matter what else may be going on at that time.

A number of other workers within the leather complex are retained on a putting-out basis, a pre-industrial scheme which has brought a lawsuit from the provincial parity committee that regulates hourly wages in the leather industry. Each cutter who works on this basis is established as a separate company, buying his leather, working his own hours and then selling his product back to the firm. Gagnon considers putting-out to be advantageous to both the enterprise and the employee who "cannot tolerate rules" and who "unlike the fellow of 18, will not be confined to fixed hours". It was one way to expand without factory space or costly bureaucratic supervision of workers and it effectively circumvented rigid salary floors.

The tannery is organized differently from the sewing factories. Two foremen[4] and a superintendent supervise production and select people for the many awaiting jobs. Orders are sent through to the superintendent on standardized forms. Rosaire Gagnon himself sets priorities on the filling of these orders. From there, orders are processed through the foremen and production begins. Friction often arises over priorities, as available skins are not always suitable for the orders on hand. After the departure of skilled

118

Clément, Gagnon had problems with the quality of his shipments and several lots of leather were returned. Expanding the sewing factories by producing leather garments and accessories was one major adaptation to the uncertainties of tanning. The sewing plants produce over half of what the company sells and operate largely with leather from the tannery.

Leather quality improved with the introduction of several skilled European craftsmen, but this created its own problems particularly in communication between local workers and the Europeans who were hired through the Federal Manpower Department. Gagnon recognizes problems in importing expertise:

> The French Canadian is reticent *vis à vis* the stranger, whoever he is, the German, the Turk, the Portugese, all of whom I have working here. There are no others who have immigrants in their factories! There is a fear . . . there are employees who said that they would not be directed by a Turk.

Despite these difficulties, Gagnon, Fortier and other *industriels* share a deep-seated conviction that specialists and experts are the answer to some of their organizational problems. Their admiration for specialists is translated into the guest invitations to C.D.E. and Richelieu meetings (see Chapter Five) and into elaborate studies of their companies done by Montreal consulting firms, subsidized by another group of experts in the provincial government's Department of Industry and Commerce.

There is a considerable element of front in the creation of what are alleged to be bureaucratic organizations. In practice, in both large stores and factories, the owners deal with their employees' small problems in a paternalistic manner; they countersign for them at the bank and assist them with financial and legal hardships. No business manager in Saint-Pascal, large or small, is completely free of these obligations; they are part of being a Pascalien of prestige and power who "meets his responsibilities". This complicates administrative acts such as dismissing long-standing employees. As Gagnon explains:

> In a place like this, we have to live with our people; it is not like Montreal. The man you have to fire, you will see in church and everywhere in the village. Due to the fact that we are so close to these people, we cannot treat them in an indifferent manner, as is done somewhat elsewhere. It is always a big deal to fire people, it brings in rivalries, families. Before firing, we must account for all of these factors.

> There was one guy who was difficult to manage, but his wife also worked for us and she is a valuable employee. He resigned for both of them and that created a double problem. It created a problem in the enterprise because his wife continued working and he thought his wife would not work. That guy created trouble and went to the neighbours. There is almost no solution; he is about 60 years old and the whole thing has quietened down.

The increased scale of the factories breaks down the particularism of the *entreprise familiale* and turns the unwritten but contractual patron-client relationship into an economic transaction. One example is the factory party. As far back as the managers can remember, they have spent liberally on employee social events and activities. In 1970 they reported a declining interest on the part of their employees and at least one enterprise decided to stop such events,since the manufacturer no longer felt a community of interest in his firm. While several small processors often can count on the benevolent labour of their employees, schemes attempting the integration of factory employees into ownership of large enterprises have met with mixed success. The widening gulf between worker and manager coincides with the beginning of worker syndicalism. However, unions as a part of the transition to industrial organization have been slow in establishing themselves in Saint-Pascal, where as recently as 1969 all factory workers were unorganized and wary of threats to their employers.

Unions

Every Saint-Pascal manufacturer emphasized that unions are ruining rural industries where communication and transportation overhead makes "Montreal wages impossible". Unlike companies which began manufacturing forty years ago, they have had less time than they might have wished to consider the advent of unions. In most industries, wages were already legally set by minimums established by union-influenced provincial wage parity committees. These were originally organized in the thirties as a corporatist, neo-fascist system once dominated by employers and clergymen who set and supervised industry-wide wage agreements. But in 1969, in response to the initiative of several experienced workers, a union election was held in the tire factory and Henri Fortier signed for three years of labour peace. Others were still able to resist unionization and even the wage policing of the provincial parity committee. Light industry takes an independent and even paternalistic position on organized labour. To quote an owner of a small enterprise:

> If I really build big, the union would come in immediately. *I can't live with them!* The union is poorly placed to know what the workers need. I have no sympathy with someone who would rather negotiate with a fellow from Montreal than talk with me. I have told this to my employees and I think they are as warned of it as I am by the manager of the bank to meet my obligations.

Similar statements are made by every factory owner in Saint-Pascal including verbal threats to move to Montreal or New Brunswick or "close my doors forever". It is impossible for me to predict if this would happen, but at the time of writing the entrepreneurial group has too much solidarity to disintegrate from a temporary economic setback. The experience of the tire factory is perhaps a better indication of what will happen to others, although other industries are more "footloose" or mobile. In practice, no manufacturer has moved or sold out since the industrialization of the town began.

Saint-Pascal and Outside Marketplaces

Not every business in Saint-Pascal is as oriented toward outside markets as the tannery or the tire recapping plant, especially the retailers who are dependent on salesmen and other intermediaries. Only the new industries have overcome some of the disadvantages of their rural location by controlling their own distribution systems. Between the autonomy of these industries and the dependency of retail merchants are various degrees of communication with outside markets and agencies. Table 4.1 summarizes these differences in the form of an external-orientation scale of Saint-Pascal businessmen that sharply differentiates local or parochial people from the smaller number who are cosmopolitan and nation directed in their everyday affairs.[5]

Even the smallest of retailers relies on suppliers from outside the Lower Saint Lawrence Region (scale step II), and even the largest of manufacturers sells some of its products in Saint-Pascal (scale step I). To obtain city goods, the small retailer does not have to leave his premises. Salesmen descend on the region beginning every Monday morning. These salesmen are French speaking and the firms they represent correspond with Pascaliens in French. In practice their unilingual clientele of local merchants has few opportunities to visit urban distributors (Table 4.1 scale steps V and VII), and regular contacts with salesmen are often their most valuable source of market information. The salesman introduces style changes, new products or technology and distribution systems. Over time the salesman-merchant relationship may develop into a strong, informal relationship with its own rules. It is not in the interest of the salesman to oversell his goods and lose his customer; the merchant, aware of the salesman's interest, relies on him for operating capital by delaying and extending payment for his merchandise. The transaction between the two has the disadvantage for the merchant of narrowly focusing his commercial networks — eliminating alternate strategies which by-pass the salesman completely. The salesman however does not have a monopoly on the introduction of national consumer culture to Saint-Pascal. Others, sometimes selling the same produce, compete for his "regular" clients. This factor prevents his broker or middleman role from becoming too powerful and allows their wide network or "territory" of clients to retain some independence.

Small family-operated manufacturing businesses are no less vulnerable to being dependent upon intermediaries. The candy factory and the small tannery, the horticultural plant and the small glove factory, all opt for arrangements with outside intermediaries who are either sales agents or wholesale jobbers in Montreal. They have few occasions to speak English or travel to marketplaces outside of Quebec. Nevertheless other small industries, the wagon factory, Landry's wool mill and the desk-maker, avoid middlemen by using mail order catalogues to reach a national market (Table 4.1: scale step IX). Mail selling also has its saturation point, and in all three cases, it restricts innovation and diversification. Ultimately, it also leads the small producer to rely on advertising agencies and on wholesalers for the goods clients request, but which they cannot produce. Several retailers have purchased large trucks and Telex (telegram) receivers which provide alternatives for by-passing middlemen.

Only two Saint-Pascal businessmen are capable of carrying on a sustained English conversation. The tannery regularly receives telephone calls in English and Rosaire Gagnon travels extensively

Table 4.1

A Scale of the External Orientation of a Sample of
Saint-Pascal Businessmen

Scale Step		Cum. No. of Respondents	Percentage of Sample	Scale Errors
I	1. Sells product or service in the region of Saint-Pascal	44	100	—
II	2. Relies on suppliers from outside the Lower Saint Lawrence region	43	97.7	—
III	3. Makes business trips to major urban centres	37	84.1	2
IV	4. Makes or receives at least one long distance call daily	33	75	2
V	5. Takes business trips to Quebec City at least once monthly	30	68.2	1
VI	6. Belongs to associations not established in Saint-Pascal			
	7. Familiar with the development plan for Eastern Quebec	21	47.7	1
VII	8. Takes business trips to Montreal at least once monthly	17	38.6	2
VIII	9. Sells product on a province-wide scale	15	34.1	1
IX	10. Sells product nation-wide			
	11. Uses a sales catalogue			
	12. Purchases supplies outside Quebec	12	27.3	6
X	13. Has a working knowledge of English which is used in business transactions	9	20.5	4
XI	14. Takes business trips outside the province[1]	4	9.1	7

Coefficient of reproducibility[2], .986   N-44   total scale errors   24

[1] Excluding Northern New Brunswick

[2] Reproducibility $= 1 - \dfrac{\text{number of errors}}{\text{number of entries}}$ (Pelto, 1970:341)

to the United States where he sends regular shipments of leather goods. In his travels, he purchases any items which he thinks his factories could make in leather in Saint-Pascal — snowmobile boots, purses, coats, hats and rifle bags. Contrasting with the tannery, Henri Fortier's tire distribution is decentralized and confined to a limited range of products distributed through his own franchised agencies, in Montreal, where local sales are managed by his brother, and in several other cities, where he has franchised dealers. Furthermore, Fortier's regionalized marketing system is almost entirely in French-speaking areas, although he relies on a few bilingual employees for communications with English-speaking suppliers (This explains one of the scale errors in Step X in Table 4.1. Fortier did not speak English).

Occasionally, the larger scale businessmen make business trips outside the province. More than visiting, travelling is an important opportunity for private communication. Members of the entrepreneurial group often take business trips together to Ontario and on occasion travel overseas to management conferences. Each trip has its regular list of stops including old friends from Saint-Pascal. On one such trip, several manufacturers asked Henri Fortier about this town that he and Rosaire Gagnon had industrialized. Fortier retorted: "Saint-Pascal? It's about 250 miles east of Montreal, monsieur, and then north!" Weeks later his reply remained fresh in his mind in a discussion about how Pascaliens situate their small industrial niche with people they meet through national networks.

Enterprise and Community Social Change

As this chapter on the new economic base of Saint-Pascal illustrates, the leaders of industrialization have not suddenly discarded traditional forms of economic organization in favour of some ideal type of rational bureaucracy. The family enterprise and patron-client ties are still found within what I earlier identified as the entrepreneurial group. However, the local and national networks and more significantly, the dominant economic values of the new economic elite are fundamentally different from those of the merchant *notables*. At one extreme, the traditional merchants with the cogs of their enterprise and social life interlinked and meshed completely into the local community are close to what Paine (1962) has called freeholders, but their acceptance of existing channels of action and existing values is incomplete and fraught with exceptions. At the other extreme, the entrepreneurial group is linked to a myriad of both regional and national networks and successfully espouses what once were locally unorthodox values. Their new dominance of community power and their large numbers of retainers and supporters have propelled them into a *status quo* that is becoming in itself the basis for an established and legitimated value system. As the next chapter illustrates, nowhere is the difference between old and new in town life more evident than in those voluntary associations that are an arena of social action and social control for the entrepreneurial group.

Footnotes

[1] The implement factory in Saint-André is a product of a post WWI industrialization that affected isolated towns and villages prior to the depression. These factories and sawmills were insufficient as a base for a dominant regional elite of industrialists, although in the thirties their nation-oriented owners such as the wagon-making Turcottes in Saint-Pascal, were associated with the local mercantile elites.

[2] See Robert Hunt's (1965) study of the developmental cycle of small businesses in rural Mexico and Dansereau's (1967) analysis of rural entrepreneurship in Eastern Quebec.

[3] Unemployment rates in the three-county area of Kamouraska, Rivière-du-Loup and Témiscouata ("the Grand Portage region") averaged over twenty percent, more than twice the Quebec average, from 1968 through 1972.

[4] One of whom is Rosaire Gagnon's 23-year-old nephew. Gagnon's younger brother supervises all tannery operations.

[5] The external–orientation scale (a Guttman scale) is separated into eleven scale steps. Starting with Step I, *each higher step incorporates all the behavioural features of those below it.* Thus Step VI, which has two variables relating to associations, is characteristic of 21 Pascaliens in my sample or 47.7 percent of the total. The one scale error in Step VI is a person who has all the attributes of a higher scale step but has not yet or will never belong to outside associations or be familiar with the development plan. No "external orientation" data from the interviews was eliminated from the scale, which may explain the larger number of "scale errors" for the most national-orientated higher scale steps. Nevertheless the scale has a significant number of items to indicate a single dimension of external orientation.

Residence built for Jacques Vencelas Taché, Seigneur of Saint-Pascal.
G.L. Gold.

The former courthouse in Kamouraska and the Centennial year post office.
G.L. Gold.

Saint-Pascal's Church and the Institut Chanoine Beaudet. Studio Jean-Paul, Saint-Pascal.

Interior of Saint-Pascal's Church before ecumenical changes. Studio Jean-Paul, Saint-Pascal.

The Turcotte farm wagon shop — original building. G. L. Gold.

The new bank and the old church. G.L. Gold.

128

The Landry wool mill and boutique. G.L. Gold.

Breaking the ground for the first secondary school (1958). Studio Jean-Paul, Saint-Pascal.

Hanging hides in the Gagnon tannery. G.L. Gold.

G.L. Gold.

Newly elected Richelieu executive meets in lounge after the dinner (Henri Fortier, first left). Studio Jean-Paul, Saint-Pascal.

The curé's benediction of the swimming pool at Friendship Inn (Auberge de l'Amitié). Studio Jean-Paul, Saint-Pascal.

The Carnaval president (right, jeweller), and treasurer (middle, tire factory management) present proceeds to Centre Social (left, skilled service worker on Carnaval committee). Studio Jean-Paul, Saint-Pascal.

A Club Richelieu mixed dinner: Pres. Henri Fortier (centre left) sits next to invited speakers; candy manufacturer and a notary in background. Studio Jean-Paul, Saint-Pascal.

132

One of the last reposoires. A Corpus Christi procession before altar at home of a director of the wagon factory (May 31, 1964). Studio Jean-Paul, Saint-Pascal.

An election tête-à-tête: Louis Saint-Laurent lending a hand in Saint-Pascal (late fifties). Studio Jean-Paul, Saint-Pascal.

Chapter Five
Sociability and the Councils of the
Entrepreneurial Group

It is tempting to hypothesize that the most externally orientated businessmen are also the basis of the town's entrepreneurial group and that social relationships in this group will be qualitatively different from those in other groups. There is support for such an assumption in Chapter Three where overlapping leadership in associations is used to identify an entrepreneurial group.

These associations, often less than voluntary in their membership (Gold, 1973), have recognized charters or objectives, bring together common interests, and ideally should have a lifespan that exceeds that of its members; as such they are what some have referred to as corporations (Brown, 1974). However, the path of Saint-Pascal's history is littered with discarded associations, many of which were casual ties of a redefinition of values by dominant elites responding to national economic and political pressures. Other associations have gone through dormant phases before being vigorously revived and, as is the case with the Industrial Society, allowed to vegetate once again. In accordance with our interest in changing leadership, it is useful to examine the conditions favouring the growth of associations and the role of these structures in maintaining group relations, social control and identity.

The starting point is an examination of group formation within the business community to find similarities and differences within what has already been described as a heterogeneous occupational group. As the pattern of this differentiation emerges it is apparent that "formal" associations are more instrumental to the unity of the entrepreneurial group than for others for whom the expressive aspect of sociability is a sufficient basis for unnamed and non-corporate coalitions.

In a discussion of these groups I will use the terms "friendship" and "sociability" almost synonymously, although friendship is applied elsewhere to intimate and private egalitarian ties which usually mark middle class social relationships (Paine, 1969). The conflict between the unity of a coalition (for this is what friendship networks are potentially) and the privacy of a two-party or dyadic relationship is aptly expressed by Suttles (1970:135) when he remarks that, "if friends invite all others into their private morality, then they lose the very special covenant they have authored . . . it is seldom a plot to which large masses can be joined". This conflict is most apparent in the ritualized friendships of the new economic elite, and least apparent in the politicized coalitions of more traditional merchants and tradesmen.

Dans la Patente — Friendship Networks

Pascaliens who belong to the same friendship network are said to be *dans la ronde* (in the circle). A *ronde* does not usually have an identity but can be thought of as a potential network or quasi-group (Boissevin, 1968). In relationship to all other social relations within the community it is a partial network (Barnes, 1968:111) through which information and various types of transactions flow (Christian, 1969:129). If the participants of this network or quasi-group are also political allies or members of the same clique,they are said to be *dans la patente*[1] (in the affair) or *avec nous* (with us). This information on sociability and networks of friends in Saint-Pascal derives from a deceptively simple question: "If you had to name about three of your best friends, who would they be?" I soon realized that the word friend (*ami*) has a number of meanings in Saint-Pascal,and in the responses I received, intimate friendships were grouped together with purely instrumental and pragmatic relationships.[2]

Clearly, friendships are part of a Pascalien's personal assets and, as such, can be a form of privileged information. Furthermore, business people and other community leaders distinguish between several different kinds of friendship, each with its own "rules of relevance and irrelevance" (Goffman, 1961:80), the understandings which define the rights and obligations in a social relationship.

These friendship choices are diagrammed in Figure 5.1 where they are shown to form three friendship networks,each of which is a partial network within the wider range of relationships in Saint-Pascal. Group boundaries are the points at which friendship

135

choices flow inward, and where, from field experience, I noted that interaction also stopped. Mutual choices, which I will define as strong ties, are linked with bold lines, and one-sided choices, which I will refer to as weak ties, are linked with dotted lines and an arrow showing the direction of choice.

Each person is also represented by his political affiliation.[3] The manner in which friendship choices follow party affiliation is striking, and indicates how some friendship sets define those who are *avec nous* in their choice of cliques and alliances; few Pascaliens of any social strata manage to avoid being identified with one or the other of the two traditional political parties.

Residence is also related to the distribution of friendship networks and of political support. The western part of town is inhabited primarily by Unionistes, and the eastern and northern parts of the community have tended to support the Liberals. Visiting is frequent between the wives in the same neighbourhood and tends to coincide with male friendship ties. This female network, on which I have very little data, is important among manufacturers and white collar managers whose wives are less involved in everyday business matters than are the wives of shopkeepers and craftsmen.

Each network in Figure 5.1 has common occupational characteristics. Network B is composed almost entirely of small merchants and tradesmen, particularly contractors, and the town doctor also falls within this group. Network C is similar to Network B in that it is also composed of merchants and tradesmen. However Network B is *rouge*, in that it includes primarily Liberal partisans, while Network C is *bleu*, supporting the Union Nationale. Both of these networks of small merchants and tradesmen are further internally unified by affinal ties as a result of numerous intermarriages between neighbouring families with similar interests.

Standing out as close-knit and relatively nonpartisan is friendship Network A which includes all of the new manufacturers and others of the entrepreneurial group. Within this network the successful Fortier (L1) and Gagnon (L2) receive the greatest number of friendship choices. They also choose each other, although they are rivals in terms of their known and expressed political affiliations. Their partisan differences are clearly subordinate to the internal unity of the manufacturing network, which is stronger than the family and political ties that developed when the town

Figure 5.1 Friendship Choices and Friendship Networks Among Businessmen and Administrators

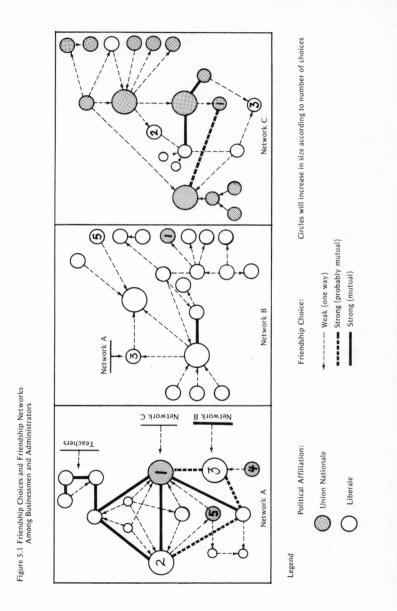

Legend

Political Affiliation:

○ (shaded) Union Nationale

○ Liberale

Friendship Choice:

------ Weak (one way)

▪▪▪▪▪ Strong (probably mutual)

▬▬▬ Strong (mutual)

Circles will increase in size according to number of choices

137

was a farm service centre. This difference became evident during the 1970 provincial election, when the collegial relationships of the manufacturers and their allies (Network A) took precedence over the partisan politics and manoeuvres of the merchants in Network B (Liberals) and in Network C (Unionistes). For example, the industrialists Fortier and Gagnon could then be seen in Friendship Inn having a quiet conversation over coffee after the Union Nationale campaign had just been launched in an adjacent room. This superficial involvement in active politics by members of Network A does not explain their legitimacy and popularity in the community — a highly politicized arena. Why, then, are some men chosen over others and what do they have to offer in exchange for the friendship which is so liberally extended to them?

Other than Fortier and Gagnon the most chosen persons are a wood merchant, Maltais, and the registrar-cum-furniture manufacturer. With the exception of the wood merchant, the three others are all marginal members of a friendship network other than that of the manufacturers (A) with which they are primarily identified. Other "stars", those with between three and five friendship choices, are favourites within their own group. The most chosen men in any of the three networks are the major employers or influential figures in Saint-Pascal — "big men" who are in a position to do favours for other people. *All* those who are chosen more than twice, and most of Network A, are members of the locally prestigious Club Richelieu, a significant affiliation that gives Network A, the entrepreneurial group, a unique corporate identity in its community.

I have said that friendships can be intimate and intrinsic, but sometimes they are also purposive and occasionally publicized. Moreover, friendship transactions tend to take place between status equals, rather than between nonequals. Thus, a friendship relationship is usually but not always horizontal and balanced. When one party consistently defines the rules of the relationship and controls the flow of value to the other party so that he might get the better of the relationship, the dominant party is a patron, not a friend (Paine, 1971). A problem arises when an outsider wishes to classify a relationship. Whether these exchanges can ever be balanced or not is usually a private matter, and information on the social accounting involved can be difficult to obtain. It would be little more than guesswork to try to classify each relationship in

Figure 5.1 as a friendship or as a patron-client tie. Moreover, a relationship which has in the past been imbalanced can become balanced, and the rules of behaviour between patron and client must be re-worked to suit a new situation of equality and friendship. Such is the case with Gagnon and Fortier, the two largest manufacturers who once sought help from local investors. After successful entrepreneurship of their own, Gagnon and Fortier were able to deal with these former patrons as status and power equals.

Friendship thus has a number of meanings to the townsmen of Saint-Pascal. To small merchants or teachers and their politically-involved colleagues, friendships are close and personal, infused with "the private morality" that characterizes North American middle-class friendships. However the scale of the small town with its large families and many intermarriages makes anonymity difficult, and in practice, who is friendly with whom, and on what terms, is often public knowledge. Furthermore, townsmen are aware of the quality of their social relationships and invest in those relationships which are of immediate or imminent use. This is reflected in the statements of the family-oriented man who sees friends as liabilities, or of the person who *needs* his friends, some of whom he has never met socially. These are not status equals, but patrons with whom they share an "obligated friendship" *(amité obligée)*.

Many friendships are highly specialized roles and are only relevant to certain activities. As friendships get more instrumental and specific they are subject to more restrictive rules. These constraints are found in the friendships of some businessmen in the entrepreneurial group (Network A) who have golf "chums" who are also marginal investors in their enterprises.

Rosaire Gagnon has a grocer friend who is his "horse friend"; he also employs the grocer's sister-in-law as his secretary, which gives them a common third party for their understanding. More important, the grocer takes care of the manufacturer's horses and *carriole* in return for a small fee for the keep of the horses. The horse owner feels free to drop into the horse-keeper's house after a long cold *carriole* ride to share a glass of gin, and the grocer feels free to invite the manufacturer to accompany him to a horse auction; but their relationship hardly carries over to the business world. It does provide a vehicle for the industrialist to get valuable information on community sentiments from a man who, in this "horse friendship", is his equal.

Another type of friendship which is common among the businessmen is "travelling friendship". This involves taking joint sales or buying trips, either for good company or the opportunity of discussion in the privacy of an automobile, or because one businessman can introduce another to a new market, to a new language area and to useful *tuyaux* (pipes or "connections"). For example, Gagnon and Fortier have attended conferences of associations such as the C.D.E. or the Club Richelieu, where they have extensive opportunities to talk with each other privately and share information on the local and national situation. Such examples again illustrate the tendency of private and concealed friendships to develop within the entrepreneurial group. Once an automobile has sped on past the parish limits, the privacy of friends is complete; but while in Saint-Pascal, a parked automobile, potential eavesdroppers and observers present the possibility of rumours of collusion. As those who are taking business trips together frequently change travelling partners, common understandings are shared throughout their network. On these occasions there is a very fine line between the local and extra-local information sources. Significantly, however many local private ties an *industriel* has, these are deemphasized in the collective rituals of the Club Richelieu.

The ritual friendship of the Club Richelieu is a third type of special friendship in which artificial primary ties function as a boundary maintenance institution that binds the entrepreneurial group together and further links them with key members of extra-local networks. In addition, the Richelieu also acts as an arena for local social control where the behaviour of other ritual friends can be monitored and, if necessary, brought into line. Before turning to the Club Richelieu and other associations, a last look at Network A provides further insight into the social construction of the entrepreneurial group.

Strong and Weak Ties

Entry into a *ronde* may be a difficult matter, for this is a commitment to one network over others and is not merely a matter of affluence or of influence. Among businessmen these friendship networks are intimately related groups of tradesmen who can be of economic service to each other without being competitors or political rivals. Economic and political rivals are divided between the two networks of tradesmen (B and C), each of which has a representative in every major type of enterprise in Saint-Pascal. The bi-partisan entrepreneurial group (A) occupies its own economic niche where the major group conflict is an ongoing game of competitive innovation between members and with other groups in the parish. Except for the supply of labour for the factories, the manufacturers and administrators, are not economic competitors. Even the large retail merchants and professionals who associate with the manufacturers do not have the competing mercantile interests of the butchers, the grocers or the service station operators of groups B and C. Individuals in *the entrepreneurial group thus seek the broadest local support they can obtain and regard as constraints any friends who unnecessarily reduce this support.* They form a *ronde* which has developed institutionalized boundaries as well as means of social control; political solidarity and the exchange of small favours are not as important here as access to information and to status.

Significantly, the entrepreneurial group receives the greatest number of mutual friendship choices. These mutual choices correspond to the conversation clusters and tête-à-têtes observable at the Club Richelieu meetings, and to travelling friends or golf partners. As strong ties, they are relationships with a high connectedness as opposed to the weak ties (in Figure 5.1) which as one-way choices have no more than a weak connectedness.[4]

While the greatest cluster of strong ties (in Figure 5.1) is within Network A, the entrepreneurial group, these strong ties are also combined with a high concentration of weak ties linking the *industriels* to the merchants in Networks B and C.*and* with contacts in major cities. This has two immediate implications for Saint-Pascal which at first seem to be contradictory.

First of all, the relatively large number of weak ties emanating *to and from the entrepreneurial group* (A) act as "local bridges" between the occupational networks in the community (Garnovetter, 1973:1364; Harary, Norman and Cartwright, 1965:198). Given the pivotal position of some of the manufacturers-contractors-investors in between local networks and regional and national networks, they can easily take on the role of brokers. The town's outside business either in marketing (cf. Table 4.1) or in politics is channeled through them. When these weak or bridging ties are sufficiently diffused, innovations and information spread with a high degree of efficiency. Given the minimum demands these ties place on others (each party need be no more than an acquaintance), they may be more effective than strong ties at overcoming social distance (Garnovetter, 1973:1967-9). That is, weak ties are more effective at "linking members of *different* small groups than strong [ties], which tend to be concentrated within particular groups" (*Ibid.*:1376). The wide network of weak ties to and from the entrepreneurial group dates back to their active involvement in the Jaciste movement and their subsequent involvement in other associations such as the Club Richelieu; it is an important factor in securing and legitimating their social position as a new elite. The extension of their network leads indirectly to the temporary social cohesion of all occupational networks within the town under their leadership.

Strong ties as such, have the special advantage of coalescing relationships *within the entrepreneurial group.* Thus, as Rosaire Gagnon has a strong relationship with Henri Fortier and another strong relationship with Louis-Georges Landry, it is unlikely that Fortier will have *no* relationship with Landry. In fact, this tie is a strong one, confirming Homan's (1950:133) assertion that frequency of contact is directly related to the strength of friendship sentiments (Garnovetter, *op. cit.*:1362). In Figure 5.1, the relationships between five people in Network A demonstrate a high degree of connectedness — the diagram is relatively symmetrical with seven known mutual choices. Moreover, my own observations indicate frequent social exchanges and strong mutual ties between several others in this network (broken bold lines).

Unlike any other cluster of business people, those of the entrepreneurial group demonstrate both a closed group of mutual choices as well as the highest number of bridge ties outside of their own friendship set. That they should be a clique and also widely connected is no mystery; together they can share information of great value and have some control over its dissemination. They can also test the reliability of sources as well as the validity of information for their own business transactions and for their own decision-making within the community. Nowhere is this strong connectedness more visible than in the Club Richelieu.

Ritual Friendship: The Club Richelieu

The leaders of Saint-Pascal's Rural Catholic Youth movement were not the only group to be admitted to the Club Richelieu. The *notables* who founded the Saint-Pascal chapter recruited these fledgling businessmen together with administrators and teachers from the newly-created regional schools. One reason for such a heterogeneous association was that the national organization required its local clubs to have a sizeable membership, and the general merchants, the notary and the doctor were insufficient personnel to launch a new organization. It was not long, however, before the *notables* lost control of the organization they had originally sponsored.

The shift in Richelieu membership is reflected in the change of the occupation of the president between 1960 and 1970. The club's first two presidents were professionals, first a notary and then a doctor. The two subsequent leaders were Louis-Georges Landry and Castonguay, two of the most active tradesmen at the time of their presidency, and the last of their generation to achieve Richelieu leadership.

In the fifth year, the club went through a period of internal conflict. The victorious faction was made up of new members who worked to effect a change in the Richelieu executive. Their efforts culminated in a leadership crisis when the regular pattern of succession from vice-president to president was interrupted by the candidacy of school administrator Hubert Leclerc, who was elected (at the expense of the pharmacist) as Richelieu president with the support of the *industriels*. Faced with a change in leadership, the occupational composition of the general membership also changed. Several professionals and a number of merchants stopped attending meetings and the Richelieu passed into the control of the *industriels* and their followers.

By 1970, one-third of the Richelieu executive committee were manufacturers and, in 1971, Henri Fortier was elected president. The largest of the Saint-Pascal manufacturers, rather than the smallest, are the most active in the Richelieu. Furthermore, more than half of the executive are former members of the Jeunesse Rurale Catholique. The opting-in to the Richelieu by the former members of the youth organizations of the 1950s did not mean a mere replacement of club leadership, but an alteration of the very nature of the elite itself. The social movement of the 1950s had become a secular socio-political force, assuming control of community institutions.

In the opinion of its own members and others in the community, the Richelieu is thought to be a restricted social club, confined to 35 of the town's citizenry, as well as two members from surrounding parishes. It is a club which "serves those in commerce better". It attempts to keep the members of all groups (other than the operators of the largest businesses) at conservative levels lest they, as a central member of the Richelieu executive carefully explained to me, "gain control" of the organization.

The entrepreneurial group, in search of support, found an eclectic definition of who could or could not be in their ranks. Table 5.1 summarizes the Richelieu membership of 1969-70, indicating the occupational composition of the club. It is no surprise that most of the seven teachers within the Richelieu are within the administrative sector of education, and may be frequently regarded as *industriels* in their own right. Other teachers who serve as club members are close friends of the administrators.

As the teachers became more numerous, there developed a widening rift between *professeur* and *homme-d'affaires.* Within the community, the *professeurs* were grouping for increased power. Thus in 1969, when *professeur* Leclerc ran for mayor against *homme d'affaire* Castonguay, both candidates were Richelieu members. The original coalition of the entrepreneurial group was being redefined and, by early 1971, fewer teachers attended meetings. Instead, new initiates came from the county police force and young businessmen "on their way". The Richelieu opted to distinguish itself from the growing educational power group, itself sensing the realization of a break in their community of interest. These occupational divisions are summarized in Table 5.1 for the membership at large and for the club's executive, in 1970.

A business person's view is that the Richelieu is virtually their only time to converse informally with each other and submit their latest activities for the approval of their colleagues. In comparison, the teachers have a nine-to-five job, and belong to a more educated and more erudite group, uninterested in the competition and problems of the business world. This reasoning is confirmed by the teachers I spoke to, who find it hard to become envious or even interested when a local manufacturer gets his picture in a magazine or begins a major expansion of his facilities. The teacher belongs to another sub-culture and, except for the administrators, his friendship is not always sought by business people.

Table 5.1

Occupational Characteristics of
The Saint-Pascal Richelieu Club in 1970

Occupation	Club Members	Executive Members
Industrialists[a]	10	3
Contractors	5	2
Merchants (automobile or television dealers)	6	1
Insurance Agents	3	2
Public Administrators[b]	3	—
School Administrators	4	1
Teachers	3	—
Professionals[c]	3	1
Total	37	10

a. Owner and manager of manufacturing-processing businesses.
b. Postmaster, registrar and Provincial Police chief.
c. Accountant, doctor and banker.

In practice, while the club is restrictive, the entrance rules are not formalized. New members are proposed to the executive committee who in turn meet to vote on offering an invitation to the outsider. Rather than describe themselves as excluded, many small businessmen claim to have been invited to meetings and claim to have been asked to be members. Their non-participation is explained on the grounds of "pressing work schedules" or a prohibitive seventy-five dollar annual subscription. Sometimes these are elaborate attempts to save face. In several cases, those who protested the most joined the club six months later, explaining that this had always been their intention. Others refused to consider the Richelieu because of personal conflict with certain members. In summary, the actual boundaries of the Richelieu are determined by those who purposely opt out of it and, ultimately, by those who are denied entrance.

Once admitted to the Richelieu, the new member will be formally referred to as "the friend _____ " (*l'ami* _____). The friendship terminology is readily extended to an initiate and occasionally to honoured guests. It formally marks membership in an exclusive social club and, by extension, affiliation with the entrepreneurial group in Saint-Pascal and adherence to the rules governing their interaction.

Since the Richelieu became the business elite's most important social activity, its membership is informally integrated with other voluntary associations, especially the Industrial Society and the Management Club (the C.D.E.). This concentration of membership is reinforced by a Richelieu rule demanding attendance at meetings. Absences are dutifully noted by the secretary on mimeographed attendance sheets, and a truant Richelieu is dropped for non participation. This is important, as the Richelieu is not simply a formal structure. The club is a focus of *industriel* solidarity; it is the outer shell of the entrepreneurial group. A discussion of the functional integration of the associations of the elite therefore begins with Richelieu rituals and how these function to promote group identity and the social control of members.

Richelieu Ritual

Richelieu members conceive of the meetings as relaxing, light-spirited social gatherings. This does not mean that Richelieu gatherings are unstructured or free from an established ritual. Deviations from accepted Richelieu practice are noted and there is usually an attempt made to adjust the misguided course of events. This ritualized sequence of activity begins before the meeting is called.

1. *The Convocation*

Meeting announcements are supposed to be mailed several days before each bi-weekly gathering by one Richelieu member who is assigned this task on a rotating basis. The bulletins are rarely straight-forward invitations to a Richelieu supper, but incorporate

146

elements of cryptic satire and burlesque humour. Sometimes they may include a series of cartoons, a poem alluding to activities of various members through pseudonyms, or a statement relating to club activities with a controversial note to it. Invariably, a good bulletin is fuel for verbal barbs at the meeting, and many members keep old bulletins as mementoes of their Richelieu activity. Should there be no bulletin, the dinner friends censure their forgetful confrère.

2. *The Bar-Room Gathering*

Meetings begin after 6 p.m. around the bar of Friendship Inn. Strangers who have been invited to participate are very obvious and within minutes they begin to meet some of the club's members. Dress also becomes noticeable. The manufacturers dress more casually than the merchants, insurance salesmen, teachers and professionals.

Members are expected to converse freely, for this is a time when a great deal of information is circulated. It is at this moment that a politician might reveal his plans for a coming election or there may be an exchange of information about business transactions, conventions and any interesting gossip. The exchange is always casual and important matters are mentioned with no obvious overtones. Serious discussions are considered out of place and tactless remarks are met with embarrassment and a harsh stare for the invader of no-man's land. This open atmosphere temporarily halts factionalism and feuding which might normally occur between some members in another context. At its extreme, this truce permits political adversaries to discuss matters of mutual interest as Richelieu friends.

Overtly it would appear as though all information circulates freely during the bar-room gathering, but in practice Richelieu members withhold any information that would benefit others at their own expense. The exchange of information is stage-managed to allow three dozen persons access to a privileged and relatively rumour-free network. It is as private as a semi-public arena could be.

The Richelieu atmosphere favours the extension and solidification of social contacts. For the insurance salesman and car dealer it is an opportunity to contact prospective clientele and cement ties with present clients. The manufacturer also feels a need for his Club Richelieu where he can find out what others are doing and introduce his out-of-town guests. Nationally, a member of the Saint-Pascal club is a Richelieu wherever he goes in urban French Canada and Richelieu membership carries a high prestige outside of the local community. Locally, the Richelieu provides an atmosphere of competitive innovation which begins when the Ami-Président rings the Richelieu bell to summon the members from the private detente of the lounge to the public arena of the dinner table. The exchange of information now shifts from business to the activities of members on a wider scale where the dinner friends reward or penalize each other according to the values of the Richelieu group.

3. *The Arrangement of Dinner Friends*

The dining room is laid out in the usual horseshoe-shaped configuration of a banquet. Facing the dinner tables is a handcrafted Richelieu emblem with "Saint-Pascal" printed below the large enclosed "R". On the head table in front of the Ami-Président is a gavel and the Richelieu bell. To one side of him is the guest speaker and on the other side the Master of Ceremonies,who handles the various arrangements for the dinner according to the national Richelieu rule book.

The usual seating plan reflects the hierarchy of the club and various social groupings within the community. This arrangement is not formally specified through rules,but established by preference and practice. The core of the entrepreneurial group, the *industriels*, cluster on one side of the table, and other groups of friends on the same or the other side of the arrangement. Teachers tend to sit towards the back of the room with the new members and a few social isolates who come to meetings but remain aloof from discussions. This seating pattern is both reinforcement and evidence of the dominant interests within the Richelieu and the marginal position of the teachers and vis-à-vis the businessmen.

4. *First Order of Business*

Unlike other parish dinner gatherings no priest is present to act as a chaplain (aumônier). The Richelieu supper usually begins without a prayer, however everyone rapidly crosses himself and if there is no initiation to intervene, a member is asked to lead the group in several refrains of the *chant Richelieu*, the Richelieu song, proclaiming the club's public goals of fraternity and service:

> Joyous workers and proud Christians, Let us unite together,
> To help the children, that they may be happy,
> And together we sing the Richelieu.
> Together we gather with gaiety, to meet real friends,
> To work for the little ones, To seek out peace and fraternity.[5]

Once the *chant* is sung, the president may bring up business items. Meanwhile, uniformed waitresses file in with the first course of the dinner.

It is at this time that each Richelieu friend who has brought guests is expected to introduce them, listing their basic credentials such as occupation and place of work. The invited speaker for the evening, the *conférencier*, is also introduced. These introductions are necessary, and if they are not made, members will make sharp cracks about the alleged inconsideration of a forgetful host. With these formalities out of the way, the Ami-Président announces the opening of the fine period *(la période des ammendes)*.

5. *The Fine Period*

The fine period is a time when members must pay for whatever they may say to the group. Licence is granted to rail on the activities of any other member, as long as the joking is not openly political or commercial. The Ami-Président recognizes each speaker and decides whether the subject under discussion should be changed or whether the speaker is out of order.

The joking is known as *taquinerie* or more informally as *taquinage*, verbal barbs the ritual friends make at each other's (and their own) expense. The "accused" is charged with various indiscretions and is permitted to defend himself, but at a certain cost. Fines are decided upon by the Ami-Président, usually in multiples of 25 cents with the total fine varying from ten cents to ten dollars. The dinner friends take turns as the fine-collector for the evening, who circulates around the tables to collect the fines; each one is ceremonially dumped into a small silver dish. The proceeds of these fines are used to support a Richelieu summer day camp in Saint-Pascal, the major "service" function of the club.

Nonetheless, joking does not begin only with the day camp in mind. *Taquinage* which brings honour, publicity and recognition for social and material achievement merits the highest fines. These high fines are usually given only to the most prosperous businessmen. *Taquinage* which is embarrassing to the attacked and touches socially incorrect behaviour merits a very low fine. The subjects for joking may be ranked in the order of the cost they incur:

Fines	Subject of Fines
(as high as $10)	a) purchase of a new automobile (paid by both buyer and seller)
$1.00 - $5.00	b) big business deals
	c) special public recognition
	d) travel
$.25 - $1.00	e) idiosyncratic behaviour of members
	f) irregularities in the seating pattern
$.25 and less	g) political activities
	h) drinking or alleged drinking during the meeting
	i) late payments of dues or poor attendance
	j) failure to wear the Richelieu pin during the meeting
low fines	k) remarks which impugn the reputation of Richelieu members or of Saint-Pascal as a
no fine	community

Taquinage serves as a subtle but direct means of social control. Material gains which are expansionary to an industry, the town or an individual are the most approved and rewarded by the group. It also ensures that businessmen buy their cars and major consumer goods locally and hire local contractors. Political discussion of any kind is discouraged, and members feel that political rifts apparent in Richelieu joking are divisive and detrimental to the club's goals. As a joking relationship,[6] *taquinage* serves as a social equalizer, releasing envy and purging personality conflicts. The most successful men come to the less successful for recognition and envy, and the less successful can use envy as a means of social control, monitoring the activities of the economically powerful. The following passage exemplifies the public accounting of the activities of Rosaire Gagnon after an interruption by his cousin the television dealer:

Maltais:	Ami-Président! I think that it is the Ami Rosaire returning from a stay in Bermuda, who . . .

Gagnon:	That's true! Its been a long time since I have had a rest. *(laughter, someone attempts to interrupt)*
Ami-Président:	*(fines both speakers 25 cents each, but not Gagnon)*
Maltais:	I said it for the good of the club. *(Interruptions and joking . . . several more fines)*
Ami-Président:	Does Ami Rosaire have an explanation to give?
Gagnon:	Yes . . . but I have been drinking certain alcoholic beverages . . . Understand that in this state, one has more imagination than usual . . . *(the Doctor throws in a quick comment, laughter)*
Ami-Président:	Ami Rosaire, from what I can gather, it is really exhorbitant to take a trip to Bermuda. For a Richelieu friend to allow himself a trip like that . . .
Someone:	A sales trip . . . *(laughter)*
Gagnon:	Ami-Président, I will cease trying to convince you that we were working in Bermuda . . . Your illusion is that we were in Bermuda to have a good time . . . We will leave you with that idea. *(That is, both Gagnon and Fortier who was still in Bermuda.)*
Ami-Président:	Will Ami Rosaire place an exemplary fine of $3.00 in the pan? *(Gagnon slowly and publicly gives the money to the fine collector.)*

The idea that the joking is always accepted without personal animosity only holds true for the duration of the meeting. The barb is further cushioned by the fact that usually (but not always) a recognized "friend" of the "accused" rises to the attack.

The openness of the barroom and dinner table removes a great deal of information from potential gossip networks; moreover group members are informed when their activities are not pleasing to other Richelieu "friends". The following is one such instance in which the accuser and the Président prepare the ground for the reply.

Mention is made of the school administration losing local autonomy. Hubert Leclerc, school administrator and defeated mayorality candidate, is asked to reply.

Leclerc:	On the level of the sector of Kamouraska, I was once *patron* but they have just removed the *patron* from Kamouraska.
Someone:	Patronage! *(no laughter, no comments, just silence)*
Leclerc:	They gave it all to Rivière-du-Loup. That's just what always happens in Kamouraska and no one speaks out! It just continues! *(silence)*
Ami-Président:	We are entering into a discussion . . . where . . . we are unable to find a Richelieu solution. I accept

what Ami Hubert has to say, that there are some claims to be made by Richelieu friends . . . but even so, this is not a matter for the Richelieu. *(no fine, no comments)*

Some members cannot accept the joking and in the face of personal attack choose not to come to meetings. Whether this withdrawal is an opting out or a forced retreat, it is an effective boundary-making mechanism within an occupational group. The withdrawal of many of the club's founding members is partially a result of the pressure generated from public joking. Others react to the joking by emulating the type of economic and social recognition which brings high fines.

Once outside of the arena of the Richelieu dinner table, some Richelieu members discuss the evening's events at length with their wives, analysing what was said about themselves and about others — tabulating their score for the evening. So, although women only attend meetings several times a year, they are well informed on what transpires at Richelieu meetings and regularly inform each other about their husbands' activities — usually through telephone gossip.

It is this kind of confrontation which can have a great deal to do with a man's self-evaluation of his status in the community. That is, joking within the Club Richelieu is one way of gauging the acquisition and withdrawal of honour and status in the community.[9] A businessman will privately admit that he was thoroughly trounced upon for a particular political involvement or he will beam with pleasureful embarrassment about being fined for expanding his business or his family.

A paradox of *taquinerie* is that while the joking encourages Richelieu to outdo each other before an arena of alleged equals it does not encourage innovation of a social or noneconomic nature. The few Richelieu friends who used the Chambre for encouraging regional development were thus deviant and, as the above case of the school administrator well illustrates, some persons are liable to be called to task for "going too far". This is the moment where the skillful innovator receives danger signals that call for a temporary withdrawal or where the more ambitious continue to social and political ruin. Guest speakers are no less liable to such scrutiny than regular dinner friends.

6. The Conférencier

After the joking has ended, the invited speaker, who is sometimes a club member, is introduced. Following a protocol established before the meeting, a designated member reads an impressive list of the speaker's credentials. When the guest finally rises, he is expected to continue the light-spirited mood of the meeting. Long tedious talks are thought to be as entertaining as the curé's sermon.

The speaker serves several different roles, all of which are integral parts of the club's activities. When a Saint-Pascal Richelieu member is the speaker, the atmosphere is very relaxed and the topic deals with particular interests and exploits of members, providing a mild form of recognition of the member and a subject for chiding and jokes. Richelieus from outside the club occasionally speak about the Richelieu movement, reminding the members that they are Richelieu, part of "an elite in the service of society".[7]

Whether local nonmembers come as dinner guests or as speakers, they are on display for the Richelieu and the Richelieu is on display for them. Unlike many other male service clubs there is nothing secret about Richelieu ritual, nor does it change appreciably when guests are present. Even initiations are public and consist of a brief oath of allegiance to the club and its objectives.

At times the final segment of a Richelieu meeting brings local guest speakers with community service positions into open interaction with members. Two explicit examples of this are the annual encouragement the Richelieu gives the Carnaval and the serious appeals received from the Centre Social's leaders to support leisure activities. As many of the members of the Richelieu are past members and participants of the Centre Social, these appeals meet with a ready response. In the one case that I have documented, the building of a lighted baseball park, instrumental action by Richelieu members closely followed an appeal by the Centre Social's director and a private meeting of the Industrial Society executive.

Another kind of local who is heard at the Richelieu is the newcomer, whether he be an anthropologist or a professor at a local school. Although never formally stated, these speakers are being carefully screened for their local objectives and viewpoints. If the speaker is at all controversial (for example, when my neighbour Turcot advocated Quebec's separation), his talk is followed by a barrage of questions and counterattacks by club leaders who wish to affirm their solidarity against the position of the guest.

The Expanded Richelieu

When an important speaker comes to town with a proposition for a new industry or service, the number of invited guests may even surpass the number of members. Another occasion for the expanded Richelieu is the bi-annual husband-wife supper that has become a gala social event. At all expanded meetings, the regular Richelieu ritual continues with the nonmembers as observers. The fact that so many townsmen have witnessed Richelieu activity reinforces the elite identity of the dinner friends in the eyes of the community. Members will make deliberate attempts to exaggerate and prolong the *taquinerie* for the benefit of the guests and their wives.[8] The after–hours accounting between a member and his wife is in this way even more significant. Pascaliens know what the Richelieu do and have no difficulty receiving such an education.

Richelieu members are themselves highly conscious of the value of publicity in reinforcing the image of Saint-Pascal and the Richelieu group. A special member of the executive assures that hardly a month will go by without large pictures of well-dressed Richelieu friends appearing in the regional newspaper, *Le Saint-Laurent.* The Richelieu stage a comedy evening during Carnaval that is well attended by other occupational groups and other social strata. Once a year Richelieu members launch a door-to-door sale of Saint-Catherine's day toffee, and come July, they turn their day camp facilities over to directors from the Centre Social.

Either as Greeks bearing gifts or as visiting dignitaries, guests will almost without exception address the Richelieu *before* speaking to other voluntary associations of the community. For example, a prospective industrialist, after visiting the "expanded Richelieu", met with the "expanded Industrial Society", repeating the same message to the same Richelieu group *plus* other interested citizens who sat in a half-empty hall awaiting the arrival of the Richelieu. This receiving order is easily achieved as the leaders of almost every other male voluntary association in Saint-Pascal are Richelieu members. It is these Richelieu members who arrange speaking engagements, and no important event escapes their attention.

Richelieu Friendship

The Club Richelieu is the largest arena of sociability for Saint-Pascal's new economic elite. It includes persons from all three friendship groups that I introduced at the beginning of the chapter, but particularly those in Network A who predominate in the club's executive committee. However, Club Richelieu as such is not a friendship group characterized by intimate dyadic ties among its members. Unlike the two groups of merchants who are *dans la ronde* or *dans la patente*, a few of whom are Richelieu members, Network A does not have frequent visiting, outdoor sporting events and common political interests. Although there are several collateral kinsmen within this group, these ties are secondary when it comes to sociability.

The mutual surveillance of the Richelieu ensures the privacy of a group but not necessarily of individuals (cf. Paine, 1973). Outside of meetings repeated public demonstrations of intimacy between any two Richelieu friends has on occasion generated rumours of collusion and the possibility of an imbalance to the (facade of) economic equality in the group. Collusion and secrecy in this context are nonetheless inevitable given the concentration of economic interests and outside investors or financial "experts" (see Chapter Four) may be the catalysts in business and social ententes that implicate several of the manufacturers.

Information, innovative competition and a corporate identity are trade-offs for the intimacy of a looser network. A manufacturer reflected in these words about his Richelieu friendships:

> It can happen, like yesterday, that a small group will be together after the Richelieu meeting. The guys would like that and say I am a great friend of theirs . Perhaps this is a false conception of what *friendship* really should be? Friendship is not simply knowing somebody in a little more depth or someone who is interested in your problems. Friendship is rather something which is free of any kind of interest, social economic or anything like that.

Walls within Walls: The C.D.E. and the Industrial Society

The Club Richelieu allowed access to the smaller and less visible arenas such as the C.D.E. and the Industrial Society executive, or for that matter any *ad hoc* committee that is of importance to the economic life of the town. Richelieu membership is not a guarantee of entrance into these core activities of the entrepreneurial group; but, given the overlapping leadership, the timing of meetings and the ease of access to most information, there is no real resistance to the participation of interested members, particularly in the regional management seminars of the Centre des Dirigeants d'Entreprise (C.D.E.).

Strictly speaking, the C.D.E. does not exist *in* Saint-Pascal, as Saint-Pascal C.D.E. members are participants in a regional branch of a national organization that promotes better business practices and solidarity among French Quebeçois business administrators. Despite the membership rules set by outsiders, the entrepreneurial group in Saint-Pascal informally decided in the mid 1960s that they represented the local "C.D.E. group". This claim to an identity has a good rationale: Pascalien Henri Fortier was the regional C.D.E. president, and Saint-Pascal sends fifteen or more delegates to regional meetings, often as large a representation as the host city of Rivière-du-Loup, five times greater in population.

The Saint-Pascal C.D.E. presence begins early in the day when a number of Pascaliens gather in Fortier's office to form car pools for the trip to Rivière-du-Loup. Even before each car leaves the town, the closed environment of the automobile becomes a beehive of enthusiastic conversation, and all of this continues on a larger scale at the C.D.E. meeting. The value of these contacts should not be underestimated. Several of the visitors are always junior administrators and small businessmen whose fifteen dollar registration fee is sponsored by one of the larger employers. In this way recruits to the entrepreneurial group have filtered through the C.D.E. and then on to other arenas of group participation. One example is the transformation of a passive auto dealer into an *industriel.* He was so changed by his C.D.E. involvement that several of his friends vividly remember the suddenness and intensity of his passion for new organizational techniques.

The C.D.E. meeting consists of a number of work sessions which revolve around a luncheon. An outside expert, often an M.B.A., is brought in by the regional leaders and the parent organization to stimulate discussion on a management topic. The very first of the regional sessions motivated six of the entrepreneurial group to apply for government subsidized C.D.E. training sessions in Saint-Pascal. After the local meetings began, the Saint-Pascal enrollment rose to twelve. In general, the C.D.E. had a special appeal for those who were already trained in group techniques through their participation in the Jaciste movements. This is partially because of the association's emphasis on participation in decision making, whether this be in business or in civic affairs. For example, participants in one regional meeting were divided into four workshops to discuss the problems of several troubled companies, one of which is a manufacturer of wood stoves (a topic close to home). When it came time for the workshops to report, the C.D.E. members from Saint-Pascal who had remained more or less together, chose interpersonal relations and goal-setting rather than financial and organizational difficulties to explain the firm's problems. Although the emphasis on personalism rather than economic criteria may also be seen as a continuation of familism or even the Catholic perception of group over individual worth (Hughes, 1943:72; Stein, 1973:48n; Taylor, 1960:43), such an emphasis is significant when one considers that a bureaucratic-human relations approach to management has been said to be absent from the authoritarian and paternalistic French-Canadian enterprise (Taylor, 1961:141). Group decision-making was absent in Saint-Pascal's traditional social institutions such as the church, its affiliated associations, parish level associations and the family.

Curé Beaudet Revisited

The élan of the C.D.E. experience is translated in one of the entre-preneurial group's first attempts at community action, an event which provides a signal comparison between the town's new secular leadership and the traditional parish authority of the curé. The venerable curé approached Jacques Maltais for a television set that could be a prize in a raffle which would raise the money to finance urgent alterations to the old parish church. On this visit, the curé did not encounter the usual sort of acquiescence; instead, Maltais insisted on bringing the matter to the attention of his "C.D.E. friends".

A meeting was soon called and, at the suggestion of Rosaire Gagnon, Maltais went to ask a reluctant curé whether he would permit Henri Fortier's brother, a layman, to appeal from the pulpit for funds at Sunday mass. There is no precedent in Saint-Pascal for such an event as this is the curé's task. But the good priest need not have hesitated because Fortier's brother is an effective speaker, as is revealed in the following text reprinted from a Club Richelieu bulletin:

> I imagine that you are surprised to see a parishioner give you a sermon! *I am here as a spokesman of a group called the C.D.E.* Now it appears that our church has recently had a face-lift and you ladies know how much that costs at Easter time. You surely appreciate the renovations! The removal of the holy table has expedited communion and certain statues have disappeared for a new decor. Our fine old church has had to update itself. Once there was a 70-year-old bank building across the road . . . today it is replaced with a new one and what a pleasure that place is to look at! That is Saint-Pascal, a place which I am proud to live in! When you look at your church, you should feel the same pride . . . *as do we of the C.D.E. who consider that the curé need no longer be the one to ask parishioners for needed money.* (emphasis added)

The speaker's integration of the C.D.E., a nonlocalized association, into the social structure of the community reflects the continuing adaptation of the entrepreneurial group to available organizational structures. Secular leadership had played its cards openly and the confrontation was bringing about a realignment of the local power structure. I doubt whether this would have been possible without the increasing dependence of the town on industry.

About the same time as the public appeal was made during mass, members of the entrepreneurial group decided to revitalize an autonomous industrial committee which had been created out of the Chambre de Commerce in 1964 (partly with their participation), and which had been largely dormant since 1966.

The Industrial Society of Saint-Pascal Inc.

Those who shared a detailed knowledge of the activities of Saint-Pascal's Industrial Society include all of the manufacturers, the administrators of the tannery and the tire factory, the four largest building contractors, the three auto dealers, several school administrators and an insurance agent — all active leaders of the town's industrial "cargo cult" and committed to the attraction and expansion of industry. A few industrial boosters are members of the original Chambre de Commerce committee, but the spark of the

158

revived Industrial Society lies with the leadership of the C.D.E. management club.

C.D.E. enthusiasm is reflected in these minutes from the first reorganization meeting:

22 October 1968

... Someone then asked the assembly whether any of the members of the Industrial Society would be against the union or fusion of the Industrial Society with the C.D.E.

Roméo Landry (an accountant) gave the following opinion: there can be no question of fusion of the C.D.E. with the Industrial Society because the C.D.E. is a management association. *It is the members of the C.D.E. who should become members of the Industrial Society.*

The members of the C.D.E. acted upon this advice: they reactivated the industrial society — with both large and small business support. Predictably the manufacturers had a heavy time commitment to their own firms, and after the first year of operations, the leadership was taken over by several merchants, a contractor and a school administrator. Meanwhile, Gagnon and Fortier, maintained close contact via their own selected representatives (their *hommes de confiance*) and through numerous impromptu visits.

Each major manufacturer chose a different way to make use of the resources of his renewed organization. Through various entrepreneurial strategies, the Industrial Society was to support and represent the town's new industrial order. While providing a front of support for the security and expansion of existing industry, it also instilled smaller and less successful men with a sense of egalitarianism and participation in economic growth over which they had little control. This is especially so for the Society's executive who represented all major industries, the schools, the Conseil Municipal and both traditional parties; all six men were members of the Club Richelieu.

The executive represented a general membership which was thought to be about one hundred, but the significance of this statistic is questionable, as the passing out membership cards and the collecting of the five dollar annual membership fees was irregular and the executive had only a vague notion of who was a member and who was not. General meetings were called about once a year and these were held to choose officers and rally support for the executive's projects.

In 1968, the first year of the Society's reactivation, at least six closed executive meetings were called and numerous other gatherings were held spontaneously in the lobby of the Post Office, at the bank or in private homes. Since then, most "formal" executive meetings are held immediately after a Richelieu supper, with only a minimum of advance notice.

Talk at the executive meetings mainly concerns projects of members of the entrepreneurial group. The largest number of projects has been presented by Rosaire Gagnon, who long promoted his idea of organizing a "leather complex" in Saint-Pascal. As can be seen by the proposed coat of arms in the photographs, Gagnon's vision of the future has had considerable support. His first approach to the group was also the Society's first major project — negotiations with the Provincial Government over the wages of Gagnon's leather cutters working on the putting-out system. In defence of Gagnon's position (non interference by Government), the Society prepared a brief for the Minister of Labour and the members of the executive personally went to Quebec with Gagnon to support his case.

Gagnon considered the Industrial Society's assistance to be useful, "a bunch of guys who can give me support when I need it", and his industry needs local allies. One intervention led to another and before long he approached his friends with a project that would use local capital to lure an Italian tannery to relocate in Saint-Pascal. This was the first in a series of attempts to develop Saint-Pascal through public subscription of capital, labour or materials.

The subscription method worked well internally in raising money for the tannery's expansion, but this and other Society attempts to obtain outside private capital were in every instance disastrous, even when the most cosmopolitan of businessmen attempted to use their influence in bringing outsiders to Saint-Pascal. External factors are a major reason for this failure. Saint-Pascal is not the only community in Eastern Quebec which is seeking new industries. Saint-Jean-Port-Joli, La Pocatière, Cabano and other newly urbanized rural towns are competing for the same industries and under the same restraints of financing outsiders with local money but without guarantees of permanency.

160

Despite these drawbacks, members of the Industrial Society decided that the town cannot rely on two industries for its future. The experience of nearby communities[9] was adequate warning of the fragility of such a situation. Members of the Industrial Society took a very serious interest in encouraging those outside manufacturers who expressed an interest in coming to Saint-Pascal. For at least three of these prospects—a shoe company, a handbag maker, and a snowmobile manufacturer—the interested parties were given a banquet (the Richelieu dinner) and a public hearing under the auspices of the Industrial Society. Besides these dealings with outsiders, attempts were made to lure producers from other parts of Kamouraska County into relocating in Saint-Pascal. In general, these efforts have been disappointing. Ambition yielded to gloom and it became difficult for the Industrial Society to maintain its credibility as an emissary of the entrepreneurial group.

The merchant members of the Industrial Society tried to come up with projects which could complement the expansion of manufacturing. An insurance salesman decided to give salesmanship courses and someone else promoted the idea of a laboratory of enterprise where C.D.E. ideas could be tested. Few of these projects materialized although Maltais' merchant committee did succeed in bringing retailers together to discuss eliminating "duplication" in retail services. Attracting new industry is not an easy thing to do and there are only a handful of men with the required connections in the cities. The Industrial Society was more successful in using its extensive local networks to promote community development projects such as a baseball park, a motel and a swimming pool. These projects brought together the local resources of the entrepreneurial group and led the Society toward becoming a political structure parallel to the *Conseil Municipal* and the *Chambre de Commerce*.

Another reason for a change in focus is that members of the new economic elite were, by 1969, having difficulty relating to each other on equitable terms. The new ideology of business introduced by the C.D.E. had failed to give everyone the same level of profitable returns. Impressive as the growth of small business had been, no one could match the success of Fortier and Gagnon. The Industrial Society desperately needed a common project to express its equality as an entrepreneurial group. This opportunity came with the construction of Friendship Inn.

Friendship, Industry and a Swimming Pool

Friendship Inn did not begin as an inn, nor did it arise out of friendship. Claude Tremblay, an inn-keeper from a neighbouring town, approached the Industrial Society to obtain backing for a project that would move his motel to a site on the projected route of the new Trans-Canada highway. Tremblay's initial negotiations with Saint-Pascal followed a familiar route. At first the entrepreneurial group found his terms too demanding. However, the one element of Tremblay's package that did interest the Industrial Society was a proposal to build a large indoor swimming pool. The executive saw the pool as a means of obtaining support for the entire project.

The pool and a restaurant were built with extensive parish support. Thirty-five local businessmen including a few school administrators subscribed $65,000 in capital and Tremblay took out a $90,000 loan from the Industrial Expansion Bank. The shareholders each promised $1500 or $2000 in cash or kind, most of which was to be paid in small monthly installments after an arrangement with the bank manager (a member of the entrepreneurial group). Twelve of the investments were made in labour, materials and land, including much of Claude Tremblay's share, through his contribution of motel units moved from his previous enterprise. Taken together, this support was adequate. Friendship Inn opened with a benediction by the curé and widespread newspaper coverage in *Le Saint-Laurent* — some of which prominently mentioned the involvement of the Industrial Society. Saint-Pascal's new bourgeoisie had been given some much needed prestige and an impressive red neon-lit monument to their cooperation.

The contributors were initially delighted to see their project realized, but their zeal was soon tempered by organizational problems within the new enterprise and its failure to become profitable immediately. The promoters spent long hours urging Tremblay to use better advertising and to offer swimming classes to non-shareholders who would pay for use of the complex. Leclerc acted as a liaison to promote swimming classes in the secondary school.

In another move to support their new project, the directors of Club Richelieu decided to hold their club meetings in Friendship Inn. Initial objections to such a move were based on the absence of a liquor licence, but these qualms were smoothed over by the opening of a clandestine bar for Richelieu members, all under the watchful eye of the (Richelieu) chief of the local Provincial Police. Nevertheless, the pool was initially unprofitable, and the sponsors decided to lease their new acquisition to the Centre Social — a strategic move for the Centre's leisure-promoting "men on their way".

It may seem rather obvious by now that the Industrial Society was hardly an indispensable force in the industrialization of Saint-Pascal. However its inability to unite the entrepreneurial group in concerted economic action reflects on the failure of the new economic elite to act as an economic coalition within their community. The Industrial Society was not the public symbol of the power or status of the *industriels*. Its operations were clandestine, ostensibly to preserve confidentiality and withhold information from potentially competitive communities or groups. This strategy proved somewhat more successful in community politics than in dealing with outside agents; but, at the local level, when the Industrial Society promoted projects which were also supported by other groups, the credit could hardly go to a single association. The Industrial Society did not have an exclusive mandate for its operations and its objectives conflicted with those of its parent organization, the Chambre.

Several teachers and small businessmen, some of whom are marginal members of the entrepreneurial group, have relied upon the Chambre to implement their objectives of regional development. To the extent that their political position on regionalism had been unpopular with the *industriels*, these members of the Chambre were concerned about what they considered to be the quasi-secret parochialism of the Industrial Society. As several of these deviants or innovators (depending on one's perspective) are also members of the Club Richelieu, they were occasionally able to follow the Industrial Society's executive meetings and act as devil's advocates of regional integration. Some of their comments at these meetings reflect the intensity of their position and the competition for legitimacy between town associations:

F _____   Never in any other movement have I seen a committee that outgrows its own association.
M _____   There's no danger. The Chambre de Commerce cannot depreciate the Industrial Society because they have worked. We also have a charter!

Thus, the Industrial Society has been a place where the representatives of the entrepreneurial group "have worked" supporting the efforts of industry as though these are a common front. Survival demanded that some common projects be successful, but this success was determined in practice by the willingness of the manufacturers to enter into financial or administrative agreements with outsiders. The limited availability of skilled labour, the fear of unionism or financial takeover by outsiders were problems which preoccupied the manufacturers of the entrepreneurial group. Combined with all other exogenous constraints such as competition and services, outside investments were often muzzled before they began. Nevertheless, the entrepreneurial team was held together, partly because it was faced with a growing opposition — some of which came from innovators who successfully remained peripheral members of the group.

Any local initiative became an "industrial" activity, especially those projects which involved the youth in the Centre Social. This particular interest in the Centre Social youth emerges from the following dialogue between Albert Levesque, a merchant and a past president of the Chambre, and two members of the Industrial Society:

Leclerc: Baseball is a little industry!
Levesque: To me, industry is something that brings in money.
             I wouldn't bother with anything that takes money
             away! Leave that for the Centre Social or the
             Chambre to organize.
Fleury: The Centre Social is composed of young people who
             cannot get their ideas across to the "establishment",
             c'est zero!
Levesque: What I remember of the Centre Social is that it is
             one fellow who was the Centre Social and the
             strategy was formed about him.
Fleury: It is the ideas of the old people that have to change,
             they do not listen to youth. The Industrial Society
             can help the Centre Social because the youth in the
             Centre carry no weight.

The paradox of Fleury's statement is that the Industrial Society did not carry very much weight either. The society only succeeded in bringing together the more successful administrators and entrepreneurs in a coalition with an ideology of equality and the assumption of a special mission in charting the future of their community.

Other associations have involved business and economic interests in Saint-Pascal without being part of the overlapping interest of the entrepreneurial group. Most in the limelight are the Chambre de Commerce Régionale and the growing Centre Social, both successful in the non-economic activities that also interest the entrepreneurial group. Significantly, their charters have been informally redefined so as to give importance to a regional and participation-orientated strategy that is not central to the values of the dominant new economic elite.

The Chambre de Commerce and the Entrepreneurial Group

The Chambre de Commerce, from its founding in 1945, was always a local organization supported and led by the most important of Saint-Pascal's merchant-artisan *notables*. Several members were invited to participate in planning sessions held during 1964 when the B.A.E.Q. was formulating the federal-provincial development plan for Eastern Quebec. Those who went returned with a planners' vision of what was to happen in future years — the plethora of small municipalities would be reduced in number, the government would move to hasten the industrialization of agriculture and of forestry, and citizen participation would be more broadly based. The persons mentioned above in the context of the critique of the Industrial society, operated small businesses and had been very active in town organizations. All three men had gained marginal acceptance into the businessmen's organizations, but they found that the concept of regional development hardly met with the acceptance of the *industriels.*

The first visible effect of the B.A.E.Q. sessions on these merchants was the regionalization of the Chambre de Commerce to include the communities in Saint-Pascal's area of influence. This had the effect of reducing the membership of Pascaliens who had supported the Chambre for its local interventions with government. It also provided another reason for the entrepreneurial group to take over the Industrial Society for the promotion of local industry — leaving several allies in the redefined Chambre. The new Chambre acts as a regional pressure group rather than the agent of local merchants. The Chambre has acted as an intermediary between the Saint-Pascal area and government, and it intervenes publicly in such matters as public works, an old age home, forestry concessions for county saw-mill operators, tourism and new regional schools. The Chambre's greatest flurry of activity came after several of its members experienced a second round of *animation sociale* sessions, this time with development workers from the Regional Development Council (C.R.D.), a public agency responsible for monitoring the B.A.E.Q. plan.[10] On the surface, the Regional Council succeeded in galvanizing the tradesmen and school administrators in the Chamber of Commerce into a more militant group, publicly demanding institutional improvements for the town. Since these sessions in *animation sociale*, the Chambre makes more effective use of advertising in the regional newspaper in Rivière-du-Loup to publicize their letters and telegrams to government offices. Their new regional identity and social involvement are different from the private and parochial operation of the *industriels* who are more interested in national markets for their products and a favourable position for their own community. Their press releases in the regional paper are confined to the Club Richelieu dinners and to the improvements and expansion of their own enterprises. To the outsider who reads the newspaper, it is the regional consciousness of the Chambre which seems to predominate in Saint-Pascal. The locals see things differently. Few Pascaliens would depreciate the dominant position of the manufacturers and their supporters, the entrepreneurial group.

Sports, Carnaval and Development

Occasionally, the routine business of a voluntary association is interrupted when a member asks, "Why did this organization ever get started?" An ideal time for such a question is during a moment of indecision in the privacy of an executive meeting. The Centre Social is one such organization whose members are constantly re-evaluating their groups activities. Members of the select Centre Social executive are all "men on their way" (*les hommes en voie*) — young businessmen, retail store employees, teachers, and an accountant from the tire factory. Activities have included providing recreation for children, building a skating cabin, and bringing dances to the village (despite the objection of the curé). Its most significant activity has been the management of Quebec's longest running winter Mardi Gras Carnaval.

The Carnaval has gradually formalized and replaced the visiting rituals and mumming of *mardi gras* (Miner, 1939:164), and since its inception has become the most important single community social event, eclipsing the Saint-Jean Baptiste Day Parade. The Carnaval President and his committee are expected to plan an extravaganza that will bring people to Saint-Pascal from as far away as isolated Sainte-Athanase. A week's festivities is the president's opportunity to make his name raising money to finance projects and to pay for a series of elaborate social evenings. The unique quality of these *fêtes* is the expectation that carnavalesque activities will cater to the free mixing of every socio-occupational group in the parish. The only parallel event with such drawing power is the 9:30 High Mass on Sunday morning. Crowning the Carnaval queen (who is chosen by lottery) is for everyone, but other evenings draw their own audiences. Some are reserved for youth, and rock bands are brought in from the large cities. The businessmen and the teachers choose their own evenings for their fullest participation, usually a Tuesday night bean feed (Le Petit' Pet)[11] and the Club Richelieu also hosts its own evening comedy show.

Businessmen sponsor the Carnaval by furnishing money, decorations, costumes and prizes. With few exceptions, the Carnaval president has been a young businessman or school administrator who begins promoting Carnaval events months before the pre-Lenten festivities begin. The president presents the Carnaval princesses at a Richelieu supper and travels from business to business making a vigorous personal appeal for money. The president's ability as a leader will be judged by how much money Carnaval clears. His success is minutely compared with that of past presidents although inclement weather is admitted as a factor affecting gate receipts. Being Carnaval president or a member of the half-dozen townsmen on the Carnaval committee (male and female members of the Centre Social executive, invited businessmen or their wives) is considered important in the social accounting by which people "take their responsibilities" and build a reservoir of honour or potential disrepute. During Carnaval, the president's personal behaviour is also under scrutiny. If his committee manages to work well as a group, this can be a base of friendships and is useful to a "man on his way". Above all, the president must not make enemies.

Since 1968, the Centre Social has redefined its objectives and extended its activities beyond Carnaval. Significantly, the reconsituated association succeeded in recruiting a number of youths who might otherwise have moved away from Saint-Pascal. Local interest in having more than just factories available was complemented by policy decisions in Quebec City and Ottawa. Government and municipal funding when added to private contributions allowed the Centre to hire a trained outsider as a full-time recreation director. With the support of the industries and supporters in the School Commission, a lighted baseball field was set up, gym equipment was purchased and a tennis court and golf clinic were organized. Then, in 1971, the Centre Social was able to attract the new regional games to Saint-Pascal. Faced with a growing demand for leisure activities, the recreation director organized local sports leagues. These draw workers and teachers into Centre Social activities, such as a volleyball league in which a barber's team played against the Volunteer Firemen, the Provincial Police and the Apostles of Hitler, a motorcycle gang. Through the financial support of Fortier, a baseball and hockey team were equipped for competition with other communities. The Centre Social in this way encouraged an expansion of the occupational base of participation in associations and provided opportunities for the crystallization of class identities.

What can be the effects of an expanding leisure organization in a small industrializing town? One obvious effect is the expansion of the social infrastructure to match the earlier growth of industry. This secondary development is a serious matter to Saint-Pascal's youth and, given the temptations to move to a larger urban centre, the politics of sports are as important to them as looking for new industries and institutions to locate in their town. Significantly, at the same time as Centre Social took over management of Friendship Inn's swimming pool, the outgoing president of the Centre (who was also president of that year's Carnaval) was initiated into the Club. Richelieu! The manufacturers, with representatives in every major voluntary association, succeed in influencing the course of local decision-making by fostering a working relationship with youth groups and with leisure associations. The teachers, who had no distinctive associations, had become influential members of these recreation groups without using them as a base for a coalition. Nonetheless, their presence is bound to affect the circulation of local leadership — a circulation in which associations have remained dormant until a spurt of activity reflects the realignment of power and status in the town and perhaps the beginning of another phase of regional leadership. As the examples of the Jacistes and the Industrial Society show, the malleability of available institutional forms permits upwardly mobile groups to adapt available structures to their own interests.

The politics of this circulation depends partially upon the distribution of formal political offices in associations and in municipal, regional and national political councils. However, since so much power and decision-making is relegated to elite councils and to parallel structures such as associations, I have until now postponed a discussion of political process in Saint-Pascal.

Footnotes

[1] *Patente* — popular name for the now defunct clandestine and ultra-nationalist Ordre de Jacques Cartier.

[2] Responses frequently extended to five and more "friends" as the question was posed in an open-ended manner. To ascertain the relationship of businessmen with other members of the community, the question was put to public figures such as the president of the school commission, a managerial worker in each of the two largest factories, the bank manager and president of the Caisse Populaire — for a total of 43 responses (41 of which are from men). There are six small businessmen who insisted that they had no friends, particularly intimate friends, because *everyone* is their "acquaintance". However, three of the six later volunteered specific replies, explaining that such a question is difficult and embarrassing to answer.

[3] Political affiliation was obtained from the interviews or from observing the 1970 provincial election campaign.

[4] *Connectedness:* a relationship between two units (individuals, groups or institutions) is *strongly connected* if every two points are mutually reachable. If a relation is such that the points are not all mutually reachable, it may be said to be *weakly connected* or *weak* (Adapted from Harary, Norman and Cartwright, 1965:405-409). If a number of possible networks are explored (visiting, travelling, kinship), the strong ties extend along the lines indicated in Figure 5.1.

[5] Travailleurs joyeux et fiers crétiens, Unissons-nous avec entrain, Aidons les enfants, qu'ils soient heureux, Et chantons le Richelieu, Nous venons avec gaieté, rencontrer de vrais amis Travailler pour les petits, chercher paix-fraternité.

[6] For two discussions of the functions of joking relationships see Radcliffe-Brown (1952 [1940], Gluckman (1965: 125ff), Handelman and Kapferer (1972).

[7] From the text of a talk given by a Richelieu International official in Rivière-du-Loup reprinted in the regional newspaper *Le Saint-Laurent.*

[8] These mixed suppers have now become more frequent as the role of women in the Richelieu slowly changes from living-room strategists to more active participants in the bi-weekly gatherings.

[9] Pascaliens were particularly aware of the dilemma of Cabano, Estcourt and Saint-Joseph. Each of these communities has had difficulty sustaining or getting industries based on primary forest products of the highlands.

[10] These committees were chosen without any understanding of the relative power of balance in the community and notably without active representation of the industrialists or the workers. Industrialization occurred to the C.R.D. executive only as an embarrassing afterthought.

[11] "The little fart".

[12] For a more complete discussion of the voluntary association concept as it applies to Saint-Pascal, see Gold (1973).

Chapter Six
Patrons and Steeples

"Think of politics as a competitive game", Bailey (1969:1) advises his readers, and this is precisely how Pascaliens perceive of *la politique*, although it is mainly the behaviour of leaders in extra-local political offices, people who can *obtain* things, who are called "politicians". The rewards at this level are tangible and the division of the community into competing teams of supporters has been more clearly visible than in strictly local-level matters.

As is the case with the entrepreneurial group and the community elites who preceded them, there is another level of political competition (not always thought of as political) where groups seeking local power are made up of individuals with claims to honour and status within the community. This local level contest is played out as much within associations as it is within formal political councils. On one hand, the increasing concentration of economic power in the town works against the need to play local power and status games by local rules; on the other hand, as long as new leaders need local backing and legitimacy to continue their economic activities, they must bend to local norms if only to have a following within their own social stratum. No business family in Saint-Pascal is totally independent of its cultural environment. As one community crisis after another has shown, there were no "free-enterprisers" immune to local social control. There are, however, many Pascaliens, especially in the entrepreneurial group, who have sufficient external support and a local following to alter the rules — although not everyone succeeds in having his way.

The Rags and the Worthy:
Reputation and Political Process[1]

Status may be a product of consensus on a man's virtues, but status ultimately lies in the appraisers of virtue, including ourselves.

171

Wealth is increasingly important in determining a person's status in Saint-Pascal; however, this appraisal will be based ultimately on moral worth, honour or disrepute. Sometimes there may be a consensus about a man's worth, while at other times, his evaluators will have come to separate conclusions. At first sight, there appears to be ambiguity over who is worthy and who is not. A closer examination shows that unshared evaluations and changing appraisals of worth are related to the process by which townspeople acquire or lose prestige and status.

Men of worth are often referred to as *gens valables*. As one townsman explains. Such persons "think and work with the community, are steadfast, reasonable in their opinions and consistent with these beliefs when it is time to act". *Gens valable* behave appropriately when they "take their responsibilities" *(prendre ses responsabilités)*. That is, regardless of wealth, a townsman "takes his responsibilities" if he correctly fulfils the role behaviour expected of him through shared normative understandings. Thus a politician campaigning for re-election announces that he will carry out the people's wishes as he is a man who "takes his responsibilities". An employer, assessing the worth of a manual labourer explains, "This man is the best of all my employees; the good fellow "takes his responsibilities." In both of these cases filling of expected responsibilities brings honour *(fait honneur)* to the socially correct individual.

Honour can accrue from both moral and financial assets. Someone who honours his moral engagements *(fait honneur à ses engagements moraux)*, lives a "good life", raises his children "as he (she) should", works for the betterment of the community, is faithful in marriage and dutifully supports his church and the curé. Honour may also be derived from financial success, either in business or in conscientious fulfillment of work. Worldly and moral bases of honour however, are increasingly in opposition with each other with the rapid accumulation of wealth by those families who control the new means of production and distribution. A *notable*, whose status is based on the traditional criteria, summarizes his sentiments on the nouveaux riches: "They have excellent reputations because their financial status has inflated their prestige, *but what are they worth?*"

Purchased honour is more fragile than that which has moral roots. A man who gains honour through wealth trades his material resources for a social product. While this exchange serves to level his wealth to that of the rest of the community, it also incurs obligations on those who have received his wealth and alienates those who have not. Townsmen are suspicious of aspiring patrons. A hasty and precipitous course toward honour and prestige may earn the social climber a bad reputation rather than a prestigious one.

One of the most severe terms for a disreputable man is a *guenille*. In everyday parlance, a *guenille* is an inanimate object, that is, a simple cloth rag, or a reusable sanitary napkin, which, until recently, could be seen blowing in the wind on the porches of parish homes. In another context, *guenille* denotes a type of person[2] — a "man who lacks sincerity in his actions" or is weak in his convictions and easily swayed. If a *guenille* is also a heavy drinker (a *soulon*), he is a person who manifests insobriety as well as insincerity.

Another term of disrepute, not quite as categorical as *guenille* is the adjective *mitaine*. Used in an inanimate sense, a *mitaine* is a mitten and also, a Protestant Church (from the English word, meeting), such as the one that was built in the village of Kamouraska after the Conquest. The animate meaning of *mitaine* is a "person without character, a man who is easily influenced" (Belisle, 1954:785).

When the situation of disrepute is a change in party allegiance, the term *vire-capot* is used to refer to someone who has voluntarily joined the opposing political team, turning his coat to a different political colour *(quelqu'un qui a viré son capot de bord)*. The terms *valable, guenille, mitaine* and *vire-capot* signify reputations which may be gained or lost. The use of these terms is dependent upon both the political position of the speaker and the political support of the person being assessed.

Acquiring and Losing Power and Prestige

The responsibilities assumed by an honour-seeker often involve the accumulation of political resources through leadership positions in associations and public institutions. In this acquisition of honour through "taking responsibilities", the social ascent or *montée*, is limited by certain ground rules. Should a man in his *montée* attempt to control what others think are too many of these resources, he may receive warning signals from his family and supporters, and from his opponents whose assets he covets and who may be eager to undermine his support through subversion (Bailey, 1969:108). These cautions are communicated to him through gossip networks (especially *via* his wife), and through more public messages such as the Club Richelieu *taquinerie*. Public confrontation is used by the social climber or his opponents only as a last resort since direct encounters may have unexpected costs. When a man receives information that he is proceeding too quickly he will, in most instances, temporarily halt his *montée* to avoid a sudden social downfall or *descente*.

These dynamics of a *montée* can be related to the Swartz, Turner and Tuden model (1966) of the political process: (1) the mobilization of political capital, (2) encounters between contestants and, (3) a showdown, which brings about (4) a realignment of political support in the local arena, and (5) the influence of countervailing power — resources which can work to restore the fallen to a position of honour and even power.

(1) A *montée* begins when a man mobilizes political capital in an attempt to gain support for his leadership position. The ascent of an individual tends to follow a set order of succession to public offices, here defined as those posts in voluntary associations which give a man prestige in the eyes of his fellow townsmen. When it comes to prestige, such posts are much more important than local political offices which are few in number and, as we shall see later, are usually marginal in effectiveness and significance. Association leaders are torn between conflicting demands of members and of national offices, and their own personal ambitions and objectives. Turnover of incumbents is rapid, and organizational goals are frequently subject to redefinition by their leaders without a widespread endorsement. Furthermore, there is an ongoing competition for leadership positions, although this will be admitted only privately. Publicly, these are said to be burdensome cargoes that are taken on because nobody else is "doing their part".

(2) The contest for leadership is rarely a public one. It is instead limited to private bargains among the competitors who use influence and persuasion to seek followers in their claims to social legitimacy. Negotiating leads to unanimity before a public selection of officers. In this way a confrontation is avoided. If there is

opposition to a leader before or after he takes office, he will often quietly resign.

(3) Some persons choose not to avoid confrontations. Their behaviour may eventually bring about an open showdown and a crisis of support that ends in the alteration of the positions of either or both parties in the dispute. Others choose confrontation after the breakdown of collusion and negotiation, or when they think they have enough support. The leaders of the entrepreneurial group, for example, successfully played their cards this way with the merchant *notables*.

(4) There are several situations in which confrontation brings about a realignment of leaders and followers. The first is the case of the innovator who decides to abrogate community norms and work toward a change in the existing structure. In the sense that he cannot achieve what he wants with established procedures or existing support, he is a deviant and marginal person. A second type of confrontation occurs when membership in nationally-linked associations causes a leader to introduce ideologies which are not easily accepted in Saint-Pascal. Both of the above situations are compounded when the social-climber is a stranger to the town. He must then counter the bias against outsiders and master the intricacies of local rules of procedure, all the while benefitting from a third party status — a facade of benevolent neutrality. One such newcomer is Hubert Leclerc, who arrived in Saint-Pascal in 1960 and soon organized a union for the teachers in the new regional secondary school.

Leclerc quickly rose through the ranks of the school system to a key personnel post where he became a patron, providing jobs and building up a following. At the same time, he introduced new teaching techniques to Saint-Pascal and worked for the modernization of the school system, particularly for increased teaching of the natural sciences. During their membership drive, in the early sixties, the *notable* leaders of the Club Richelieu invited Leclerc to join the Saint-Pascal chapter. Once active in the new organization, Leclerc received the support of the young manufacturers (locals) to challenge the *notable* leadership of the club. The confrontation was successful and Leclerc branched out into other organizations, seeking leadership positions in each one. He then made his move into municipal politics. Approaching the municipal ruling group, he gained a town seat through another confrontation (see below — "Unanimity and Local Elections"). Leclerc by this time was virtually accepted as a member of the entrepreneurial group, although not without certain tension.

With honour accumulating, Leclerc began to consolidate his achievements. He organized a gala evening to fête his accomplishments, which proved to be the last of a series of events which had generated opposition and eroded support. All were part of a *montée* gained at the expense of Leclerc's status as a *gens valable*. He had already received warnings of his improper conduct, but chose to ignore their implications. Rumours then spread that he was an alcoholic and the Provincial Police began to follow his car. Calculating that he was still in his *montée*, Leclerc announced himself as a candidate for mayor. Although they were seeking a youthful candidate, the entrepreneurial group refused to support Leclerc and his teacher following could not prevent an electoral defeat. At this time, a follower noted that Leclerc would have fallen already if it were not for his influential administrative post.

The last crisis, according to several members of the Richelieu Club, came when Leclerc invited the bishop for the 25th anniversary of the Chevaliers de Colomb (for which he was serving as club president or Grand Chevalier), but the organizers "forgot" to grant Leclerc the honours of past Grands Chevaliers, each of whom received a memento for his past service. Discouraged by the desertion of his supporters, Leclerc drank several glasses of gin and rose to condemn the ineptness of fellow club members. In response, some of them left the room while others threatened to retaliate with violence . . . The next morning, various organizations are said to have received resignations from Leclerc, several of which had been mailed days earlier! Leclerc's honour was debased in private conversations; even his sanity was questioned. Having lost his sobriety and sincerity, Leclerc temporarily acquired disrepute in the appraisal of a growing number of former allies and opponents.

(5) Most such showdowns are followed by major shifts in allegiance and support. In the case of the innovative outsider Leclerc, followers drifted away from him. Disappointed with some Pascaliens, he took the initiative to transfer to a more challenging administrative post in a nearby city and sold his suburban-style home to an incoming civil servant.

Informal social control was the means of redress used in Leclerc's case. The outcome of the dispute was no surprise as both sides had been prepared to contend with any eventuality. However, in this as in all such trouble cases, the restoration of peace is as important as the need to end the conflict. The redressive mechanisms used to bring about peace are rarely extra-local, and invocation of the institutions of the larger system is only a last resort. The loser does not always have to leave; Leclerc certainly could have remained in Saint-Pascal and quietly weathered out the storm. Departure is not as easy for the many townsmen whose livelihood is intimately related to a local clientele. Even if a defect in such a person's worth becomes public, he is always able to regain some of his lost status and reconstitute his presentation of self to others in the town. The dishonoured may try to *reprendre* (bring back) or *racheter* (buy back) honour. In this attempt at vindication, a person is aided by whatever economic and social assets he has left in the community; in recovery, the fallen may well become a valuable ally to a former foe.

Such is the case of Albert Levesque, an innovative grocer who actively espoused political, religious and municipal reform leading the Carnaval, the Centre Sociale, the Chambre and the Lacordaire League (temperance). However, in doing so, he made his share of enemies who helped bring about his temporary downfall. Levesque is no more of a drinking man, than anyone else in Saint-Pascal (an occasional beer or dry gin), but most others had not accumulated as many foes, especially in the Provincial Police detachment. In the tense atmosphere on the eve of an election, Levesque found himself involved in campaigning for one of the candidates. Later, his car was followed on trips through the county and he was arrested twice for reckless driving, the second time after an angry struggle with the arresting officer. The accused was tried, convicted and released on payment of a $500 bond for "good behaviour" As it was time for election fever, grocery sales dwindled. The innovator had been brought into line through social control although the court system had intervened to serve local ends.

Levesque had to stall his *montée* in Saint-Pascal and endure the wrath of gossip which branded him as a *mitaine* and more, but, as in most such cases, the supposedly soft man had economic and political strengths through kith and kin who could help him rebuild his honour and reputation. After his trial, he did not move away from Saint-Pascal where he owed some money to local businessmen. Instead, he returned home and with the help of his son rapidly reestablished his clientele. After some months had elapsed, several town leaders began to suggest that Levesque was not such a bad fellow after all, and perhaps he should have been given a hearing in the first place. Later on, Levesque was able to "take back" his honour and responsibilities, and he reentered local politics, cautiously gathering support for his projects and waiting before launching further plans for the town.

Both these examples illustrate the political process by which Pascaliens seek social positions and thereby honour and status and sometimes power. Pitt-Rivers (1965:22) writes that: "Honour . . . provides the nexus between the ideals of a society and their reproduction in the individual through his aspiration to personify them. As such, it implies not merely habitual preference for a given mode of conduct, but the entitlement to a certain treatment in return. The right to pride is the right to status." In Saint-Pascal honour is not simply accorded; those who claim it must enforce their claim with a sufficient audience who will listen and respect them. Wherever possible, support is acquired privately, since a public confrontation risks an irretrievable loss of prestige. "On the field of honour, might is right" (*Ibid.*:25). There are, however, some high status Pascaliens who are neither mighty nor righteous. They are not strangers who sought a rapid acceptance, or locals with large families united behind them. They are however well connected in urban centres and have gained special access to bureaucratic networks. Some, such as the sons of white collar and supervisory workers (see Chapter Four), are highly respected for their involvement as *marguilliers* or for other community and religious responsibilities.

Patrons and Mediators

"Saints" as Mediators and Brokers

These townspeople have an asset of detachment that, when combined with an exemplary moral status, gives them an acceptability as "saints" who can override factional differences between individuals and social groups. Several have established a reputation as mediators, working for the good of all without overt political considerations, while still furthering their own policies and position.

One such "saint" received an advanced classical education before becoming postmaster and, much later, mayor. His wide-ranging activity in religious and secular organizations earned him special recognition from the Pope. One of his community functions has been that of president of the regional and local school commissions, where he was able to defuse a complicated factional struggle while still achieving the inevitable objectives of the faction which desired centralization of the school system. He was also the leader of the group who successfully sponsored the movement for a nursing home and staffed it with an order of nuns. Through the diversity of his associational activities, he had bridged an organizational gap across generations. His role is that of a mediator and a broker rather than that of a patron who has economic or political power over his clients. He is best known for his ability to restore harmony and unanimity. With every service or good deed a "saint" may also profit, building an unassailable position of modest material comfort, high status and some power.

Other "saints" include the parish priest and the Federal Member of Parliament, neither of whom come from a large family "clan" which is identified with a political colour or its position on a long standing local feud. They are thus relatively above reproach even though, a generation earlier, their parents may have been "strangers".

The role of mediator cannot easily be filled by members of antagonistic families. What the "saints" lack in economic resources and kinship ties, they gain by a certain neutrality in pragmatic matters and useful networks to the outside. Their moral qualities give them the charisma to attract a responsive and sometimes loyal following. They incorporate all of the qualities of high status in the Saint-Pascal which, as a function of prestige, are related to participation in both the sacred and secular aspects of parish life.

Patrons and "Obligated Friendship"

Some persons are able to attract a following quite independent of their moral attributes. In practice, this is a continuing exchange of mutually desired resources. The flow of favours in at least one direction is often material, while the return for the favour — the balance or equivalence of the relationship — is either unspecified, or so structured as to perpetuate the tie to the advantage of one or both parties. The power holder in the relationship, the patron who may or may not initiate the relationship, can ideally call on his "friends" or clients for favours when these are needed.

Sometimes these demands are excessive and Pascaliens say that a demanding patron can make his friendships "sing" for him (*faire chanter*) to obtain the return presentation when it is needed. The debt to be repaid can either be a financial debt (*dette financière*), or a debt of gratitude (*dette de reconnaissance*), such as politicians may publicly call for during an election. Pascaliens call a particularly demanding or scheming patron a *patroneux*, the *eux* suffix added to the everyday word *patron* (boss) as a derogatory diminutive.

Clients may owe their patrons a debt of gratitude even though they rarely or never, socialize with them. The client's return for favours granted may be symbolic — a personal validation through identification with and recognition of someone with power and prestige, or juridical — a vote on election day (Lemieux, 1973:191). Their gratitude may be a recognition of a favour, such as a job, a letter written, a small loan with a long repayment schedule or even public honours.

The need for a patron is not constant and depends on a client's need for political, social and economic resources and the willingness to incur a debt. Some examples of prestations by patrons to clients are: a provincial deputy supplying funds to a penniless tradesman to start a small business, and then receiving repayment and requesting him to honour his commitments by publicly presenting a merit plaque to his patron at a banquet which his patron has arranged; a provincial deputy supporting a supplier in the everyday business of obtaining government contracts and then calling in his debts at election time despite other commitments.

In both of the above examples there is a fine line between the unbalanced reciprocity of patron-client ties and the balanced reciprocity of colleague contracts. The terms are private and are liable to generate envy if they become public information. Awarding favours is thus a sensitive matter. Assisting one party may alienate another and reduce a patron's own stock of supporters. Such is the case in the school board and in small businesses, where administrators are often careful to avoid hiring too many members of any single large family to the detriment of others with whom they must still do business.

Clientship between businessmen often involves large sums of money. In Chapter Four, I noted that only a few local businessmen had the capital for the expansion of new industry, and that in soliciting loans clients are quite aware that they tread a delicate balance between assistance and control. Large sums must be paid back quickly, in cash, and not in shares of new enterprise as is often the first request. Here the collegiality of the manufacturers has proven to be mutually useful; rather than obligate each other financially, they enviously watch each other, aware that takeover of one man's enterprise means danger to the others. To them this could signal a breakup of the existing balance between entrepreneurs that would seriously disrupt the arena in which they are rewarded for their success and kept abreast of opportunities.

Formally, at least, not all political decisions in Saint-Pascal are made by patrons. Both the Town and Paroisse have municipal governments, and the responsibilities of these governments have increased dramatically with the presence of the new factories.

Municipal Politics in Saint-Pascal

Since 1936, the parish of Saint-Pascal has been politically divided; the municipality of the Paroisse encircles that of the Ville. The split resulted from a farm-village factional dispute rather than from any topographic feature of the landscape. The farmers refused to pay taxes for village services such as street lighting, and village leaders requested a division of the parish into two municipalities, neither of which can be said to constitute an autonomous community. The rural parishioner continues to resist annexation and taxes for "services we do not need". Town leaders have come to regret the fission, especially after Saint-Pascal acquired the status of a town (*ville*) in 1966. They complain that people in the rural Paroisse share the centralized amenities of the Ville without paying for them. A further point of contention is that Fortier's tire factory, Landry's wool mill, Clément Gagnon's small tannery and Fleury's horticultural business lie only yards outside the town limits. The Paroisse, its population constantly diminishing, has depended on tax income from these industries and has had to negotiate a fire protection agreement with the Ville.

Both Ville and Paroisse are governed by elected municipal *conseils.* The more active of the two, the Conseil de Ville, is staffed with six elected councillors (*échevins*), an elected mayor, and an appointed secretary treasurer. In 1969, while Castonguay's sons administered the day-to-day business of his trucking firm, he was able to serve as both town mayor and provincial deputy. He worked closely with the municipal secretary, the town's only permanent administrative employee who, in 1970, had held his position for almost ten years.

The six *échevins* show up for conseil meetings, but do little committee work between sessions. They are merchants, factory managers and school administrators representing every local strata with influence in the community. A photographer is the only small merchant on the Conseil; he has for company a contractor and an accountant who works for the tire plant (the accountant's employer, Henri Fortier, was the previous occupant of his council seat). Two other *échevins* have administrative posts in the school system. This composition of the *conseil* allows the three largest employers in Saint-Pascal—the tire factory, the tannery and the schools commission a firm grip on municipal politics.

The composition of the *conseil* also tends to reflect the government that holds provincial office so that when the provincial deputy is a Pascalien, he has also been the town's mayor. The previous deputy, a Liberal physician, had been the mayor of La Pocatière; the deputy before him had been the mayor of Mount-Carmel. A mayor in government is seen as an added advantage in the community's competition with other towns for the limited resources available to protect and expand the town's institutional assets. Townsmen explain that it is natural that the *conseil* should side with the government as this will give them more leverage in getting provincial grants (*octrois*) for the municipality.

The mayor and his Conseil are elected for a term of four years. Be this as it may, each change in provincial government between 1945 and 1966 was accompanied by a corresponding change in Saint-Pascal's mayor and *échevins.* Mayor Castonguay, a Union Nationale leader, was an exception when he stayed in municipal office for two years of the Liberal government even after he was defeated as provincial deputy. This was partly because he had just won an overwhelming mandate to the *mairie* only four months before the provincial election. He was replaced as mayor four years later by the postmaster-president of the school commission.

Conseil meetings, held in the council chamber of the county registry office, are known to be quite dull. At the beginning of the session a brief prayer is said for Saint-Pascal, and all present turn toward the municipal coat of arms on the south wall and cross themselves. From then on, it is quick sailing as the Conseil follows an agenda prepared by the municipal secretary and the mayor. Other than the *échevins* the Conseil room is empty and silent unless an important civic issue musters a group of interested spectators; such issues rarely arise and when they do, the mayor and his cadre of *échevins* tend to speak with one voice.

The mayor meets with the other 17 mayors of the county in the Conseil de Comté. which governs the unorganized parts of the county. These joint meetings are generally ill-attended and most of the work is done by a permanent secretary. However, in 1972, government threats to reduce the flow of resources to Kamouraska county and the leadership of the defeated Social Credit candidate who was also mayor of nearby Mount-Carmel, transformed the Conseil du Comté into a county-level pressure group to pressure and resist electoral planners in Quebec and in Ottawa.

In general, the mandate of both local and county councils is severely restricted by the administrative responsibilities of the provincial government for most municipal services. What remains are local roadworks, lighting, sewer systems, water systems and lawsuits. Low taxes and a minimal municipal administration are the preoccupation of the Conseil which has maintained a conservative municipal budget and a skeleton staff of municipal employees. Furthermore, provincial government proposals for regional government and "rationalization as services" suggest the prospect of diminishing autonomy for the independent-minded rural paroisse and of its further integration into Quebec's urban system.

Unanimity and Local Elections

Saint-Pascal's local elections are rarely contested. A contested vote indicates a serious disagreement which could be resolved in no other manner. Thus elections to the school board, to the various committees of the Caisse Populaire and often to the Conseil are won by acclamation. Occasionally an *échevin* is contested, but the mayor's candidate has always won. No incumbent mayor has ever been defeated at the polls, as social pressures have always brought about a resignation before an electoral confrontation of this order. Even when Hubert Leclerc challenged Castonguay for the *mairie*, people who would rather have seen a new mayor, voted to support the incumbent claiming either that this was their obligation or that Castonguay was too important a person to be defeated in this manner.

The according of prestige and disrepute has been suggested as one way in which the small community maintains consensus and deals with threats to its shared values. However, maintenance of surface harmony in community matters is in direct opposition to the open factionalism which accompanies provincial elections, where prizes are related to an externally determined set of rules. A local observer explains: "in a milieu where everyone knows each other (*tout le monde se connait*), you know if people are with you; elections are not necessary". Factionalism exists, but it is rarely made public (except via gossip networks, which have value as political weapons and "leaks" to get town reaction). Reading the minutes of voluntary associations, one would never expect that anyone has disagreed, since the secretary summarily concludes that the proposal under discussion was "resolved in unanimity". Challenges do occur, but mainly as private confrontations where the scale of conflict is reduced as much as possible. A good example of the privacy of most local political processes is the way in which Hubert Leclerc obtained his seat on the *conseil*. This is Leclerc's version of the confrontation:

> In 1967, Castonguay ran for mayor with the help of the "C.D.E. group" and several invited supporters. Henri Fortier, the tire manufacturer, headed the group of twenty. I was a stranger to the "C.D.E. group", but I wanted to be on the *conseil*.
>
> I went to the municipal secretary and asked him for two filing forms, one for mayor and the other for *échevin*. Then I went to Henri Fortier's office, but not before I was told that I was insulting, as Castonguay should run without opposition.
>
> Fortier already knew of the matter and he was furious. He agreed to let one of his candidates go and allow me to run for seat number four. I said that this is fine, but would he second my nomination and Castonguay be the first to sign it. I left with a stiff warning from Fortier, but the covenant was sealed and Castonguay was as good as elected.

It was not until the next election that Leclerc found that he could not beat Castonguay when the election was contested.

To an outsider, these power plays may seem "undemocratic". Saint-Pascal's politics sometimes preserves incompetence in public office by rewarding the acquiescent behaviour of followers; it all depends whose politics one is prepared to accept. Men with radical ideas, who are innovators, receive few friendship choices and have been kept away from circles of political decision-making. An honourable man who has political support and who follows social conventions is assured perpetual re-election and even the opportunity to select his successor. This type of unanimity keeps the town running smoothly, but radical change is effectively paralyzed by social convention. Decision-making is avoided if there is a good chance of opposition. A subject is bantered about the meeting room. If it seems agreeable to all, it is passed; if not, it is shelved for a time when opposition would be diminished (such as when an opponent is away on a business trip). Innovative ideas in this way tend not to be acted on unless they have considerable private currency.

Low Risk Ideology

The avoidance of risks which could upset unanimity is part of a general avoidance of actions which might risk scarce resources. The low tax ideology found in municipal politics is one example of low risk thinking. In the early 1960s, a bitter battle raged in the parish over whether the schools should be modernized and centralized within the village. Centralization and curriculum changes were to close all the rural schools and decrease the amount of religious instruction; neither change was in the interest of conservative farmers and townsmen. The issue escalated into a public confrontation between both factions, and one of the surface issues (although by no means the most relevant) was the farmer's resistance to higher school taxes. In retrospect, the opponents agree that sentiment was also a major issue, but with taxes, the relative costs of centralization could be calculated.

The Conseil spends much of its time obtaining and spending grants from the various ministries. Such bureaucratic functions are less ominous since they do not constitute a threat to raise taxes. Any indication to the contrary can be a lethal political weapon. When Leclerc challenged Castonguay to the mayorality, gossip networks and an open letter were used to infer that if Leclerc were elected, taxes would go up. Such restrictions effectively limit the ability of the municipal councils to be anything more than extensions of government ministries. The Conseil will speak out when Saint-Pascal's institutions are threatened by government or neighbouring communities, or when an opportunity is present to obtain a valued resource from the outside. Even here, if the new resource means a risk for influential men, the whole development may be blocked. As Vidlich and Bensman (1958) found in the American town of Springdale, municipal government has been effectively paralyzed by both external and internal constraints.

The *esprit de clocher*

Earlier I referred to the strong notion of localism which protects the good life for the parish as an *esprit de clocher* — parochialism or, literally, "the spirit of the steeple". The 18 municipalities Kamouraska County are in intense competition for the resources distributed by outside agencies in this domain; one community's gain is thought to be a neighbour's loss.

The deputy can be a collaborator in perpetuating this localism and a community may stand to gain by having the deputy elected from the ranks of its citizens. Once elected, he and his team of supporters must produce new resources for the town. If they do not do so, the deputy is liable to reproach by individuals and by voluntary associations. In a recent example the Chambre de Commerce in Saint-Pascal asked the deputy why *he* was building a hospital for nearby Saint-Pacôme in Western Kamouraska and not for Saint-Pascal in the east. The hospital soon became a provincial election promise, but after the deputy lost the election, the opposition took over in Quebec City, and Saint-Pascal's hospital project was back at its starting point. On these issues, partisan divisions are ignored and the deputy is supported as a fellow townsman rather than a *rouge* or a *bleu*. If he does not favour the people of his town, he is subject to defections from the ranks of his own clients.[4] The provincial Liberal deputy since 1970, a poultry grower from neighbouring Saint-Philippe-de-Neri, has thus far avoided becoming mayor of his village, but he is still expected to obtain resources for those who helped him be elected.

The results of inter-community rivalry are often expensive. Saint-Pascal's industrial growth and resulting water pollution has led to a long and costly lawsuit by neighbouring Kamouraska, which receives Saint-Pascal's effluent. This long standing dispute is however of less importance than competition between Eastern Kamouraska County (Saint-Pascal) and Western Kamouraska County (La Pocatière). Many Pascaliens feel that some institutions given to their Western rival are rightfully theirs, and were lost on account of the favouritism of the former Liberal deputy from La Pocatière. One such grudge is a centennial year cultural centre that Saint-Pascal requested and then lost to its western rival. More serious is being deprived of a liquor store.[5] Animosity between the two sectors at one time was expressed openly at rowdy hockey matches, but gradually the hockey leagues were rearranged to include member teams from friendly parishes.[6] The Pascaliens have not always been losers in inter-community rivalry. During other administrations Saint-Pascal obtained the County Registry Office and the County Seat *(chef lieu)*, the roads garage, the provincial police detachment and also the county health office. The planners in the capital think of these services in terms of master plans and central place arithmetic. Kamouraskiens, familiar with the *esprit de clocher* within the county, are liable to think differently.

The instrument of support in inter-town struggles is the *mémoire* or brief which tends to follow a characteristic format. Saint-Pascal's leaders have drawn up *mémoires* on such subjects as obtaining the old people's home, centralizing milk production in their parish, obtaining a snowmobile plant from a prospective manufacturer and a cultural centre.

The *mémoire* always begins with a stock description of the location of the parish emphasizing its centrality and its drawing power. The next section deals with the benefit of locating in Saint-Pascal. The last part of the brief usually contains supporting letters from all or of most of the *conseils* of each of the 12 surrounding municipalities of Eastern Kamouraska County. Of course, the mémoire is only one component in the competition; the personal networks of leaders are usually more important. It is also common to see the communities ranged between Saint-Pascal and La Pocatière choosing sides — Mount-Carmel in Eastern Kamouraska has been known to support La Pocatière to the west instead of its more immediate neighbour Saint-Pascal.

The planners for Eastern Quebec have recommended that the county's municipalities be fused to centralize services and to give them improved bargaining power with central institutions (B.A.E.Q., 1966) In practice, local communities such as Saint-Pascal jealously guard their autonomy. Saint-Pascal's experience indicates that cooperation is possible when there is little risk to the supporters and if advantages will accrue without an increase in taxes.

Toward a Regional Conscience

Advocates of municipal centralization began a strong campaign in the mid-sixties to build support for their cause, but most were forced by their peers to retreat or even withdraw from active social life. Their efforts initially met with no support from the entrepreneurial group and their open promotion of reorganization generated resentment in neighbouring municipalities. The campaign was continued underground by the small groups of businessmen and administrators in the Chambre de Commerce. Gradually they obtained support from the town and the expanding industries who then began to see the benefits of centralization. Otherwise, in everyday local politics, it was "unanimously" ignored, as is any divisive community issue.

Regional integration proceeds slowly. The pooling of some municipal services such as water and fire protection is already recognized as necessary. Village councils, floundering in lethargy and lack of expertise, inevitably must rely on outside technical experts, usually salesmen. This is horticulturist Fleury's description of how Saint-Philippe-de-Néri five miles from Saint-Pascal went into the fire protection business without her neighbours:

It took an hour and a half just to read the list of options they wanted on the truck. The truck is so large that they have no garage to put it in. They will have to use a barn. They don't even have a water supply that the hoses can handle.

188

> Thirty percent of the truck is paid for with a government subsidy.
> If they had asked Saint-Pascal to provide them with this service, they
> might have obtained a subsidy for 60 percent of the cost. That is
> why we are underdeveloped.

A first attempt to alter this *esprit de clocher* was a short-lived
committee that emanated from the social animation sessions of
the Regional Development Council for Eastern Quebec. From the
beginning, outside "animators" urged that the committees be
deliberately focused away from particular local problems. This
emphasis was explained by one of these government paid group
leaders as a "problem of developing a regional conscience . . . The
territory needs a strong urban centre, so it can fight larger cities".
The attempt at so-called *animation sociale* deceived some of its
first supporters, who considered the regional benefit to be of
questionable value for their community.

> I became angry seeing things slip from us . . . . You put your confi-
> dence in the government and in these structures. Yet there is some-
> thing lacking at such a high level. There is some value in keeping the
> *esprit de clocher.*

In the spring of 1971, the issue of centralization resurfaced under
threat of a government reorganization which would split the county and link it with the urban community of the city of Rivière-du-
Loup. Following the type of segmentary opposition which consti-
tutes inter-community support, all of the mayors of the county
united against the government. The reasons given were financial:

> The mayors of the county refuse to leave the present limits of
> Kamouraska County where they are full citizens. The separation
> would be of no benefit to the tax payers if they would be further
> impoverished by buying increased taxes for services which are more
> apparent than real.
> The mayors add that a brainwashing is now going on through
> written propaganda and information sessions conducted by partial
> animators, recruited in 'civil servant land' (*fonctionnarisme*) paid
> with taxpayers money to sell them a reorganization project against
> the will of the rural population. This is equivalent to a prostitution
> of democracy. (*Le Saint-Laurent*, May 26, 1971:1-2)

The reader should have no problem putting this in an ideological
and historical perspective. Changing political boundaries, for exam-

ple, is a potential threat to politicians concerned about their own control over the resources in their ridings or, as is the case with the constant expansion of the boundaries of the federal riding of Kamouraska, the continued existence of their ridings. Urbanization can only benefit the majority of the entrepreneurial group, by widening their area of influence. It is the federal and provincial deputies[8] — traditional intermediaries between community and supra-regional government — who had the most to lose, along with the old rural middle class of small merchants and the farmers whose needs they once served.

National Trends in the Sixties

Until 1962 a basic political dualism pervaded the politics of rural Quebec. Third parties had made few inroads despite the various attempts of the Social Credit Union des Electeurs to institutionalize their political action committees and form a populist government in Quebec as had been done in Alberta and in British Columbia during and after the depression. (cf. Stein, 1973:54-74) In power from 1944 until 1960 under Duplessis' leadership, and then again from 1966 to 1970 initially under the leadership of Daniel Johnson, the Union Nationale[9] (the *bleus*) had interests that attracted clerical and petty bourgeois support for the maintenance of French-Canadian nationalist ideologies, especially before 1960. Jean Lesage's Liberals defeated the Unionistes in 1960 after disorganization fell upon the Duplessis political machine following the death of their chief. The Liberals returned in 1970 to annihilate the Unionistes at the polls.

The Créditistes (Ralliement Créditiste) made their first inroads on traditional dualism in the federal election of 1962, capturing 26 of Quebec's 75 seats (26 percent of the popular vote in Quebec [Stein, 1973:86]), including the federal seat for Kamouraska where deputy Pelletier, a lumberjack and union organizer living in Saint-Pascal, began his career in federal politics. Throughout the 1960's there was an informal organizational entente between Pelletier, at the federal level, and the Unionistes such as Castonguay) at the provincial level. This entente began to disintegrate at the end of the decade with the defection of a key Unioniste to the newly created provincial Créditistes. Saint-Pascal's voters were quite sensitive to these national power shifts, for, except in 1970 when fellow townsman Castonguay was the unsuccessful candidate, a majority of Pascaliens voted for the party that won their riding and on a provincial level, the party that formed the government.

Political Parties and National Politics

Blues and Reds: The Breakdown of Political Dualism

Within the town, political affiliation is a label that most people cannot conceal, especially community leaders who are called upon at election time to demonstrate their loyalties. Whole families and whole *rangs* are identified as blue or red in provincial electoral contests — even those families who have been Créditistes. With the exception of the entrepreneurial group which is mixed in its allegiances, coalitions and networks in Saint-Pascal have closely followed partisan lines.

At election time, militants of one party will cast the other party as fools and heretics, emphasizing personality differences as political faults. Thus a Liberal party organizer (his party out of power), after carefully explaining to me his understanding of obligated friendship, concludes, "All this is quite true, but only as members of the Union Nationale make friends this way."

As Lemieux (1962:333) noted in the early sixties, the opposition casts broadsides at the government candidate on his inability to handle elected office, but the government candidate can point to the ability of his party to *obtain* things for voters. As voters in Saint-Pascal were privately reminded on the eve of the 1970 election, a government candidate will deliver favours whether he is elected or not! It's his party that will be in power, as both sides emphatically claim.

Men of means in Saint-Pascal are expected to contribute to the *caisse electorale* (campaign fund) of their political party. Together they form the political teams of the candidates. At this level the lines have been so tightly drawn that when a *chef de file* of one political team becomes a *vire-capot* and changes party, he represents a political threat to all factions. A *vire-capot* is publicly dishonoured by the members of the party of his ascribed colour, and may even be distrusted by the party he has newly adopted. Nevertheless, *chefs de file* do change political cloaks especially when their patron faces a loss of electoral support or if his party is threatened on a national level.

In practice, at the level of local leadership in Saint-Pascal, there were no significant differences between the two traditional provincial parties. However the national elimination of the Union Nationale in the 1973 election left a power vacuum in the opposition that has not yet been taken up by either the Parti Québecois which seems to have the support of teachers and some white collar and blue collar voters, or the Créditistes who, with a strong candidate at the provincial level, could probably obtain considerable lower middle class support. The result is difficult to predict, but barring the merger of several parties, political dualism at all levels has temporarily disappeared in Saint-Pascal. The provincial liberal deputy could, in 1973, *include all of the entrepreneurial group* among his public supporters — a conversion that began with the Unioniste defeat of 1970 and with the rise of the separatist Parti Québecois. The opposition is divided along class lines and between the left and the right of the political spectrum, two oppositions that were once not very meaningful.

The Deputy as Patron

It would be incorrect to think of the patronage system in Kamouraska County simply as political corruption. In Eastern Quebec, patronage has long been a part of all institutional life — political, educational, commercial and social providing essential links between an underdeveloped bureaucracy, and life at the level of the parish. The term *patronage* is a more recent label for what people have always called *protection.* There are many politically protected positions which once changed the morning after the elections, such as the *gratte* who cruised the county roads with a mechanical grader and the *cantonnier* who distributed road work as a representative of the party in power (Miner, 1939:57). The deputies and their local level leaders (*chefs de file*) are the dominant partners in patron-client exchanges.

In Saint-Pascal the prestations of political patrons have usually been material — liquor, gravel, culverts and roadwork, contracts and jobs in road maintenance, hydro work and other tasks calling for mainly seasonal, unskilled or semi-skilled labour. The greater the number of party faithful (clients) who can receive prestations from a patron, the greater the opportunity of the patron to assure himself a juridical return in votes and in delegated power. Thus it is in the patron's interest to make his prestations divisible, maximizing his supporters and minimizing the accumulation of power among his *chefs de file* (cf. Lemieux, 1973:193).

Since Kamouraska's deputies have usually been of the government party, supporters of the opposition party are likely to be co-opted into supporting the *deputé's* political colour, as they were dragged *("hâlés")* over to his party *(Ibid.*:195). This whole process has worked to redistribute government services to individuals and groups through the non-bureaucratic channels of the patron. This patronage is not necessarily interpreted as being moral or immoral, but rather as amoral, as an uneven exchange. The scale of patronage determines whether the exchange is between the patron and a group or an important obligated friend or between the patron and one of many potential supporters and voters.

Gros patronage (big patronage) is what the Kamouraskiens refer to when an office-holder extends prestations of an important material nature; the client will usually be a group such as a whole community that is "given" a new road or a hospital by their provincial deputy. This type of patronage has become more important in provincial politics in recent years while the Créditiste federal member of parliament has taken over some of the *petit patronage* (small patronage) that was once provincial.

Petit patronage is seen as a series of little favours which carry the request for a diffuse and on-going repayment, but the accounts may never be drawn up. A certain amount of *petit patronage* is seen as the sign of a good deputy. In practice such patronage is an extension of small administrative favours, services, material goods as well as the immaterial prestations of prestige, esteem and friendship coming from a man of great personal reputation. *Petit patronage* is more than the pre-election delivery of several *poches* of potatoes and culvert pipe on the door step of a needy farmer, it is a complex series of many-stranded coalitions (Wolf, 1966:81) which have tied together the different social classes of rural Québec. The patron, possessing the differential resources partly given to him by an urban society, is able to skirt the anonymity and complexity of urban life by providing an informal social service, and takes on a broker role short-circuiting the bureaucracy if not removing the reasons for its existence (Lemieux, 1967).

The Politics of Asphalt: Political Patron vs Bureaucracy

The comprehensiveness of the patronage system has eroded since 1960, especially in provincial politics. Nevertheless, throughout the sixties, several deputies made intensive efforts to build wide-scale political support through patronage. They met with only modest success, since the extension of government services into the county seriously threatened the broker role of the deputy as the effective channel to the bureaucracy in the capital. Outsiders in the civil service blatantly refused to honour the rules of the patronage system. For example, when the placement officer Cloutier came to Saint-Pascal from Quebec City, it was not long before the deputy called him and suggested that it might be appropriate that new jobs be funnelled through the deputy's office rather than the placement bureau. The new civil servant found the situation amusing and subsequently failed to produce for his potential patron. His reward system is situated outside the sphere of deputy-client relations in his department's criteria of bureaucratic universalism.

In another instance, a supporter of the opposition party was telephoned by the deputy after an election victory. He was instructed to relinquish his construction job with the hydro company as he should know what happens after the government has changed hands. The worker did not step aside and when the patron's designates turned up at the construction site, the foreman, a young Montrealer, sent them packing.

At the time of my research, both the provincial deputy for Kamouraska County and the federal deputy for Islet and Kamouraska lived in Saint-Pascal, and both men were accessible to the town people. The deputies, especially the provincial representative, convey a public image as men who are personally responsible for bringing in good things from outside their riding. Unlike the curé whose interests are parochial, the deputy has to balance the interests of his supporters in many parishes. This single person could not possibly bypass an expanding bureaucracy. In many areas, from police services to liquor sales, good things came direct-ly· from the ministries, and deputies began to find it more difficult to convince voters that public spending was a result of their intervention and generosity. Nonetheless *gros patronage* in its broadest sense was an important campaign strategy of *both* national parties during the 1970 provincial election.

The Union Nationale incumbant Castonguay repeatedly reminded every parish in his riding of the money he had brought them during his term of office. One such list was distributed as a mailbox circular. A selection of its contents speaks for itself:

My Accomplishments for Kamouraska, 1966-70

Saint-Pascal

Minister of Municipal Affairs

Grants	Water and Sewage	$	55,435.00	(*Each* construction
	Winter Works		22,396.43	job is listed and expenses
	Fire		28,128.44	are itemized and geographically located)
. . . other monies . . .				
	Villa Saint-Pascal		550,000.00	(opened in 1968)
	Hôpital Saint-Pascal		650,000.00	(Promised before the election, never opened)

Minister of Highways

	Total	715,526.79	
. . . including . . .	lights	744.21	
	asphalt	97,686.00	
	Grand Total	$2,364,232.37	

The candidate concludes:

This is why I have the firm conviction that the population of Kamouraska County will show its gratitude to him who has been its most faithful and devoted servant.

He was defeated! But this was more on account of the Créditiste presence and the defection of Union Nationale *Chefs-de-file* than the ingratitude of the voters. Within a year of his election, the new deputy (a Liberal) promptly published a similar list of accomplishments. As one merchant explains, the message of both candidates is:

> I have grabbed this for you. I have taken it from others; without *me* you would not have it. For what I have done for you, you have a *debt of gratitude (reconnaissance)* to see to my re-election.

Rather than being a unique case, the deputy is one of several powerful patrons each with a large roster of clients. The deputy's patronage is just more public and visible. Both federal and provincial deputies are close to public life in Saint-Pascal, leading the procession of *notables* during the opening night of Carnaval, sitting at the head table for parish supper, present at Club Richelieu gatherings and lead speaker for dedication of any new public works whether or not it was built with government funds or ever built at all. Federal deputy Pelletier carries his "deputy as leading citizen" role into his everyday transactions with Pascaliens.

Petit Patronage and the Universalistic Prestations of the Créditistes

Deputy Pelletier has become an acclaimed spokesman for the little man as well as for the Douglasite Social Credit formula of increasing consumer purchasing power through dividends and a reduction of government spending. Once active in the militantly Catholic Bérets Blancs, he continues to support the legitimacy of traditional French–Canadian values, but overtly this is done on a non-partisan basis. He perceives of his position in the same way as do other "old guard Créditiste MP's (who) had long adopted the parliamentary style of delegates rather than representatives; that is, they saw their role in parliament as representing their constituents rather than the country at large" (Stein, 1973:117). In practice, many Liberal and Union Nationale deputies have used similar strategies in being universalistic brokers and patrons to all their constituents (Lemieux, 1973:196).

"In the seventies, *petit patronage* is less important than the search for major institutional inputs into the county, that is, *gros patronage*". The contractor whom I am quoting is identifying the relationship between a patron and a group (usually a town or village) as the essential of *gros patronage*, where liquor stores, unemployment offices, highway garages and baseball diamonds are the prestations sought by the economic elite of local communities. In 1970, the provincial political arena was looked to for the newly-available largesse of deputies and ministers. Federal largesse on any significant scale — economic expansion grants or agricultural subsidies — was announced by distant Federal ministers or by relatively unknown civil servants. At the same time, Federal transfer payments such as subsidies, social and unemployment insurance and welfare expanded at a geometric rate. For the working man, one codemaster for this distant and confusing bureaucracy is the Créditiste federal deputy, who acts as broker or middleman for things from the outside — the small prizes of *petit patronage.*

Pelletier sees his responsibilities as "an interpreter of badly-made laws for ill-informed people". On weekends, his Saint-Pascal home is crowded with petitioners from his riding, each with an individual small request for assistance. Most of these are swiftly taken care of and followed up with a letter from his Ottawa office. The requests include everything from passport applications, work permits and subsidy information to support a winter carnival in Témiscouata County and glasses for a local boy attending school in Ottawa. These solicitations often involve dual jurisdiction and the federal deputy is prepared to arrange things at both federal and provincial levels. His task begins with the problems brought to him, rather than in the formal character of his office. As a man who solves problems at all levels and for all petitioners, he speaks for his people in Ottawa. He is almost a "saint" — relatively free of partisanship: a permanent representative in Ottawa.

Footnotes

[1] The material in this section was first prepared as part of a paper (Gold, 1970) presented at the American Anthropological Association meeting in San Diego, and at a special seminar at the University of Toronto. I am grateful for insightful comments received from Larry Chrissman, Mike Levin and Renaud Santerre.

[2] Dionne (1909:370), defines *guenille* as a "man without character, a man who is soft"; another definition is that of *vaurien* or a "worth-nothing" (La Société du Bon Parler Français, 1930:386).

[3] Barth (1959) found a similar type of mediator, whom he refers to as a

saint, among the Swat Pathans. The opposition between the transactional leadership of chiefs and the moral leadership of saints is carried further by F.G. Bailey (1969). The moral leadership of the "saints" is not nearly as significant as the role of the patrons and far less important than the leadership of nineteenth century priests such as Alphonse Beaudet (Chapter Three).

[4] This is sometimes a very difficult proposition for the deputy who must retain his out-of-town support.

[5] The liquor store was later "obtained" by the provincial deputy in 1974.

[6] Frankenberg (1957) has related the role of football matches in playing out the animosities between Welsh villages. Hockey games are used to create a social no-man's land between French villages in Manitoba and again between French and Menonite villages (Yvette Herold, private communication).

[7] *Amination sociale* — popular action committees with the objective of participatory involvement in social change. After extensive use of the technique in Eastern Quebec by the B.A.E.Q. planners, it was picked up, often in highly vulgarized form, by hundreds of other organizations. For a critique of participatory planning in Quebec see Gagnon (1973).

[8] In French these are referred to as the *deputé provincial* and the *deputé fédéral*. I am not using the usual English translations — federal member of parliament and provincial member of the National Assembly because in Saint-Pascal they are usually known as "the deputies".

[9] A party founded in 1935 by Maurice Duplessis from the remnants of the Quebec Conservative party and several renegade Liberals. See Quinn (1963) for an informative treatment of the Union Nationale.

Chapter Seven
Development without Modernization?

"There is no room for two arenas in Kamouraska County"
              headline, *Le Saint-Laurent*, March 14, 1973
"There is always room for Small Industry"
              editorial, *Le Saint-Laurent*, October 24, 1973

The choice between factories and arenas is an appropriate ending to our analysis of the industrialization of Saint-Pascal. The new factories remain under the individual control of the industrial middle class or by local standards, the regional elite. The allocation of public resources for new institutions such as arenas is decided upon privately by planners' reports submitted to the provincial government, and by the *gros patronage* of the deputy who publicly "gives" prestations to his constituents. Saint-Pascal chose not to go its own way in the construction of winter sports facilities with only the profits of their Carnaval.

In the case of an arena or in that of a factory, large scale institutional additions are intelligible in the context of the redefined vocation of the agricultural service centre. Economic changes resulting from the surplus of semisubsistance agriculture have led to new demands that are not met easily from the local surplus of industrial capitalism.

The sons of downwardly-mobile artisans redefined Saint-Pascal's mercantile resources to begin a period of expansionary industrial capitalism. Free of external control in the initial stages, the town became atypical of many Quebec communities in that its elite was less dependent on outside economic interests. Saint-Pascal is, nevertheless, representative of small urban service centres in Quebec that have similar postwar associations, occupational groups and political formations. Also similar I suspect, are the social relationships among the economic leaders and the dominant liberal ideologies which were introduced under their tutelage. This generalization is based on sampling the content of regional newspapers — the reaction to the film and the first research reports on

199

Saint-Pascal (Gold, 1972:1973). It can be validated only by further study of leadership groups in the context of other types of urban communities. Relatively little social research has been done in the more traditional type of industrialized service centre (cf. Falardeau, 1964 (1953):109). The opening of planned frontier towns such as Radisson and Mount Wright shows quite dramatically that the possibilities of new community types are far from exhausted. A comparison remains to be done between transformed farm centres like Saint-Pascal and the single industry town which has "no lingering myths of days gone by . . . community jobs and lives depend upon twentieth-century science and technology" (Lucas, 1971:28).

Saint-Pascal's new leaders are the most recent regional elite to form a team that has managed community-nation negotiations. After the realization of the common goals that bring coalitions together, each previous elite — seigneurial, clerical and mercantile — declined in importance. Their downfall or their retreat into obscurity, has always been initiated by another occupational group with whom they initially collaborated, sometimes to preserve their own routinized or threatened status. In this saga of elite circulation there has been an oscillation between national and local or regionally-orientated leadership groups.

On several occasions I have played the role of the historical determinist in suggesting a coming confrontation between the new elite and technocratic or blue collar coalitions. However there are a number of possible scenarios for future leadership in Saint-Pascal, and there is no reason why these will not follow national trends in Quebec.

A first possibility is the continual absorption of "young men on their way" into the Club Richelieu and into other councils of the entrepreneurial group. Several innovative leaders in their twenties and thirties have already taken a greater interest in the development of social infrastructure and by implication, a willingness to make alliances with persons in other occupations. This could lead to a reorientation of the town's common interest associations without any visible confrontation from incumbent leaders. Other possible outcomes of this same scenario are an organizational split, or the sudden regeneration of another long dormant association, or the creation of entirely new associations. A second possible scenario would be that of the newly unionized workers coming into conflict over community leadership and forming a parallel power structure, perhaps together with teachers and small merchants. The first of the two scenarios seems to be the most likely, but predictions about the politics of intergroup relations locally or nationally, cannot be made easily.

The arena provides an example of the complexity of alliances. After it was "given" to La Pocatière, businessmen were as disappointed in this loss to Saint-Pascal as they were when small industries could not be persuaded to locate in their town. For years several of the "young men on their way" had sought action on an arena and time had brought about a concensus that the town needed more institutions "to keep people from moving away". But the arena was not launched by the entrepreneurial group as a joint capitalistic venture as was Friendship Inn. The municipal *conseil* was left with the task of dealing directly with the provincial government.

Anthropologists working in the Western Mediterranean have succinctly referred to *modernization* as a process that perpetuates dependence "by which an underdeveloped region changes in response to inputs (ideologies, behavioural codes, commodities and institutional models) from already established industrial centres". In contrast, development is defined as the acquisition (*by an underdeveloped region*) of "an autonomous and diversified industrial economy on its own terms" (Schneider, Schneider and Hansen, 1972:340). Others have maintained that the increase in differentiation and in complexity of community institutions is linear so that both commercial and general institutional complexity grow at approximately the same rate. Thus Young and Fujimoto are able to conclude that "the creation of new towns is increasingly frequent in the modern world, but certainly none of these communities is such a new place" (1965:351).

Changes in Saint-Pascal have not followed the pattern of many non-industrialized regions in the western world. Instead they fall into a different category of community where local level industrialization precedes and then is followed by institutional modernization. Even in 1970 the emergent objectives of Saint-Pascal's leadership were to correct the disparity of being a town that had experienced development without modernization. While factories were bulging with expanded workshops in Saint-Pascal, shopping centres, hospitals and arenas were being "obtained" or initiated locally in other less industrialized communities.

Saint-Pascal conceivably could *develop* its social infrastructure in the same way as it developed its industry, that is, with local resources. But the leaders of this development would have to be capable of resource appropriation in highly technical and bureaucratic fields. This expertise was not available locally for the development of industry and probably institutional modernization also will come through the brokerage of outside experts. Some experts are foisted on the region, such as the civil servants attached to the Office for the Development of Eastern Quebec (O.D.E.Q.), while others are invited by the regional elite to incorporate themselves into local institutions. Were a sufficient number of strangers able to become part of the regional leadership, they could redefine the charter of coalitions and institutions in which they participate. However, as I explained in Chapter Five, there are corporate walls which distinguish the entrepreneurial group as more than a coalition and these can prevent short-run intrusion by outsiders.

The entrepreneurial group is the first coalition of its kind in the history of Saint-Pascal and similar regional centres. The social organization of the group is characteristic of that of a new commercial-industrial bourgeoisie. Its community-nation networks are unlike those of the early nineteenth-century seigneurial elite which had little economic power, and its use of associations in occupational and in class terms is more explicit and instrumental than was the case with the mercantile-professional elite who preceded them. Control of factories that are unprecedented year-around inputs into the regional economy, is equally or more effective than the strong moral leadership of the nineteenth-century priest-leader such as Alphonse Beaudet. Thus in economic terms alone, the new elite can appropriate more local resources than the groups it has supplanted. Significantly, the impact of the new group is more than economic.

The ideology of industrial capitalist development is nurtured by associations such as the C.D.E. and the Club Richelieu, expressly and overtly by the former and more discreetly and covertly by the latter. Associations also provide an arena for the management of *industriel* identity and a reasonably effective means of informal social control and accounting. In this way, the coalition acquires a class ideology and a corporate cloak. Its associations are more synonymous with corporate groups having a wide value-based charter than they are with 'voluntary' associations. Information flows more easily within this arena than across the markers which set off its members with the identity of a separate reference group (Ross, 1975). Barth, following Goffman (1959), applies these criteria to interaction in bounded systems such as ethnic groups: "If people agree about these prescriptions, their agreement on codes and values need not extend beyond that which is relevant to the social situations in which they interact." (Barth, 1969:16) The entrepreneurial group has developed an ideology of group friendship that influences the range of permissible semiprivate and public behaviour between individuals.

In one way innovation is encouraged by the challenge of formalized sociability and by envy within the group. Paradoxically however, formalized competitive innovation discourages spontaneous innovation in areas that are outside the values generated by accepted behaviour patterns (Barth, 1966:14). Entrepreneurial roles, making value flow where there are constraints to its passage (Barth, 1962), become difficult to take on *within* the entrepreneurial group. With the gradual withdrawal of the original successful leaders and with the decline of their charisma, the group loses its role models. The rituals of competition could become less important as the group seeks ways of making corporate decisions about its milieu. It is at this point that formerly marginal members of the entrepreneurial group come to the fore — persons who are nodal or bridges to other local networks and coalitions that have resources to offer. Group values are then liable to be redefined as new relationships are worked out with the community (cf. Barth, 1966:15).

Since 1960, a number of new organizations have been introduced to Saint-Pascal mainly as offshoots of the leisure activities of the Centre Social. Each association brings with it a set of outside assets and constraints, like the *taquinerie* of the Club Richelieu, which can be used by the members to achieve more than the purely expressive ends of the original association. Some occupational groups have not gone through the process of using the malleability of associations to fit their common interests. In the case of the teachers and the workers who are in constant interaction with their peers as opposed to the businessmen who are occupational coalitions, primarily unions. The management of communication within blue and white collar common interest groups in Saint-Pascal and in Quebec remains to be studied.

In the first chapter, I emphasize the doubts of some Pascaliens about the viability of sustained industrial growth. These doubts reappear in the fourth chapter in the context of a growing state capitalism. Underlying the leaders' uncertainty is a delayed realization that increasing economic scale and industrial homogeneity may not be secure strategies for the future of a small service centre. To be more pessimistic, there seem to be few local means available to brake and control the steamroller of rural industrialization. Pressures within upwardly-mobile groups insist on the continued expansion of their particular niche until it is over-extended and headed for catastrophe. It is not sufficient to say that expansionary ideologies were not present in preindustrial or peripheral regions of Quebec where "the citizen's role in rural industry takes precedence over the role of the entrepreneur" (Dansereau, 1967:22). This conventional wisdom on French Canadian industrialization must be placed within the context of the milieu in which enterprise operates. In Saint-Pascal the citizens' role has determined where the profits of entrepreneurial activity were directed (Gold, 1974). In the context of elite decisions, a convent school and an arena may hold the same status as a tannery or a tire factory.

Appendix

The Interview Sample

Since I was interested primarily in the new industries and in sociability among the various owners and managers, all of the manufacturers, building contractors, and high volume retailers are included in the sample. Also included are all three general merchants, the last of the merchant *notables*. Added are numerous small merchants, and independent tradesmen from butchers to the undertaker who were randomly selected from a census of businesses with street visibility or a telephone listing. The occupational composition of the representative sample is summarized in Table A.

Forty-four of these forty-six persons were interviewed within the first six months of the project. To achieve greater representation in networks, questions on associations and sociability were also asked to a small group of professionals from the school system, the bank and the public service agencies. The bank is also treated as a separate business even though it is not a comparable unit: bank personnel are part of a transient 'civil service' and the Saint-Pascal branch is controlled by a head office in Montreal.

When double ownerships are accounted for, the sample includes 61.1 per cent of the town's businessmen, and 100 per cent of the manufacturers.

Sex — All except two of the business persons are males. The two female managers are in business because of the death or illness of their husbands, and expressed little interest in business as an occupation.

Age — The ages of the sample range from 27 to 63.

Scale — The businesses surveyed include all of the town's major employers and all firms which could have a major sales and distribution network. Table B demonstrates the wide range of annual net sales of the businesses that were surveyed. Twenty thousand dollars annually is a minimum figure for a company in acceptable financial health and the three businesses which show less than twenty thousand dollars in sales were tottering at the brink of insolvency. Sample selection is thus biased against the smallest businesses.

The survival rate of all businesses is high compared to urban small commerce where often fewer than 50 per cent of new enterprises make their first year. This stability is probably related to the family business, a low-risk operation where the owner is fortified against calamity by low overhead and sometimes by an alternate occupation.

The sales figures in Table B are based only on unverified respondent estimates, but they are sufficient to demonstrate the extent of Saint-Pascal's sustained economic growth.

Table A

The Interview Sample

	Population	Final Interview Sample
Manufacturers and Processors	11	11
Merchants		
general stores	3	3
furniture and appliances	1	1
auto dealers[1]	4	4
chain stores	2	2
pharmacies	1	1
agricultural machinery[1]	4	2
cloth merchant	1	1
jewelers	2	1
saws and outdoor equipment	2	1
butchers	3	1
grocers[2]	4	1
clothing stores	3	1
Trades and Services		
general contractors	2	2
plumbing contractors	2	1
electrical contractors	2	1
printers	1	1
photographers	1	1
millers	3	1*
dry cleaners	1	1
shoe repair	3	1
undertakers	1	1
barbers	2	0
others	3	0
transport companies	2	1*
insurance agents	4	1
hotels and pensions	3[3]	1
banks	1	1
Total	72 (100%)	44 (61.1%)

[1] All of the auto dealers also operate large gas and service stations.

[2] All of the general stores also sell groceries.

*Other merchants of this type are included within another category. Sawmill operators and pulp contractors are not included in the census: their business is largely in outlying parishes.

[3] Not included in this list are two restaurants not located in hotels or in rooming houses, one a small snack bar and another an old bus converted into a stationary canteen.

Table B

Saint-Pascal Businesses
Arranged by Increase in Net Sales 1964-1969

Net Sales	Number of businesses		Percentage Increase 1964-1969			
(Chiffre d'affaires)	in 1964	in 1969	0	1—50%	51+%	new
$1,000,000-	1	3	—	—	2	1
$500,000-$1,000,000	2	5	—	1	2	1
$250,000-$499,000	4	8	2	2	2	2
$100,000-$249,000	10	10	1	3	5	1
$50,000-$99,000	6	4	1	1	3	—
$15,000-$49,000	6	4	2	—	—	—
less than $15,000	6	3	3	—	—	—
Subtotal	35	37	9	7	14	5
No Information	4	7	—	—	—	2
Total	39	44	9	7	14	7

Bibliography

Aubey, Robert
1969 Entrepreneurial Formation in El Salvador. Explorations in Economic History 6:268-285.

Aubey, Robert, John Kyle and Arnold Strickon
1974 Investment Behaviour and Elite Social Structure in Latin America. Journal of Interamerican Studies and World Affairs 16:71-95.

Bailey, F.G.
1969 Stratagems and Spoils. Oxford: Blackwell.

Barbeau, Marius
1918 Le pays de gourganes. Transactions of the Royal Society of Canada 3rd series, Vol. 2:193-225.

Barnard, Julienne
1961 a. Mémoires Chapais. Tome I:1744-1848. Montreal: Fides.
1961 b. Mémoires Chapais. Tome II:1848-1875. Montreal: Fides.

Barnes, J.A.
1968 Networks in Political Process. in Local Level Politics. Marc J. Swartz ed. Chicago: Aldine.

Barth, Fredrik
1959 Political Leadership Among Swat Pathans. London: Athlone Press.
1963 The Role of the Entrepreneur in Social Change in Northern Norway. Bergen: Univ. Press.
1966 Models of Social Organization (Occ. Pap. R. Anth. Inst. 23). London: Royal Anthropological Institute.
1969 Ethnic Groups and Boundaries. Boston: Little and Brown.

Belshaw, Cyril
1955 The Cultural Milieu of the Entrepreneur: A Critical Essay. Explorations in Entrepreneurial History 7:144-146.

Benedict, Burton
1968 Family Firms and Economic Development. Southwestern Journal of Anthropology 24:1-19.

Bennett, John W.
1967 Microcosm and Macrocosm Relationships in North American Agrarian Society. American Anthropologist 69:441-454.
1969 Northern Plainsmen: Adaptive Strategy and Agrarian Life. Chicago: Aldine.

Blanchard, Raoul
1935 L'Est du Canada-français. (2 Vols.) Montreal: Beauchemin.

Bloom, Gordon F. and Herbert R. Northrup
1965 Economics of Labor Relations. fifth ed., Homewood: Richard D. Irwin.

Bohannan, Paul
1955 Some Principles of Exchange and Investment Among the Tiv. American Anthropologist 57:60-70.

Bossé, Eveline
1971 Joseph-Charles Taché [1820-1894]. Un grand réprésentant de l'élite canadienne-française. Québec: Garneau.

Breton, Yvan
1973 A Comparative Study of Work Groups in an Eastern Canadian Peasant Fishing Community: Bilateral Kinship and Adaptive Processes. Ethnology 12:393-418.

Brown, D.E.
1974 Corporations and Social Classification. Current Anthropology 15:29-52.

Bureau d'Aménagement de l'Est du Québec (B.A.E.Q.)
1966 Plan du développement de la région-pilote: Bas-Saint-Laurent, Gaspésie et les Iles-de-la-Madeleine. 10 vols, Mont Joli: B.A.E.Q. .

Christian, William
1969 Divided Island, Faction and Unity on Saint Pierre. Cambridge: Harvard University Press.

Congregation de Notre Dame (C.N.D.)
1947 a. & b. L'oeuvre d'un grand éducateur. 2 vols, Montreal: Congregation de Notre Dame.

Cook, Ramsey, ed.
1969 French-Canadian Nationalism. Toronto: Macmillan of Canada.

Dansereau, Francine
1967 Etude de l'entrepreneurship dans une région à développement marginal. Unpublished M.A. thesis, Université de Montréal (page numbers cited are from a mimeographed B.A.E.Q. report).

Davis, J.
1973 Forms and Norms: the Economy of Social Relations. Man 8:159-176.

Dionne, N.-E.
1904 Le parler populaire des Canadiens-français. Quebec: Laflamme et Proulx.

Dumont, Fernand
1963 Recherche sur les groupements religieux. Social Compass 10:171-192.

Dumont, Fernand, Jean-Paul Montminy and Jean Hamelin
1971 Idéologies au Canada français, 1850-1900. Québec: Les Presses de l'Université Laval.

Dumont, Fernand, Jean Hamelin, Fernand Harvey and Jean-Paul Montminy
1974 Idéologies au Canada français, 1900-1929. Québec: Les Presses de l'Université Laval.

Falardeau, Jean Charles
1953 The Changing Social Structures of Contemporary French-Canadian Society. in J.C. Falardeau ed. Essais sur le Québec contemporain. Québec: Les Presses de l'Université Laval.
1960 Les Canadiens français et leur idéologie. in Mason Wade ed. Canadian Dualism/La dualité canadienne. Toronto & Quebec: University of Toronto Press and Les Presses de l'Université Laval.
1965 L'origine de l'ascension des hommes d'affaires dans la société canadienne-française. Recherches Sociographiques 6:33-45.

Faucher, Albert
1973 Québec en Amérique au XIXè siècle: essai sur les caractères économiques de la Laurentie. Montreal: Fides.

Frankenberg, Ronald
1957 Village on the Border. London: Cohen & West.

Gagnon, Gabriel
1973(1970) Les Iles-de-la Madeleine: Elements for an Anthropology of Participation. in G.L. Gold and M.A. Tremblay eds. Communities and Culture in French Canada. Toronto: Holt, Rinehart and Winston of Canada. (trans. from Recherches Sociographiques 11,3,:223-234.

Gagnon, Lysiane
1969 Les conclusions du Rapport B.B.: De Durham à Laurendeau-Dunton: variations sur le thème de la dualité canadienne. in Robert Comeau ed. Economie québécoise. Québec: Les Presses de l'Université du Québec.

Garigue, Philippe
1962 Organisation sociale et valeurs culturelles canadiennes-françaises. Canadian Journal of Economics and Political Science 28:189-203.

Garnovetter, Marc
1973 The Strength of Weak Ties. American Journal of Sociology. 78:1360-1380.

Gaspé, Philippe Aubert de
1866 Mémoires. Ottawa: Desbarats.

Geertz, Clifford
1962 Peddlars and Princes. Chicago: University of Chicago Press.

Gérin, Léon
1897 L'habitant de Saint-Justin. Transactions of the Royal Society of Canada (second series) 4:139-216.
1938 Le type économique et social des Canadiens. Montréal: Editions de l'A.C.F. .

Glade, William P.
1967 Approaches to a Theory of Entrepreneurial Formation. Explorations in Entrepreneurial History N.S. 4:245-259.

Gluckman, Max
1965 Politics, Law and Ritual in Tribal Society. Chicago: Aldine.

Gold, Gerald L.
1972a The Emergence of a Commercial Bourgeoisie in a French Canadian Town, unpublished Ph.D. Thesis, Minneapolis: University of Minnesota.
1972b Saint-Pascal. 16mm sound, colour film. Toronto: McGraw Hill-Ryerson (produced by Department of Audio-visual Services, University of Guelph).
1973 Voluntary Associations and a New Economic Elite in a French Canadian Town. in Gerald L. Gold and Marc-Adélard Tremblay eds. Communities and Culture in French Canada. Toronto: Holt, Rinehart and Winston of Canada Ltd.

1974 Merchants and Industrialists: Dependency and Control in a Quebec Regional Elite. Paper given at the annual meeting of the Canadian Sociology and Anthropology Association, August, 1974.

Goffman, Erving
1971(1959) The Presentation of Self in Everyday Life. Middlesex: Penguin Books.
1961 Encounters, Two Studies in the Sociology of Interaction. Indianapolis: Bobbs-Merrill.

Jocas, Yves de and Guy Rocher
1961 Inter-generation Occupational Mobility in the Province of Quebec. in B.R. Blishen, F.E. Jones, K.D. Naegele, J. Porter eds. Canadian Society. (Toronto: Macmillan Co. of Canada).

Handelman, Don and Bruce Kapferer
1972 Forms of Joking Activity: a Comparative Approach. American Anthropologist 74:484-517.

Harary, Frank, R.Z. Norman, and D. Cartwright
1965 Structural Models. An Introduction to the Theory of Directed Graphs. New York: John Wiley.

Hébert, Anne
1973 Kamouraska. (English Translation), Toronto: Musson.

Hughes, Everett C.
1938 Industry and the Rural System in Quebec. Canadian Journal of Economics and Political Science 4:341-349.
1943 French Canada in Transition. Chicago: University of Chicago Press.
1963 The Natural History of a Research Project: French Canada. Anthropologica 5:225-239.

Hunt, Robert
1965 The Developmental Cycle of the Family Business in Rural Mexico. in June Helm ed. Essays in Economic Anthropology. Proc. 1965 Annual Spring Meeting, American Ethnological Society. Seattle: University of Washington Press. Pp. 54-79.

Kluckhohn, Clyde
1958 The Evolution of Contemporary American Values. Daedalus 87:78-109.

Lamarche, Jacques A.
1966 Réflexion d'un adulte sur sa jeunesse nationaliste. Cahiers de cité libre. 2:51-57.

Lapointe, Gérard
1960 Etude du diocèse de Ste-Anne-de-la-Pocatière: Analyse de la structure sociale. Québec: Centre de Recherches en Sociologie Religieuse.

Lemieux, Vincent
1967 Le patronage politique. paper delivered at the 35th annual meeting of ACFAS (Association Canadienne français des Arts et des Sciences) Sherbrooke. Nov. 1967.
1973(1970) Political Patronage on the Ile d'Orléans. in G.L. Gold and M.-A. Tremblay eds. Communities and Culture in French Canada. Toronto: Holt, Rinehart and Winston of Canada. (translated from L'Homme 10:22-44)

LeMoine, Sir James MacPherson
1872 L'album du touriste: archaeologie, histoire, littérature, sport. Québec: A. Coté.

Liebenstein, Harvey
1957 Economic Backwardness and Economic Growth. New York: John Wiley & Sons.

Lucas, Rex
1973 Minetown, Milltown, Railtown, Life in Canadian Communities of a Single Industry. Toronto: University of Toronto Press.

Michaud, Marcel
1950 Monographie de la Caisse Populaire de Saint Pascal de Kamouraska. unpublished M.A. thesis. Université Laval.

Miner, Horace
1939 St. Denis. A French Canadian Parish. Chicago: University of Chicago Press.

Moreux, Colette
1969 Fin d'une religion? Monographie d'une paroisse canadienne-française. Montreal: Les Presses de l'Université de Montréal.

Nash, Manning
1958 Machine Age Maya: The Industrialization of a Guatemalan Community. Chicago: University of Chicago Press.

Paine, Robert
1962 Entrepreneurial Activity Without its Profits. in Fredrik Barth ed. The Role of the Entrepreneur in Social Change in Northern Norway. Bergen: Norwegian University Press.

1969 In Search of Friendship: an Exploratory Analysis in 'Middle-class Culture. Man 4:505-524.
1971 A Theory of Patronage and Brokerage. in Robert Paine ed. Patrons and Brokers in the East Aectic. Saint-John's: Institute of Social and Economic Research.
1973 Scale and Personal Dimension in Society. (mimeographed) Burg-Wartenstein Symposium No. 55: Scale and Social Organization.

Paradis, Alexandre
1948 Kamouraska (1674-1948). Québec: C.S. Grandbois.

Pareto, Vilfredo
1968(1901) The Rise and Fall of Elites (H. Zetterberg ed.). Tottowa: Bedminister Press (translated from Un applicazione de teorie sociologiche. Revista Italiana di Sociologia. 1901:402-456).

Pelto, Pertti
1970 Anthropological Research, The Structure of Inquiry. New York: Harper & Row.

Pitt Rivers, J.
1965 Honour and Shame. in J. Perstiany ed. Honour and Shame: the Values of Mediterranean Society. London: Wedienfield & Nicolson.

Porter, John
1965 The Vertical Mosaic, An Analysis of Social Class and Power in Canada. Toronto. University of Toronto Press.

Quinn, Herbert F.
1963 The Union Nationale: A Study in Quebec Nationalism. Toronto: University of Toronto Press.

Radcliffe-Brown, A.R.
1952 Structure and Function in Primitive Society: Essays and Addresses. Glencoe: The Free Press.

Rioux, Marcel
1964 Remarks on the Socio-Cultural Development of French Canada. in Marcel Rioux and Yves Martin eds. French Canadian Society. Toronto: McClelland and Stewart Carleton Library. (trans. from: Contributions à l'étude des sciences de l'homme 4 (1959):144-159.
1969 La question du Québec. Paris: Editions Seghers.
1973 On the Development of Ideologies in Quebec. in Communities and Culture in French Canada. G.L. Gold and M.-A. Tremblay eds. Toronto: Holt, Rinehart and Winston of Canada. (trans. from Revue de l'Institut de Sociologie. No. 1 (1968):95-124.)
1974 Les Québecois. Paris: Seghers.

Ross, Jennie-Keith
1975 Social Borders: Definitions of Diversity. Current Anthropology 16:

Saint-Germain, Maurice
1973 Une économie a libérer, le Québec analysé par ses structures économiques. Montreal: Les Presses de l'Université de Montréal.

Schneider, Peter T.
1973 Coalition Formation and Colonialism in Western Sicily. Arch. European Sociology 13:255-267.

Schneider, Peter, Jane Schneider and Edward Hansen
1972 Modernization and Development, the Role of Non-corporate Groups in the European Mediterranean. Comparative Studies in Society and History 14:328-350.

Schumpeter, Joseph A.
1934 The Theory of Economic Development: An Inquiry into Profits, Capital, Credit, Interest, and the Business Cycle. Cambridge: Harvard University Press.

Société du Bon Parler Français (La)
1930 Glossaire du parler français au Canada. Québec: L'Action Sociale Limitée.

Stein, Michael B.
1973 The Dynamics of Right-Wing Protest: A Political Analysis of Social Credit in Quebec. Toronto: University of Toronto Press.

Strathern, Andrew
1972 The Entrepreneurial Model of Social Activities: from Norway to New Guinea. Ethnology II:368-380.

Suttles, Gerald D.
1970 Friendship as a Social Institution. in George J. McCall et al eds. Social Relationships. Chicago: Aldine.

Swartz, Marc J., Victor W. Rurner, and Arthur Tuden eds.
1966 Political Anthropology. Chicago: Aldine.

Taylor, Norman W.
1960 The Effects of Industrialization — Its Opportunities and Consequences Upon French Canadian Society. Journal of Economic History 20:638-647.
1964(1961) The French-Canadian Industrial Entrepreneur and His Social Environment. *in* French Canadian Society, Marcel Rioux and Yves Martin eds. Toronto: McClelland and Stewart (trans. from Recherches Sociographiques 2:123-150.)
1965 Entrepreneurship and Traditional Elites: the Case of a Dualistic Society. Explorations in Entrepreneurial History N.S., 2:232-234.

Tocqueville, Alexis de (J.P. Mayer ed.)
1960 Journey to America. New Haven: Yale University Press.

Tremblay, Marc-Adélard
1950 La ferme familiale du Comté de Kamouraska. unpublished M.A. thesis, Université Laval.

Trudeau, Pierre Elliott
1956 La grève de l'amiante: une étape vers la révolution industrielle au Québec. Montreal: Editions Cité Libre.

Trudel, Marcel
1955 Chiniquy. Trois Rivières: Editions du Bien Public.

Verdon, Michel
1973 Anthropologie de la colonisation au Québec. Montreal: Les Presses de l'Université de Montréal.

Vidich, Arthur and J. Bensman
1958 Small Town in Mass Society: Class, Power and Religion in a Rural Community. Princeton, Princeton University Press.

Warner, W. Lloyd
1949 Democracy in Jonesville. New York: Harper.

Wolf, Eric
1966 Peasants. Englewood Cliffs: Prentice Hall.

Young, Frank W., and Isao Fujimoto
1965 Social Differentiation in Latin American Communities. Economic Development and Culture Change 12:344-352.

Index

215